Plantation Church

Plantation Church

*How African American Religion
Was Born in Caribbean Slavery*

NOEL LEO ERSKINE

OXFORD
UNIVERSITY PRESS

OXFORD
UNIVERSITY PRESS

Oxford University Press is a department of the University of Oxford.
It furthers the University's objective of excellence in research, scholarship,
and education by publishing worldwide.

Oxford   New York
Auckland   Cape Town   Dar es Salaam   Hong Kong   Karachi
Kuala Lumpur   Madrid   Melbourne   Mexico City   Nairobi
New Delhi   Shanghai   Taipei   Toronto

With offices in
Argentina   Austria   Brazil   Chile   Czech Republic   France   Greece
Guatemala   Hungary   Italy   Japan   Poland   Portugal   Singapore
South Korea   Switzerland   Thailand   Turkey   Ukraine   Vietnam

Oxford is a registered trade mark of Oxford University Press
in the UK and certain other countries.

Published in the United States of America by
Oxford University Press
198 Madison Avenue, New York, NY 10016

© Oxford University Press 2014

CIP data is on file at the LOC

9780195369144
9780195369137 (pbk.)

For James H. Cone
Doktorvater
Mentor and Friend
And in Memory of
Reverend U.N. Leo Erskine
My First Teacher of Caribbean Theology

Contents

Preface

THIS BOOK WAS born and came to maturity in several communities on both sides of the Atlantic. It had its genesis in rural Jamaica, West Indies, where my grandparents, who were children of slaves, practiced their version of African church in the mountains of Jamaica. This sparked in me a curiosity to investigate Black churches and their practices that facilitated survival "a long ways from home." While my grandparents were devoted to African expressions of faith and life, my parents, on the other hand, attended schools and churches where Jesus, not Africa, was the controlling motif and point of entry into cosmology and theology. The theology and worldviews of my parents were shaped by missionaries. But even in this context Africa was not abandoned as its memory lingered; its presence was experienced in rituals and music in their worshipping community. There was a constant struggle between Africa and Europe for the souls of Black people. It is in this crucible between Africa and Jesus, enculturation and acculturation, that the parameters for this investigation—Black churches and slavery in the Caribbean and the United States—unfolds.

My experience as pastor of churches in Harlem, New York; Atlanta, Georgia; and Jamaica, West Indies, provides another context for an examination of Black churches; coupled with this is my vocation as student and teacher of Black ecclesiologies, in both the Caribbean and the United States of America.

The reader will note that the understanding of church that emerges throughout this manuscript presupposes the historical and cultural priority of the Black religious experience in the Caribbean. The Black religious experience began in the Caribbean and not in the United States of America. Because of this, the view of Black churches that emerges presses beyond nation-state constructions of church as well as the notions of church informed primarily by the United States. The methodology that informs this investigation is intercultural and interregional as it highlights different ways of being church on both sides of the Atlantic. One goal is that fresh models of church emerge and illustrate the making of a Black Christianity. What emerges are cross-cultural ways of understanding Black churches and rethinking the language and grammar of how Black churches have been understood in the "Americas" and the priority of extending the notion of Black churches beyond the United States. Another aim of this project is to investigate the meaning of Black churches when people of African descent are culturally and politically in the majority. The converse is also important—what is the meaning of Black churches when people of African descent are culturally and politically in the minority?

The reader from the United States context may be surprised that this book is not primarily about traditional Black churches that pattern Christian expressions of church such as the African Methodist Episcopal or African Methodist Episcopal Zion or other iterations of Black Christian churches. While these are acknowledged, much of the emphasis is on what Dr. Du Bois called African churches. This emphasis opens the door to probe the role of the African preacher and medicine practitioner during the era of slavery and to question what was the role of African mythologies and cosmologies in helping enslaved persons win the war against plantation slavery in the Caribbean and the United States.

This book is in many ways a community project. Colleagues on both sides of the Atlantic have been instrumental in reading, editing, and shaping drafts of the manuscript. In the Laney Graduate School at Emory University, my colleagues have read and responded to several drafts of the book. Faculty colleagues at the Candler School of Theology and the Society for the Study of Black Religion have also given invaluable feedback to presentations. To faculty and administrators at the United Graduate School of Theology at Yonsei University in Seoul, Korea, I offer expressions of thanks for their hospitality during my sabbatical and their invitation for me to present chapters in a symposium at the Graduate School. Research for this book took me to theological schools in Barbados, Trinidad, Jamaica, and Cuba. Field trips took me to Haiti, the Virgin Islands, Ghana, Nigeria, and Kenya. Candler School of Theology provided financial assistance that made these trips possible. I am most grateful for this assistance.

To generations of graduate students at Emory University who took my class on cross-cultural theologies and helped in shaping the final product I am grateful. This project would not have happened without the patience and editorial skills of my editor Theo Calderara. I am indebted to my wife, Glenda, for reading, suggesting changes, and making space for me to write. Her care for details is invaluable.

Noel Leo Erskine

Plantation Church

Introduction: Remembering Ancestors

AS I LOOK back on the roots of Black churches in my own experience, I recall that Grandpa Tatta who spent much time in the fields, tending sugarcane, smoking his pipe, and communing with nature, said it was important to learn to worship outdoors because trees and streams point beyond themselves to the world of spirit. He observed that it was impossible to make it in a cruel world of suffering and oppression without the agency of ancestors, who are encountered in babbling streams and the beauty of nature. One reason that in African culture baptisms had to be in rivers was the stream represented the healing quality of the spirit world, and the encounter with spirit would awaken the love for freedom hidden in our innermost being. The recognition of spirit hidden in the beauty of nature and within ourselves would awaken feelings of love and joy and point to the "life force" that enlightens all reality. For Grandpa Tatta the Black church was not yet a Christian church; it was an African church. This church embraced the spirit in all things and taught that one could meet spirit under a tree, in the fields, at the market as well as in a church under a cross. This was in the tradition of Afro-Caribbean people who take their religion with them to the fields, to the market, or to a sanctuary. The African church as it emerged in the Caribbean was not only a community of persons joined together in a common bond and purpose to worship and acknowledge a higher deity, but church became the celebration of Black sacred space in which there was a continuous interaction between the world of ancestors and the physical world. Black churches included a place for the respect of nature, the acknowledgment of its beauty, and the recognition of the organic relationship between the natural and human worlds. African churches included Black sacred space to listen to a voice in "a burning bush" or in the song of a bird. Listening to spirit included listening to things—streams, nature, birds, and animals. In Grandpa Tatta's church it was more important to listen to things than to people. To worship was to create sacred space to listen to the promptings of spirit and to experience the awakening of a new consciousness of freedom, love, and the courage to hope in the face of excruciating suffering.

Grandfather explained to us, children, that the sugar mill on the homestead, and a commitment to grow what the family ate, was passed on from his father, who was born during the time of slavery and insisted that they should live close to the land and from the land.

Slavery was abolished in Jamaica in 1838. This was true of English colonies in the Caribbean, but in Cuba only ninety miles away, slavery continued until 1886 and in Brazil until 1888. Grand father Tatta was raised during the time of slavery in the Caribbean, and spending time in the woods, communing with nature, and recalling his father's resolve to be self-reliant was one way of remembering Africa and the traditions that sustained them during the time of slavery.

Grandma Mum spent much time weaving baskets and would occasionally attend the Baptist church because she said she liked to sing, dance, testify, and be possessed by the spirit. I knew then as a youngster in Jamaica, and while spending summers with grandparents, that I wanted to see the world through their eyes and to learn from them how they created an alternative existence against the cruel world of suffering and subordination. I wondered what it was like for my great-grandparents to have been slaves; what were the stories and traditions that helped them make it through the cruel world of slavery? How much of Africa did they remember? What were the roles of ancestors and other spirits? Grandpa Tatta and Grandma Mum were like African priests in the village who mediated between life and death, providing healing for the sick and consolation for the sorrowing, and allowing their encounter with ancestors to provide a window to an awakening to a new consciousness.

When Grandma Mum died, at her funeral we sang her favorite song, "Sweet Beulah Land." Grandpa Tatta said Sweet Beulah Land was Africa. Grandma Mum believed when she died her spirit would fly across the oceans back to Africa to be with her ancestors. Africa provided the frame of reference for faith and culture. In the African church there was a theology of spirit; they believed the divine suffused all reality and that healing included the physical and spiritual realms. All of reality was considered divine and the bearer of the holy. During the era of slavery most Black churches throughout the Caribbean were African churches.

An enigma was my father, Grandpa Tatta's and Grandma Mum's son, Leo, who said that he chose Jesus rather than Africa as the point of departure for faith and life because the Jesus people throughout the Caribbean built schools and hospitals, and sent missionaries to Africa. While Grandpa Tatta began his day in the fields communing with nature, smoking his pipe, and engaging spirits, my father began his day singing, "Nobody knows the trouble I've seen, nobody knows but Jesus. Sometimes I am up sometimes I am down, Oh Yes Lord, sometimes I am almost to the ground, Oh Yes Lord." At other times he would sing, "I am so glad trouble don't last always, hallelujah, I am so glad trouble don't last always." Father said Jesus was the hallelujah in the midst of trouble that pointed the way out of oppression and slavery and prevented the master from winning the war against Black humanity or from decimating their lives. At the end of the day enslaved people won the war against their humanity; slavery came to an end largely because of the agency of Black churches.

I asked my father why was he not in the tradition of Grandpa Tatta, telling stories about Africa and worshipping in sacred spaces down by the river or in the cane fields listening for the sound of the holy. He pointed out that he was immensely influenced by the African American George Liele who was born in Virginia, in the United States in 1750 to African parents, sold into slavery in different states, and ended up in Savannah, Georgia, where his master, Henry Sharp, allowed him to preach in a local Baptist church and to boat along the Savannah River where he would visit enslaved persons on plantations and would recite verses of Christian hymns as a witness of his faith. He traveled by boat to Silver Bluff, South Carolina, where he was one of the early leaders who founded a Black Baptist Church there about 1773 and in 1777 founded a Baptist church, in Savannah, Georgia. After the American War with Great Britain there were several British loyalists in the Savannah region who chose not to live there under American rule and instead migrated to the Caribbean. Among them was Colonel Moses Kirkland, the commander of the British forces in the Savannah area who loaned George Liele the fare to Jamaica with an understanding that he would be indentured to him until he repaid the loan. They arrived in Jamaica in January 1783 and Liele began preaching there shortly after his arrival. Liele named his church the Ethiopian Baptist Church. This church became the parent church of several Baptist churches throughout the island. My father became a minister in this church and I followed in his footsteps serving as pastor prior to my travel to the United States to study with Professor James Cone at Union Theological Seminary in New York.

Although I sided with my father, I could not forget my grandparents, Grandpa Tatta and Grandma Mum, and their central question, "Where do you stand in relation to Africa?" I believe that my decision to pursue doctoral studies with James Cone was a way to remember my grandparents.

Africa and Jesus

Two approaches to survival and liberation begin to emerge. On the one hand there was the question of Africa, raised by Grandpa Tatta and Grandma Mum: "Where do you stand in relation to Africa?" To remember the forests and the streams and to meet ancestors down by the river was to remember Africa. The unwillingness to separate the sacred and the secular, to take one's religion to the field or to the market, kept the memory of Africa alive.

On the other hand there was the question of Jesus; where do you stand in relation to Jesus was in many ways also a question about Europe, since the Jesus presented to enslaved persons was often through the lens of European missionaries. This created a tension between Jesus and European culture making it difficult to distinguish between Jesus and the master's culture. Often Jesus was a stranger and a foreigner to slaves in the Caribbean, as he had a European accent, was dressed like a European, and resembled one. This Jesus was often a problem for enslaved people as they were taught that Jesus was gentle, meek, mild, and obedient; therefore, they should seek in their relationships with the master to emulate the qualities of Jesus.

George Liele who started the Baptist Church in the Caribbean and through the naming of his church remembered Africa crafted theology and church polity between both African and European poles. In Chapter 6 we look at a church covenant presented to the congregations in Jamaica in which Liele straddles the fence between Africa and Europe.

What modified the European approach to Jesus was that enslaved Africans remembered Africa. Africa provided the framework for clarifying and planning their destiny. On both sides of the Atlantic a majority of enslaved Africans were like Grandma Mum, who went to church because they remembered Africa; they liked to dance, to sing, to testify, and to be possessed by spirit power. Jesus as presented by missionaries was transformed by many enslaved persons into an African spirit. African religion did not disappear when it came in contact with Christianity. Christian saints and spirits were baptized into African culture and religion.

Black churches became communities of faith bound together by their histories of suffering and slavery in the Caribbean and the United States. The focal point of this religious story was, at first, African churches formed by Africa's children who survived the Middle Passage and hammered out a faith and theology in the crucible between Africa and Jesus. Although many of these churches took on the "veneer of Christianity" they were at heart African churches. There were several marks of an African church:

1. The embrace of African worldviews informed by the question, "where do you stand in relation to Africa?"
2. Highlighting of the continuous interaction between the physical and spiritual worlds, noting the ways in which the sacred and secular are fused together.
3. An openness and embrace of the *novum* in history in the quest for survival and liberation. There was a praxiological focus on liberation with an understanding that spirit provided the basis of authority often through the bodies of believers.
4. Acknowledgment of evil forces in the world and the need to be protected from evil through the aegis of ancestors and the ministry of a medicine man/woman or priest. The plantation was often seen as site for evil.
5. The importance of dance, "redemption songs," as instruments of liberation.
6. Recognition that in these Black churches the spirit often takes over the bodies of believers. To be possessed by the spirit often means that one's body becomes an altar and a medium through which the spirit communicates. This is illustrated in Rastafari, Revivalism, Vodou, and Obeah.

While missionaries emphasized the memorizing of the Lord's Prayer, the Ten Commandments, and passages in the Bible that emphasized submissiveness and subordination, the main reason many enslaved persons attended a mission church had to do with reasons similar to those of Grandma Mum. They loved singing, dancing, and spirit possession; later it had to do with drumming and Black preaching. Black people often had their own agenda which was very different from that of missionaries. One agenda item of enslaved persons was to use religion, African or Christian, or a combination as a tool for dismantling the shackles of slavery. They reinterpreted Christian symbols and myths in an African frame of reference without losing the essentials of their native beliefs. An important aspect of African genius was the ability to maintain the integrity of their religious worldviews while at the same time they were open to the new that the sociological and theological environment suggested. Africans were not locked into an either-or frame of reference; their way of life and approach to the life and death issues that slavery engendered made them practice "a both and" approach to problem solving. This was why—and still is the case in Black churches whether in the Caribbean islands or on the American mainland—there is a firm commitment to combine Africa and Jesus. It is the beginning of Creolization—the melding of African and Christian worldviews. This is illustrated in the practice of Vodou in Haiti or in Louisiana, where Catholic saints provide a covering for African deities. This is also the case of Obeah in Jamaica where a cross is worn as charm and the Bible is used as a source of authority.

Methodology

Scholars as diverse as W.E.B. Du Bois, Carter G. Woodson, Gayraud Wilmore, Lewin Williams, Eric Williams, and Albert Raboteau attest to this turn to Black churches by Africa's children and the life they lived in the crucible between enculturation and acculturation—life lived in the tension between the memory of Africa and the promise that Jesus represents. There are two points of distinction between the approach of these scholars and the one this project advocates. While these scholars describe the turn to religion by Africa's children in the Caribbean and the United States, their analysis is primarily intraregional highlighting an articulation and exposition of Black churches in each region. This approach does not push beyond the nation/state framework. Consequently, this project with its comparative-historical emphasis presses beyond the nation/state paradigm and raises intercultural and interregional questions with implications for gender, race, and class in the understanding and meaning of Black churches on either side of the Atlantic. This comparative-historical analysis opens up the possibility of rethinking the language and grammar of how Black churches have been understood in the Americas and extends the notion of church beyond the United States. The conversation among Africans concerning their memory of Africa and their interpretation of Jesus juxtaposes Africa and Europe in a search for fresh models of church that place its stamp on the making of a Black Christianity. The forging of a Black Christianity from sources African and European presses the question of the meaning of Black churches when people of African descent are culturally and politically in the majority. And the converse is pertinent. What is the meaning of Black churches when people of African descent are a cultural and political minority?

This means that the focus of this book is not a chronological accounting of historical periods as they relate to Black churches, but the choosing of decisive moments in history in which these churches were established and served as agencies of freedom. This study also notes ways in which these churches resisted cultural patterns of oppression and adapted to historical circumstance in the quest for survival and liberation.

This study notes that the Black religious experience began south of the border in the Caribbean. Both the historical priority and the cultural and political majority of enslaved persons in the Caribbean allow the Caribbean experience to frame much of the discussion and the understanding of Black churches that emerged on both sides of the Atlantic. The reader is reminded that the Black experience did not originate in slavery but has its genesis in Africa. Chapter 1 begins with Africa's children's experience of migration, displacement, and resistance. The story of slavery in the New World documents the involuntary displacement of about 12 million Africans who were stolen from their homeland and taken to the Americas to forced labor, often in shackles, on plantations in which the White master or overseer dictated ultimate decisions concerning life and death. The question of identity was always central. It was their African-ness and the experience of migration through the Middle Passage that provided a hermeneutic of resistance in a strange land a "long ways from home." Their presence in the New World exposed Africans to Christian teaching of Jesus as Christianity was often the only religion allowed on plantations. What is of interest is that Africans did not reject the religion of their oppressors but were willing to consider it, if it eventuated in their survival and liberation.

Chapter 2 highlights African roots and begins to translate that background into the New World context, and explains ways in which the memory of Africa informs the culture of Black churches. A lively discussion ensues among African theologians concerning creation stories, providence and sin, and an emergent theology of spirits. Both Kwesi Dickson and John Mbiti explore African views of time, freedom, and destiny. It is noted that both enemies and friends are under the protection of God and no harm may befall one without the will of the supreme deity. One is often heard to pray, "God remove from his back. That is, stop protecting him." We examine Africa's role in the formation of a Black ecclesiology. Chapter 3 points to the reality of the Black religious experience which began south of the border. It points to the priority of the Caribbean experience historically as we are informed that slavery began in the Caribbean as early as 1502 and the Caribbean experience was far-reaching in shaping the Black religious experience in the United States.[1] Throughout this book particular mention will be made of the role of Haiti as the first Black independent republic in the New World liberated by enslaved persons and its importance as a symbol of freedom for oppressed Black people. W.E.B. Du Bois underscores the centrality and priority of the Caribbean experience: "American Negroes, to a much larger extent than they realize, are not only blood relatives to the West Indians but under deep obligations to them for many things. For instance, without the Haitian Revolt, there would have been no emancipation in America as early as 1863. I, myself, am of West Indian descent and am proud of the fact."[2]

Chapter 4 examines the phenomenon of the plantation church as we note Dr. Du Bois's claim that the new which confronted enslaved people in the

Americas was the reality of the plantation in which Africans had to make adjustments as this was a context in which the rule of the master was supreme. It is in this chapter that we see Africans in the New World tapping into their understanding of good and evil in the formulation of a creolized religion. One of the evils of existence on the plantations was that Africans were not introduced to any concept of voluntary labor. Work was enforced and the circumstances of slavery made work demeaning. Combined with this was the lack of respect accorded women on plantations. The plantation is examined as a framework for oppression and a site of resistance and liberation engendered by Black churches. We note the exercise of the power of the master class in seeking to obliterate the memory of Africa, and enslaved persons used slave religion to carve out Black sacred spaces of survival and liberation.

In Chapter 5, The Making of the Black World, Black churches emerge as centers of resistance as enslaved persons confronted a world organized with their demise and destruction in mind. These churches became means and sources of utilizing supernatural forces and places where the spirit would lead the worshippers in strategies of resistance to break the power of oppression. Black churches served as sites of resistance where plans for the over throw of slavery were often conceptualized and executed. The leadership of Toussaint L'Ouverture, Gabriel Prosser, Denmark Vesey, and Nat Turner are examined. Black churches came to the fore as centers of a pragmatic theology. The goals were freedom and winning the wars of dehumanization and desacralization against human beings made in the image of God. Leaders of Black churches on both sides of the Atlantic discovered that the God of their ancestors was the God of the Bible and this gave them a new confidence to read and interpret the Bible for themselves. They began to embrace the Bible as a resource for winning the war against dehumanization and an important tool in dismantling the house of slavery which was artfully built by the slave master. Chapter 6 pulls the themes and threads together in asking for the meaning of the Black religious experience as it looks toward the creolization of Black churches, noting that this experience is more than an examination of religious practices and rituals; it is the search for the meaning of what it takes to be human in a context of displacement and epistemic violence. The creolization of Black churches carved out in the crucible between Africa and Jesus is highlighted as one of the lasting contributions of Black churches.

When it is remembered that Africa's children came to the New World in large numbers during the sixteenth century through the transatlantic slave trade and settled in the Caribbean over a hundred years prior to the first Africans landing in Jamestown, Virginia, in 1619, it is surprising that so little work has been done to document the interaction between these peoples. It is widely known that because slavery was the vehicle that brought African peoples to the New World, their history has been one of displacement and dislocation. What is not equally known is the nature of the religious experience that created Black sacred spaces and provided an alternative experience against the cruel world of slavery on both sides of the Atlantic. Black churches created a culture of resistance as Denmark Vesey in North Carolina and Nat Turner in Virginia facilitated a culture of resistance in the 1830s. In many of the colonies, Nanny and Sam Sharp in Jamaica, Cuffy in Guyana, and Morales in Cuba organized uprisings. The culture of resistance was dramatized in the island of Haiti, the largest sugar plantation in the Caribbean, when Toussaint L'Ouverture, a slave, led the resistance under the slogan of the French revolution, "Liberty, Equality and Fraternity." Haitians rebelled for freedom and Haiti became an independent republic in 1804.

This manuscript investigates the role of Black churches, which were at first African rather than Christian churches, in creating a culture of resistance in search of the virtues of freedom, equality, and humanity. We begin with stories of migration, displacement, and resistance.

I

Migration, Displacement, Resistance

THIS PROJECT IS a comparative analysis and exposition of Black churches in the Caribbean and the United States. My own reality in churches in these regions provides the impetus for this investigation. I was born and baptized in a church founded by the African American George Liele who after serving churches in Savannah, Georgia, in 1782, migrated to Jamaica, West Indies, and began the Ethiopian Baptist Church in the capital city, Kingston. The Ethiopian Baptist Church became the parent of several churches throughout the island and the region. This church created Black sacred space for oppressed people in their search for empowerment and dignity in the face of forces that sought to tear the self apart.

As a young man I attended theological seminary in Jamaica and became a minister and teacher in this church following in the footsteps of my father. It seemed to me, then, that if I were to serve the Caribbean in a way that put the liberative agenda of the gospel in conversation with a society that was harsh for most of its citizens, then to be situated within the church was most propitious. The church in the Caribbean has had a paradoxical relationship to society. At times the church used the Bible to challenge the assumptions on which "slaveocracy" thrived and at other times the church and the Bible became instruments of oppression. Often the God presented by the church was not invested in the lives of ordinary people and therefore not in the alleviation of the harsh suffering and grinding poverty that faced these people. Especially from the perspective of the missionaries who often sought to do the bidding of the planter class, the Bible was presented through the cultural lens of people in power. This seemed to be the case when the Baptist Church in Great Britain sent out instructions to its missionaries in Jamaica.:

> You are going to people in a state of slavery and require to beware lest your feelings should lead you to say or do anything inconsistent with Christian duty. Most of the servants whom the Apostle Paul addressed

in his epistles to the churches were slaves, and he exhorts them to be obedient to their masters in singleness of heart, fearing God, and this not only to the good and Gentile.[1]

This was also true of instructions given to missionaries in the Wesleyan Methodist and Moravian churches. Consistent with notions of Christian duty in the colonial Caribbean was the upholding of the institution of slavery.

This also meant honoring the Eurocentric hermeneutics that supported the system of oppression for Black and poor people. The truth is that the hermeneutics the foreign agencies advocated represented a certain social class that was certainly not neutral in biblical interpretation. It represented an investment in the colonial economic system. The interpretation the Scriptures advocated was on the side of the planter class and against the masses of poor people. In this setting and with this approach to the Scriptures, which did not recognize the Eurocentric ideological captivity of the Scriptures to the brokers of power, the Bible was able to liberate neither the oppressor class nor the oppressed. The Bible was read in a way that affirmed the blindness and insensitivity of the church to the suffering masses. Help had to come from outside the mainline churches, as oppressed people took matters in their own hands by interpreting the Christianity handed to them by missionaries and mainline churches from an African frame of reference. Black people created their own understanding of church and saw God through their own lens. In many ways George Liele, who began the tradition in the Caribbean of relating the church to Africa gave oppressed people permission to relate Christianity to African religious practices and to make Africa the point of departure for their understanding of church. This way of viewing one's context and world is certainly not unique to the Caribbean, but it is true throughout the African Diaspora. The truth seems to be that in their capture and journey through the Middle Passage to plantations throughout the American colonies enslaved persons lost vital aspects of their religion that were compensated for in grafting Christian tenets to their African beliefs. Through memory, individual and collective, they were able to fill in the gaps as they embraced elements of the Christian faith. This is evident in the study of Vodou, in Haiti and Louisiana, where Catholic saints are given African names; in the practice of Santeria, in Cuba; and with the Shouter Baptists, in Trinidad, where ancestors and deities are given African names. In these contexts there is an African worldview and ethos that informs and suffuses religion in European colonies in the New World. This worldview informs and instructs religion, art, music, and the people's way of life.

Unlike Africa's children who were brought to the New World in chains against their will to work on plantations, I, along with thousands of other residents from the Caribbean, migrated to the United States to further my education and to work as an immigrant in the twentieth century. In a profound sense, the United States is a land of immigrants. Unlike Africa's children who were brought involuntarily to the Caribbean and American colonies over three centuries, from the sixteenth through the nineteenth, those of us who came to the United States in the twentieth century in search of education and jobs did not come in chains, nor were we coerced: we came voluntarily. Our journey across the Atlantic was unlike those who traveled the Middle Passage and in the process had their humanity compromised as they were regarded and treated as chattel by their captors and owners. In their article, "The Middle Passage," Malcolm Cowley and Daniel P. Mannix give a vivid description of the journey of human cargo across the Atlantic to the New World by Africa's children, who became architects and founders of the Black church.

> As soon as an assortment of naked slaves was carried aboard a Guinea-man, the men were shackled two by two, the right wrist and ankle of one to the left wrist and ankle of another; then they were sent below. The women—usually regarded as fair prey for the sailors—were allowed to wander by day almost anywhere on the vessel, though they spent the night between decks, in a space portioned off from that of the men. All the slaves were forced to sleep without covering on bare wooden floors. . . . In a stormy passage the skin over their elbows might be worn away to the bare bones. . . . "It is pitiful, . . . to see how they crowd those poor wretches, six hundred and fifty or seven hundred in a ship, the men standing in the hold ty'd to stakes, the women between decks and those that are with child in the great cabin and the children in the steeridge which in that hot climate occasions an intolerable stench."[2]

The Black church was formed through the traffic across the Atlantic of Africa's children packed like sardines and treated as human cargo. It was for all intents and purposes a chattel church. In a book on Black churches, it is imperative to note that Christians were leaders in the traffic of Africa's children across the Atlantic for sale and work as beasts of burden on plantations in the New World. Many scholars consider it something of a mystery that Africa's children would turn to the religion of their oppressors and seek the favor of the gods of their oppressor in their search for survival and liberation. Much of this book seeks an answer to this mystery and an exposition of the ways in which Africa's children whether in the Caribbean or in the American colonies merged African and Christian worldviews in the elaboration and explication of their faith. How has the religion of the oppressed and this chattel church served as source and resource of empowerment in a context of epistemic violence? How could enslaved persons in European colonies speak of God during and after slavery, and why did they speak of God? How did these people deal with the absence and presence of the God of their ancestors?

I discovered early that the histories of African peoples of the United States and the Caribbean are intertwined through the experience of the Middle Passage and their subsequent suffering in the New World. The Black community on both sides of the Atlantic is marked by a history of enslavement and oppression. It is widely agreed that enslaved persons were often taken to the Caribbean prior to their voyage to the United States, and this opened up a new history in which the presence of Africans in the New World created an African Diaspora. There was a tension between their existence here in the New World and there in Africa, their home of origin. *Here* in the New World they longed for *there*, their home, Africa—the forests, the ancestors, family, gods, and culture. In a profound sense, the traffic between the Caribbean and the United States mirrored in a small way the painful distance for enslaved Africans who were brought to the New World in shackles and forced to create a new existence "a long ways from home." For the vast majority of Africans, unfortunately, the journey to the New World as human cargo was one way. Very few were able to return home to Africa, and so slaves would sing of feeling "like a motherless child a long ways from home." Or again they would sing of not being able to hear anyone pray and for others the drums were silenced. The inability of many Africans to return to Africa, the silencing of the drums, and the rendering illegal their African religious practices point to the eventual loss of language and much of the culture of Africans in the New World. This loss of language illustrates the profundity of the oppression of Africans in the New World and their constant search for identity. A sense of rejection confronted Black people at every level, even in the Christian church, where they were often humiliated, as they would be required to sit in the balcony or on pews painted black at the back of the sanctuary. This humiliation and rejection made them readily identify with Jesus the Christ who they understood to be rejected by his own people and in the end suffered crucifixion at their hands. As enslaved persons identified with the suffering and rejection of Jesus they would sing: "Were you there when they crucified my Lord, Were you there when they crucified my Lord, Sometimes it causes me to tremble, tremble, Sometimes it causes me to tremble."

As they were unable to return to Africa, it was important for them to maintain contact interregionally, as we will see in the search for an answer to slavery and the confidence that the medicine man and priest would not lose their liberative and healing powers in this new setting. Because Africans were unable to return to the homeland, the search for community took Africans in the New World to Jamaica, Trinidad, Haiti, the Bahamas, Canada, and from these places to the American colonies in search of community with each other. In a profound sense, even the formation of the chattel church was itself an expression of the search for community, an attempt by enslaved persons to acquire equilibrium in a culture of displacement and dislocation.

This interrelationship between the Caribbean and the United States finds expression in a request by the Free Methodists of Haiti who needed help from the African Methodist Church under the leadership of Richard Allen. "Because the Wesleyans refused to ordain native Haitians, the Free Methodists were formed in Haiti. The Episcopalians started under Reverend, later Bishop J. C. Holly who led 111 persons from New Haven, Connecticut, in May 1871; they were given lands about 3 miles from Port-au-Prince at Drouilland."[3] Bishop R.R. Wright Jr. points out that as early as 1823 African Americans, including Baptists, Seventh-day Adventists, Pentecostals, and members of the Church of God in Christ churches, traveled to the Caribbean to participate in the development of that region.

It should not be surprising then that President Boyer of Haiti "sought to induce a large number of African-Americans to come to Haiti, especially to work on farms. He promised to each a certain allotment of land, and encouraged them to make Haiti their permanent home and to become citizens."[4]

President Boyer sought the cooperation of the African American church and wrote to the founder of the African Methodist Episcopal Church, Bishop Richard Allen, with his request. In reply Bishop Allen stated:

To his Excellency Jean Pierre Boyer, President of the Republic of Haiti
    Port-au-Prince, Haiti
    August 23, 1823
    Sir
    It is with deep sentiments and the most ardent respect of gratitude that I am addressing you the following lines. My heart burns affectionately in acknowledging the kind offer you have made to these poor oppressed people here in the United States, by offering them an asylum where they can enjoy liberty and equality. In spite of great opposition, I invited people to assemble in my church (Bethel) and explained to them your propositions. I found that they were willing to

accept them. I then prepared a book to inscribe the names of those who were willing to embark for your island. I have on my list over 500 names ready to embark as soon as the necessary provisions can be made, plus those who have already embarked. . . . I have no doubt soon there will be thousands who are willing to come to your country in spite of the efforts of the white inhabitants who are trying to stop them. . . .

> With sentiments of the greatest respect
> Very truly yours
> Richard Allen[5]

Life Together as Shipmates

Although Africans in the diaspora could not return to Africa in large numbers, they were able to facilitate cooperation with each other, no doubt, because they had similar dreams of liberation, economic justice, and empowerment in a strange and different setting. In the language of Psalm 137 they had to "sing the Lord's song in a strange land." Although they hailed from different tribes and regions, there were many aspects of African culture that were universal—for example, respect for the dead and the place of the ancestors in the daily affairs of the community along with the reality that the Supreme Being was not directly involved in the daily activities of life. The main location of the Supreme Being was outside of this world. The will of the Supreme Deity was made clear through his assistants, the ancestors and lesser deities. This was one reason that made Christianity readily accessible to Africans; they were able to see Jesus, the Holy Spirit, saints, and angels as emissaries of the High God who were assigned to carry out His will. There were several points of contact to serve as a bridge for community: the importance of music, dance, religion, prayer, and belief in a world suffused by spirit power. There are scholars who mention that an added reality was the experience of being a "shipmate" across the Atlantic. This experience of being shackled together and squeezed into the same cramped space, as they traveled across the Atlantic shackled to each other, formed a bond among Africans who were chained to each other. This was especially the case among members of the same sex as men and women were separated on the voyage. Africans who recognized each other on this common journey referred to each other as shipmate. In their book, *The Birth of African-American Culture*, Sidney W. Mintz and Richard Price attribute this bonding among shipmates as the beginning of African American culture and the commitment to community among persons of various tribes and ethnicities. According to Mintz and Price, the Middle Passage was not merely a negative experience, as enslaved persons were not passive in that context. In the face of dehumanization and humiliation they reached out to each other and formed a social bonding and network that may be traced in contexts as different as Trinidad, Suriname, Jamaica, and the United States. "The bond between shipmates, those who shared passage on the same slaver, is the most striking example. In widely scattered parts of Afro-America, the 'shipmate' relationship became a major principle of social organization and continued for decades and even centuries to shape ongoing social relations."[6] These scholars point out that in Jamaica, the term "shipmate" was transposed to "brother" or "sister" and was regarded as the most affectionate and dearest term. "So strong were the bonds between shipmates that sexual intercourse between them, . . . was considered incestuous."[7] Shipmates regularly regarded each other's children as their own and the children in turn referred to their parents' shipmates as "Uncle" or "Aunt." "In Suriname, . . . the equivalent term "sippi" was at first used between people who had actually shared the experience of transport in a single vessel; later, it began to be used between two slaves who belonged to a single plantation, preserving the essential notion of fellow sufferers who have a special bond."[8] Today throughout the Caribbean the term is used between persons who find themselves in similar circumstances of misfortune. This notion of "shipmates" signals the importance of Black faith among Africa's children forging their own identity. When it is remembered that slave ships often docked in the Caribbean and provided an occasion for slaves to be acculturated in the Caribbean prior to their journey and introduction to plantation life in the colonies on the American mainland, the term "shipmates" (brothers and sisters) is both symbolically and literally true in relation to Afro-Caribbean and African American people.

As brothers and sisters, Afro-Caribbeans and African Americans share a common history of oppression and a common goal of liberation. Further, the basic fact of our existence is poverty, which plagues the majority of Black folks whether in the Caribbean or in the United States. What is especially hurtful for brothers and sisters in the United States is that they live in the midst of an economy of abundance, yet their unemployment rates are twice that of White people. Martin Luther King Jr. described the plight of African Americans as constituting "an island of poverty in an ocean of plenty." For Black people in both the Caribbean and the American mainland, poverty has become the central problem in the twenty-first century as we have witnessed record numbers of home foreclosures and jobs lost in the first couple of years of President Obama's administration. With the advent of the first African American president, there was widespread hope both in the Caribbean and in the United States that the cycle of poverty and hopelessness that has been emblematic of the style of life of the majority of Black citizens under previous administrations would be alleviated. But the redistribution of resources and goods and opportunities for which oppressed people prayed has not materialized. Granted, the Black church in the twenty-first century, whether in the Caribbean or in the United States, is certainly not a chattel church as was the case from the sixteenth through the nineteenth centuries. It remains, however, the church of the poor. It remains the church of those who live on the margins of society. In Black churches in the United States it is not unusual to hear people pray of their desire to make the American dream their own. They ask: "When will my miracle happen?" "Why is my miracle taking so long?" Because of the reality of cable television, these prayers and worship services are piped into Caribbean homes, and people there also view the church as an escape hatch and God as the provider of their material needs. Perhaps one way forward is the engendering of a spirit of community, in which each views the other as shipmate or has an understanding of each as brother or sister. This may be one way for the empowerment of the church-community. C. Eric Lincoln puts the issue in perspective for us: "The black Christians in white churches were cramped by their style and stifled by the requirements of racial conformity. Though they were finally in 'church,' it was demonstrably not 'their' church, a communication that spoke pointedly and consistently through the sermons, the prayers, the spiritual suppression, and the absence of fellowship. In the white churches the Africans were offered a God who had cursed them and ordained their travail and debasement in perpetuity. . . . Hence, it was inevitable that black Christians would heed the call to 'come ye out from among them.' "[9] The sentiments expressed by Lincoln find credence both in the Caribbean and in the United States, where in many mainline churches the people who exercise power, whether in terms of polity or finances, are not among the Black poor. This certainly cuts across the notion of shipmates, as realities of class and gender bracket this notion of brothers and sisters seeking to build communities of liberation and empowerment.

The Black person in the United States has discovered as we in the Caribbean did a long time ago that our poverty is not due to our indolence or lack of creativity; the truth is that our poverty is contrived. There is a history to colonialism, exploitation, and domination. The truth is that we have been made poor. Our poverty is a consequence of the relationship of the "colonizer and the colonized." Our poverty was engendered by the master-slave relationship that characterized the lives of enslaved Black people in the Caribbean and the United States for over 300 years. The cycle of dependence and imitation needs to be broken, and one of the spaces where this was attempted with relative success was in the Black church, even if for some time it was a chattel church. Evils done to Black people in the public sector sometimes seem insurmountable. For example, a fixture of plantation life was the havoc wreaked on the Black community in the attempt to destroy the family. When we look at the plight of the Black male, whether in the Caribbean or in the American colonies on the mainland, we see a history in which the oppressor provided for the Black man's family, protected his family, and found ways, too numerous to mention, to emasculate him. The Black man was reduced to being a boy as he internalized a negative self-image of his oppressor. The protracted oppression made Black people turn on each other as enemies rather than to each other as shipmates. The situation was even worse for the Black woman. She was an object of frequent rape, violence, and abuse by the master. Often her family was sold away from her and she too had to work in fields from sun up until sun down. She too was brutally flogged by the master, sometimes while pregnant. As we will note when we review the history of oppression, the church, whether free or chattel, was often conflicted. There were times in the chattel church in the Caribbean and the United States, members, and sometimes preachers, in the church led rebellions in an attempt to initiate change. But most of the time the church faithfully walked alongside the oppressed and went along with the system.

Framing the Question for Liberation

I would like to turn to the relationship of the Christian church with Indians in the Caribbean and the American mainland noting that the relationship of Europeans with oppressed peoples in the Americas began not with Africans but with Indians.

In his *The Devastation of the Indies,* Bartolome de Las Casas raised a number of pertinent questions that may help us frame our investigation of the encounter between European and Amerindians and people of African descent. The first priest to be ordained in the New World, Las Casas raises these questions of the church, the Roman Catholic Church, not only to make the case of liberation for the Indians and generations of oppressed people of African descent but as a hermeneutic of liberation within the church itself. He asks, should Indians have the same rights as Euro-Americans? Further, do Indians have intrinsic rights to their land and culture? How has the Christian gospel addressed non-Western people and regarded their cultures? To what extent did the eradication of non-Western populations and culture compromise the Christian gospel?[10]

To ponder these questions from the vantage point of the twenty-first century, the answers seem rather obvious; but when looked at in the context of their original framework in the sixteenth century, when non-Western peoples were seen as ignorant and uncivilized, the questions force Christians to acknowledge the existence of the other, and have within them a shaming effect. One of the problems with the first question is that the priest acknowledges that the very humanity of the Indian was in question, and by implication the humanity of the European Christian. The intent of the first question—is the Indian a human being in the same way as the European—posits the European as the standard of humanity. It is clear from the question posed that the cleric takes sides with the European against the oppressed Indian. Even in the twenty-first century this is still the case for many Christians who privilege the European over against people of color. In the text, Las Casas addressed his fellow Spaniards as Christians; he presupposed a *respublica christiana*. Much of European civilization was understood as rooted in the Christian religion. There was a melding and fusing of Christianity with European culture. To be Western and European was at the same time to be Christian, and the corollary was that to be non-Western was to be heathen or infidel. Many Europeans at the time would answer that Indians and certainly later Africans could not have the same rights as Euro-Americans because they were neither Christians nor Western. The implication was that if they became Christian their status would change and this was tested later, especially by enslaved Africans who converted to Christianity in large numbers only to discover that they were still regarded as inferior. This question led to another: if Indians and Euro-Americans do not have the same rights, granted the cultural and ideological gap between them, what can be done to change the equation? Later this proved to be a central question in the emergence of the chattel church. How may this church move from the status of chattel to human? Of course, the master class was afraid of dealing forthrightly with this question, and the chief way in which it was answered later was that the change of status from heathen to Christian or infidel to Christian did not change the ontological status of the enslaved in relation to God or master. There were implications for freedom hidden in the question. What many in the master class failed to understand was that the freeing of the other, Indian or African, also included the freedom of the master. To abolish the master-slave relationship would free both enslaved and enslaver. Bartolome de Las Casas was not at this time advocating the overthrow of the system of oppression. He was advocating more humane treatment for the Indians within the system of slavery. When it is remembered that Las Casas first entered the Caribbean as a twenty-eight-year-old missionary representing the Spanish state and church, it is remarkable that he emerged as the protector of the Indians. In an attempt to understand the church and its relationship to First Americans, we look further at another question posed by the protector of the Indians: how has the Christian gospel addressed non-Western peoples and their culture? The question was addressed to the American scene and focused specifically on First Americans. The immediate context was Hispaniola where Indians were forced to work in the fields and in mines, not for their own benefit but for that of their oppressors. "Their life which had been so happy had become toilsome and sad, and in something approaching despair they struggled to release themselves. But neither their own efforts nor Isabella's instructions had any lasting effect. They had become, and they continued to be, slaves."[11]

The Spanish state instituted a system known as *repartimiento*, the practice of giving Indians to colonizers who were referred to as *encomenderos*. This system of *repartimiento* meant that Indians did not belong to individuals but to the state and were assigned by the governor to masters he thought best for the Indians. The task of the colonizer was to Christianize and civilize the Indians in an attempt to domesticate them. The main responsibility of making Indians Christian was a task which the church embraced. In a profound sense we could say that perhaps the first missionary was Columbus, who came to the West Indies with the blessing of crown and church and it was his hope to bring the peoples of these new lands not only within the pale of the state but within the purview of the church."Everything worked against the Indians. At the outset the Spaniards had not been consciously brutal; they were too few in numbers to run risks. . . . Columbus finding volunteers for the colony difficult to recruit, had looked to Spanish jails for fresh blood. The criminals transported to Hispaniola at his suggestion, besides providing a source of continual disaffection, carried out with them a grudge against society which they vented on the Indians. . . . The Indians died off like flies. It is said that the native population of Hispaniola fell in the first fifteen years of Spanish occupation from one million to sixty thousand inhabitants."[12]

As early as 1514 Las Casas began to preach publicly against the injustice of the entire structure of the *encomiendia*. He gave up his own slaves and suggested that a change of heart was required for people who exercised power over the first Americans. "He ceaselessly denounced the officials who oversaw Spain's American outposts and who slaughtered and enslaved thousands of natives for their own financial benefits."[13] Another priest who spoke out against the cruelty meted out to the Indians by the Spaniards was Father Antonio Montesino. Speaking from John 1:23 he said his fellow countrymen were committing a mortal sin against the Indians "because they kept the Indians in such a state of cruel and horrible servitude, violating every right and law, oppressing and exploiting them without feeding them or treating their illnesses caused by excessive and forced labor, leaving them to die or killing them to maintain the daily intake of gold."[14] Shortly after 1508 the islands of Puerto Rico, Jamaica, and Cuba were captured by Spain and the *encomiendia* system was introduced in these countries. King Fernando in a letter written June 6, 1511, expressed his desire and hope that the abuses of the *encomiendia* system experienced in Hispaniola would not be repeated in Jamaica. The king observed that if Catholic education were taught to the indigenous peoples there would be great improvement.[15]

Both Antonio Montesino and Las Casas, who became close friends, worked assiduously for the amelioration of the plight of the Indians. In 1516 Las Casas was appointed procurator and protector of all Indians by Francisco Cardinal Jimenez de Cisneroa. Great progress was made in Indian communities with churches, schools, and hospitals, and the introduction of livestock into their communities. "Thus, the priority should have been to save their lives, even without the Indians being baptized, since this would have been better than to leave them in the *encomiendas,* where they probably would have been baptized but would have died quickly. The *encomienda* system should therefore have been abolished and the capture of Indian as slaves prohibited in the Bahamas, the Lesser Antilles and on the Venezuelan coast."[16]

But this dream was too ambitious to be true. In 1518 when Rodrigo de Figuero was appointed governor, *Juez supreme de las Indians,*[17] a study he commissioned, acknowledged that the mission to the Indians was unsuccessful. One of the obstacles that were not surmounted was the inability of the colonists to learn the native languages of the Indians. "In the end, after concluding his investigation on 5 November 1519, Figueroa authorized the enslavement of Carib tribes in the region and in December gave concessions to slave traders to include Arawak tribes."[18] One of the misperceptions of Europeans was that Indians in the Caribbean were passive and spineless people. It is instructive that Governor Figueroa gave orders for the enslavement of the Caribs who were the fiercest among the Indians. To show the extent of his determination to oppress the Indians he included the peaceful and passive Arawaks. The Indians along the coast of Venezuela rebelled and burned the convents of Cumani and Chiribichi and killed two Dominicans. Later that year, the Indians launched a surprise attack on Cumani, killing five persons.[19]

These rebellions by the Indians coupled with the passion of the Spaniards to dominate the region, made Las Casas's dream of peaceful coexistence between Indians and colonists impossible. The dilemma that Las Casas faced was the reality that although the Catholic Church proffered a theology that advocated respect for the dignity of Indian people and the notion that they too were made in the image of God, there was no attempt by the church to change the system of slavery. Lewin Williams, in his *Caribbean Theology*, points out that the sympathies of the church were no match for the cruelty of the colonial power.

> Colonial power had begun its work of destruction and despite all the plunder and death prompted by colonial greed, the church did not disclaim its partnership with the state. Later when, because of the demise of the Indians, the decision was taken to import Africans to the New World to take up where the Indians had left off . . . the missionary church gave more than its sanction.[20]

About fifty years after the conquest of the Indian lands in the Caribbean, the Indians as a people were almost extinct. Many Indians pointed out that although the Catholic Church failed to prevail against the colonial powers through its missionaries, the church was often an advocate on their behalf. "In the meanwhile, the number of Indians continued to decrease in La Espanola. Yet in 1577, it was confirmed that some of them were still alive. . . . At the beginning of the seventeenth century, the extinction of the original population of the island was final. . . . The same happened in Puerto Rico. On 11 March 1549, Bishop Bastidas wrote that there were less than 50 native Indians and that he was paying special attention to them."[21] There is no doubt that the Catholic Church tried to minister, and through advocacy, sought to soften the plight of the Indian people under Imperial domination. At a conference presided over by Bishop Angulo in Santo Domingo which aimed at providing regulations for Christian work among the Indians the following were approved:

(a) For adults to receive the sacrament of baptism they had to know "Our father," "Hail Mary," "the Creed" and the "ten commandments"; they were also required to believe in the effectiveness of baptism and be willing to live a life free from sin.

(b) Indians were also obliged to receive the sacrament of confession and the Holy Eucharist once per year. The priest was required to instruct them in the meaning of these sacraments. Holy Communion was also to be given to the sick.

(c) The clergy was expected to be familiar with the marriage practices of the Indians. The church observed that because their marriages were monogamous they had the sanction of divine right. Further, clergy were expected to be kind and courteous to the Indians. In addition to religious duties they also had educational and cultural duties through the use of Christian doctrine. Priests were required to teach children to read and write in Spanish and instruct Indians to order their lives in a civilized way. "As in other Spanish-American synods, the provincial council of Santo Domingo was also in favor of setting up Indian communities, since it was thought that this measure meant more favorable conditions for Christian civilization."[22]

The Introduction of Africans as Slaves in the New World

While it is true that Las Casas was not the first to advocate the importation of Africans as slaves in the Caribbean, it is rather unfortunate that due to his frustration of how cruelly Indians were treated by fellow Christians and in many instances exterminated, "in 1517 and in 1531 Las Casas advocated this importation 'in exchange for Indian freedom,' believing that Africans were more able to survive heavy labor."[23] Las Casas who had lived in the Caribbean since 1502, saw firsthand the cruelty meted out to the Indians by his fellow Spanish compatriots and Christians. He made their protection and advocacy his life's mission but his pleadings on their behalf were complicated by the fact that he also accepted land and slaves under the Spanish system of *repartimientos*, which made him as Christian and colonist, responsible for the civilizing, Christianizing, and humanizing of the Indians. Like other colonists, he sent them to the mines to seek gold to make a quick profit. While he was an example in his personal relationship with the Indians, he did not in the first twelve years question or condemn the structure and the economic system of slavery. As a first step he pleaded with the governor on behalf of the Indians and after pointing out the cruelty of the system relinquished his own slaves. In 1515 he traveled to Spain and in subsequent years pleaded for an amelioration of the system that was killing off the Indians. Not meeting with success in his proposals in 1517 he suggested the importation of Africans to the authorities in Spain. He argued that Africans were more suited to plantation work and that one African would be able to do the work of four Indians. "When Las Casas suggested that each Spanish resident in Hispaniola should be allowed to import a small number of Negro slaves for himself, Charles V saw much virtue in the suggestion, and promptly bestowed on one of his Flemish favorites a patent to supply the four Spanish settlements of Hispaniola, Cuba, Jamaica and Puerto Rico with four thousand Negroes annually."[24] The eighteenth-century historian Bryan Edwards, in *The History, Civil and Commercial, of the British Colonies in the West Indies*, wonders how a church leader could will the enslavement of one race of people while advocating the release from slavery of another. He writes:

> The concurrence of the emperor to this measure was obtained at the solicitation of Bartholomew de Las Casas, Bishop of Chiapa, the celebrated protector of the Indians; and the conduct of this great prelate on that occasion has been the subject of much censure. . . . While he contended . . . for the liberty of the people born in one quarter of the globe, he labored to enslave the inhabitants of another region and in the warmth and zeal to save the Americans from the yoke, pronounced it to be lawful and expedient to impose one, still heavier, upon the Africans.[25]

Earlier we noted a question posed by the actions of Bartolome de Las Casas, "How has the Christian gospel addressed non-Western peoples and cultures"? Edwards answers the question in relation to the action of Las Casas, who, in pleading for the release of First Americans from the degradation of slavery at the same time advocates the enslavement of Africans. It is true that in his later book *The History of the Indies* Las Casas expresses his deep regret and repentance for proposing the continued enslavement of African people.

However, the action of this prelate of the church places Black people and the church irrevocably together in the New World. The church's action makes it responsible for the presence of Black people in the Americas, their abuse, and their struggle for freedom and dignity.

Our brief overview of the Catholic Church's care for the well-being of First Americans indicates that there was sensitivity among the clergy concerning the plight of the Indians. Las Casas made advocacy on their behalf his life's work. A cursory review of the church's actions on behalf of Africans indicates that there was less sensitivity. "It was not by chance that the municipal council of Santo Domingo, on 1 December 1531, accused the bishop of negligence in his religious attention to the Blacks."[26] Synods in Puerto Rico in 1645 and in Cuba in 1680 stated that it was most difficult to improve the deficiencies of the Christian education of African slaves. The synods "managed to promote certain improvements while restricting the widespread belief that Africans were barbarians and incapable of receiving the gospel. . . . In light of the scant attention paid to the blacks by the church, it was not surprising that they kept their traditional African religions. No member of the clergy knew any of the original languages of the slaves; but . . . [the slaves] remembered their ancestors, their gods and so kept their secret link with their lost homeland."[27]

Lewin Williams reminds us of the roots of the church's prejudice toward Africans. In the papal permission of 1503 for the enslavement of Africans the Catholic Church stated: "being as they are hardened in their habits of idolatry and cannibalism, it is agreed that I [the pope] should issue this decree. . . . I hereby give license and permission . . . to capture them . . . paying us the share that belongs to us and to sell them and utilize their services without incurring any penalty thereby, because if the Christians bring them to these lands and make use of their services they will be more easily converted to our faith."[28] Historian Dale Bisnauth wonders if this papal bull may well have had its origin from "the chancery of Ferdinand and Isabella, the Spanish sovereigns." In any case he observes that Pope Alexander VI both in his "private and public life made the title 'Vicar of Christ' the most appalling mockery that has ever been perpetrated in the name of religion."[29] The history of African and European relationships in the region indicates that Africans saw through the hypocrisy of the church.

A measure of creolization took place as Africans adapted elements of the Christian faith to their native religions. For the most part they remembered Africa, the ancestors, the forests, their gods and thereby maintained their link with their ancestral homeland. As late as the latter part of the eighteenth century a bishop in Cuba charged that he was shocked at the indifference of slaves to the church service.

> He charged that many were not attending mass on holy days and Sundays before they began work on their own properties, and that others were not seriously learning their own lessons. In both situations he wanted the civil authorities to intervene and in the latter case even wanted to go so far as to incorporate physical punishment for laxity. He proposed that instead of the gentle method of instruction, the local clergy should adopt "the method which clerical teachers of New Spain and Peru teach their Indians," that is by using the whip on them in front of their fellow communicants if they forgot their lessons.[30]

Although this stern reaction of the bishop in Cuba may have been unusual, the attitude of enslaved Africans in the Caribbean was not. For example, in Jamaica even after emancipation in 1838 Africans found Christian marriage oppressive as compared to African traditions and customs, which led missionaries to complain of their incorrigible ways.

> The wife had specific responsibilities within the family. She was in charge of marketing. She would serve her husband by cooking his

meal, waiting on him, and then eating alone. While the Black woman was willing to accept this lifestyle with its heavy responsibility, she was unwilling to accept Christian marriage. The Christian concept of marriage was unknown to Black people prior to the coming of the missionary, and black people refused to change their practice of concubinage for it. The Black woman also tended to regard Christian marriage as a mark of subordination and slavery to the male. A large percentage of Black Jamaica still rejects Christian marriage.[31]

Oppressed people in the Caribbean were able to see clearly that the established churches were not on their side. The truth is the churches were in harmony with the planter class, and in many cases missionaries were paid by the planter class. It was often the case that only rare individuals had the courage to stand with enslaved people and challenge the institution of slavery in either the seventeenth or the eighteenth centuries. This remains one of the sad chapters in the history of the church in this region.

Spain was not the only country that exploited Africans in slavery in the Caribbean and sought the well-being of their souls through baptism, even if they were unwilling to risk and proffer a theology that would ensure the freedom of their bodies. Portugal and France followed the lead of Spain by often advocating baptism for enslaved people and often passing laws to ensure their humane treatment. If the Roman Catholic influence and theology was dominant in the Spanish, French, and Portuguese colonies, the Protestant ethic and theology was more prevalent in the English, Dutch, and Danish contexts. In these contexts a central question that emerged was, can an enslaved person become Christian? It was this question that made the planter class suspicious of nonconformist missionaries. Baptist, Methodist, and Moravian missionaries saw their responsibilities as saving the souls of enslaved people throughout the Caribbean. The Church of England along with the Roman Catholic churches understood religion to be a matter of the exercise of the intellect and doubted the ability of Black people to participate. The churches that regarded religion as a matter of the heart saw their task of making enslaved people "Christian." To make enslaved persons Christian would have benefits for both the enslaved and the enslavers. For slaves to become Christian would mean that they would be obedient and would seek to serve their master as they serve God, and this would mean that the master would brutalize the slave less. Further, to Christianize the slave would have the net result that the slave would be more industrious and would run away less. This would also make the master more humane, as a Christian slave would produce a gentler, kinder master. We note in following chapters that enslaved persons in the Americas would not give up their dancing, drumming, ancestor worship, spirit possession, obeah, and other African ways of relating to the world. The bottom line was missionaries came to realize that there was a connection between higher sugar prices and cruel treatment of slaves. Slavery and Christianity were incompatible. It became increasingly clear that for planters, and later for missionaries, the priority was for sugar and profits

> With the introduction of sugar into the Caribbean, the islands underwent a dramatic change. Between 1640 and 1655 they were transformed into sugar colonies. Small farms gave way to large plantations; tobacco was superseded by sugar; many small farmers and indentured laborers were ousted to make room for African slaves. When Jamaica was acquired by the English and St. Domingue by the French, they too became sugar colonies. The Dutch were excluded from trading with the English islands from 1651 and with the French islands from 1664. But the English began their own slave trade which lasted from 1651 to 1808 and which introduced an estimated 1,900,000 Africans to the Caribbean. The French trade in slaves lasted from 1664 to 1830, transporting some 1,650,000 Africans. Meanwhile, the Dutch brought another 900,000 to the Guianas, Curacao, Aruba, Bon Aire and St. Eustatius.[32]

Western Europe extended its boundaries in the Caribbean for economic gain, and as the economic powers sought to make profits through the plantation economy in which millions of Africans were enslaved, it was the job of the missionary to use the God of Christianity to make Africans accept their lot as slaves on plantations "a long ways from home."

Robert Peart, a Muslim who became a member of the Old Carmel Moravian Church in 1813, was arraigned before the magistrates to determine what effect Christianity had on Black people: "To the first question, as to the instruction received, Robert replied: 'We are told to believe in God, who sees us everywhere, and in His Son Jesus Christ, and to pray to him to take us to heaven.' 'Well what more?' 'We must not tell lies' 'What more?' We must not run away and rob Massa of his work.' . . . Thereupon the judges declared themselves satisfied, and let the slaves go."[33]

In his classic text *The Negro Church*[34] the sociologist W.E.B. Du Bois points out that one of the new realities that confronted Black people in the Americas was the social innovation of the plantation. The plantation was substituted for clan and tribal life of Africa. The political power of the African chief was transferred to the White master. "The clan had lost its ties of blood relationship and became simply an aggregation of individuals on a plot of ground, with common rules and customs, common dwellings, and a certain communism in property. The two greatest changes, however, were, first, the enforcement of severe and unremitting toil, and, second, the establishment of a new polygamy—a new family."[35]

It is important to remember that the only religion the masters allowed on the plantation was Christianity. One assumption Europeans made was that Africans had no religion, unlike the Indians before them. Christianity was the religion Europeans brought with them to the New World. One of the promises Columbus made to the church and crown of Spain was that the meaning and purpose of his expeditions to the Americas was to bring the heathen within the pale of the church. Christianity was a religion that the Europeans controlled, and embedded in their version of Christianity was inequality and the inferiority of other peoples in relation to Europeans.

Africa as Controlling Metaphor

Enslaved people remembered Africa, and the memory of Africa became a controlling metaphor and organizing principle for Africans in the New World as they countered the hegemonic conditions imposed on them by their masters. They remembered the forests and they relived this experience of the forests through the practice of religious rituals in the brush arbors, often down by the riverside. The memory of ancestors and a sense that their spirits accompanied them to plantations in the New World served as sites of a new consciousness. This awakening convinced them that they would survive through running away to the forests or through suicides that would reunite them with families and the Africa they remembered. It was primarily through religious rituals and the carving out of Black sacred spaces that enslaved persons were able to affirm self and create a world over against the world proffered by the master for their families. With the creation of the Black church through the memory of Africa engendered by the African priest and medicine man, they prevented slavery and the enslaved condition from dominating their consciousness and robbing them of their creativity to dream a new world and new churches. Du Bois reminds us that this was by no means at first a Christian church but an African church created and controlled by Africans. It was the community's memory of Africa that provided a site for dreaming and planning the emergence of new churches, whether in Haiti, South Carolina, or Barbados. There were more than eleven million persons who were transported via the Middle Passage to plantations in the New World. Although they represented different belief systems and spoke different languages, they were able through collective memory to forge new social circles and new ecclesial communities in order to survive.

On arrival in the New World, Africans were sold as human cargo and became slaves owned and controlled by the planter class. Throughout the region, drumming, dancing, and religious practices that remembered Africa were forbidden. Enslaved persons were forbidden even to use their own languages or to give their children African names. The master class devised many means to erase the memory of Africa. It is interesting that as the African priest/medicine man/woman emerged on plantations throughout the New World, Christians believed that the antidote to African ways and practices, indeed to African religion, was to baptize the African priest. They were convinced that baptism would neutralize his gifts. In many cases, enslaved people were baptized by European clergy before boarding the ship, or on deck as the ship set sail through the Middle Passage en route to plantations in the Caribbean at first, and later to the American mainland. The practice of baptizing enslaved persons was used as a basis for justifying slavery by arguing that a Christian slave is to be preferred to a heathen infidel even if that infidel is free.

On plantations in the New World, masters were careful to separate enslaved persons from their tribes, clans, and language groups to keep communication among them to a minimum. Despite this practice enslaved persons were able to communicate, as many of their dialects came from the same basic language structure. In his *Myth of the Negro Past*, Melville Herskovits calls attention to this ability of enslaved persons to relate and communicate in spite of the difficulties of tribal affiliations and language barriers. Earlier in this chapter we noted that a number of commonalities existed among enslaved Africans in terms of their approach to religion. All African peoples who were transported to plantations in the Americas believed in a high God who was not involved in the daily affairs of their lives. Although this high God is believed to have created the world, he lives outside the world perhaps somewhere in the sky. The absence of this high God in the affairs of people is compensated for by the secondary deities who mediate between people and the high God. Additionally, African peoples who endured and survived the Middle Passage believed in the worship of ancestor spirits and in kinship lineage and the value of the extended family. In "The Creation of Afro-Caribbean Religions and Their Incorporation of Christian Elements," Bettina Schmidt points out that during the early years of slavery in the Caribbean, enslaved Africans were able to create new religions as they combined elements of their faith in this alien environment. Although African customs and practices were forbidden, Africans were able to invest the content of their

African beliefs in the worship of Christian saints. "Hence, African slaves began to use Christian iconography and symbols in order to hide their [African] beliefs and practices. Under the shield of Catholic saints, African deities were able to survive the long period of oppression. . . . After slavery these *cabildos* founded houses or temples, so-called 'Casas de Santos' (Houses of the Saints) which became important support networks for former slaves. When, for instance, former slaves left the plantations and arrived in a town, they looked for a *casa de santos* for help, in particular for a house of the saint they already worshipped on the plantation."[36] At the core or center of the rituals of these newfound religions in the Caribbean was the belief in a high God who created humankind and the created order; also at the center of the new expression of their faith was belief in the intermediary deities, and ancestor spirits. African peoples naturally tend toward a hierarchical faith, having lived with the reality of the king, the queen mother, and the African chief. When this is coupled with the influence of the Catholic Church, one can get a sense of the complex nature of religious rituals with the centrality of the spirit world and the need for a mediator between human beings and the spiritual world. In this worldview, incantation or divination, the communication of the divine or the spiritual with the human, is of first importance. It is in this context that the role of the priest/medicine man/woman is essential. Later on, as the faith developed, not only were the priest and medicine man/woman the ones to mediate between the spirit world and humans, but the spirit would posses whom it pleased and they would become messengers of the divine. I witnessed this recently during a field trip in Trinidad at a ceremony of the Shango religion, as Oshun the Orisha of love possessed a woman who brought gifts to him and through her spoke to the worshippers. I also witnessed this firsthand through women of the Revivalist faith in Jamaica, who under the possession of the spirit would warn the community of impending disasters that would always come to pass. "This practice allows the direct communication with the spirits while they are incorporated in a human body. This practice is in the center of the collective reunions and celebrations which often attract outsiders to the religion. In combination with music and dance, religious manifestations are one of the main characteristics of Afro-Caribbean religions."[37] These traits are true of Black church practices on both sides of the Atlantic. "They are pivotal focal points for understanding African forms of logic and spirituality, especially with regard to experiences of fortune and misfortune, well-being and disease, life and death. These features are present in the religious traditions of Haitian, Dominican, and Louisianan Vodun as well as Cuban, Brazillian, Trinidadian, Puerto Rican, and U.S. Orisha communities."[38] It is clear that there was more than a reciprocal relationship between the gods of Africa and the saints enslaved people encountered through Christianity in the New World. Something new happened as enslaved persons were willing to use elements of the master's religion to help trigger and sustain the memory of Africa. The religion of the slave was more than an adaptation of African religious practices to the situation of bondage on plantations in the Americas. It was more than a blending of African religious practices with elements of Christianity. It was all of these and more, and the more had to do with the creation of new religions in which Africa provided the organizing principle and religion confronted Black people with the central question, "Where do you stand in relation to Africa." Dr. Du Bois in *The Negro Church* points out that this was at first an African church which was born in the Caribbean. The advent of Christianity among the enslaved population, at first in the American colonies and later in the Caribbean, raised an equally important question, "Where do we stand in relation to Jesus?" Africa and Jesus set the framework for this text.

We turn to African roots noting that African identity began in the African homeland and not in the New World slavery.

2

The Memory of Africa

IN THE LAST chapter it was noted that most of Africa's children who were brought to the New World for forced labor on plantations formed Black churches. A majority of enslaved persons were unable to return home to Africa. The formation of Black churches was their chief way of constituting self and restoring their shattered histories in the wake of dislocation and displacement in a strange land. Black churches provided psychic and social space for the creation of worldviews and a sense of community that helped them survive in an alien land.

Many African Americans and Afro-Caribbean people have sought to make the journey home to Africa for their ancestors. With Bob Marley we chant "We are going home to our father's land." Of course, we go a little further than Bob Marley and affirm that Africa is not only our fatherland but literally, also, our motherland.

A few years ago, I took this journey to West Africa, Ile-Ife in Nigeria. As the engines of the plane shattered the quiet of the African countryside, I said, "Africa at last." I along with others made this trip for many of the ancestors trapped on plantations in the New World who were unable physically to journey home. As the plane taxied on African soil I wondered if my father, who had joined the great company of the ancestors some thirty years prior, knew that I was home in Africa. In mother Africa I remembered my father. Childhood memories surfaced and I recalled the morning of my baptism. There were many of us children dressed in white robes who met at the church at 4 A.M. in the village of Trinityville, in St. Thomas, Jamaica. The church had its theological roots in the traditions and teachings of the African American George Liele, who in 1783 arrived in Kingston, Jamaica, from Savannah, Georgia, and founded the first Baptist church that he named the Ethiopian Baptist Church. Jamaicans were proud to be members of a church that had its roots in the teaching of this great African American.

I recalled my baptism. I recalled the gathering at the church in the early morning: drumming which remembered Africa called us to worship, and moved by the spirit, we sang, danced, and testified. Children were taught that we were not allowed to dance unless the mothers of the church gave permission by dancing first. We knew we would be reprimanded by the mothers if we danced out of turn. After much praying, drumming, dancing, and testifying in the spirit we set out, with the mothers leading, to the river where we would encounter the spirit and have our sins washed away. At the river, the drums filled, with the spirit, were possessed by an incredible energy. It was a numinous experience and we were lost in wonder and awe. I was led into the river by the water mother to be immersed by my father who was uncontrollably filled with the spirit. At the river we met the spirit of ancestors who had traveled across the waters to the New World. The river reminded us of the waters that carried the ancestors from Africa to the New World. On releasing me after my immersion in the river, I emerged with the force of the spirit to clapping, drumming, and dancing. The water mother guided me safely to the changing booth.

In Africa I remembered water, river, baptism, and ancestors. It was as if the ancestors took over my consciousness. On African soil I remembered my father leaving to join the ancestors.

My teacher John Mbiti taught that the ancestors know everything. The ancestors are our communion of saints who provide a connection to "the power without beginning." According to Mbiti, the ancestors channel this power to Africa's children and provide the means to protect the present, guarantee the future, and allay our fears and anxieties of the past. It is this ancestral channel of spiritual power through which flows the life force that animates the world and makes it come alive. The ancestors were the key to spiritual energy and the power without beginning. Unable to return home to Africa the ancestors would sing:

> *Sometimes, I feel like a motherless child*
> *Sometimes, I feel like a motherless child*
> *A long ways from home.*

At other times they would sing:

> *An' I couldn't hear nobody pray, O Lord*
> *O, way down yonder by myself*
> *I couldn't hear nobody pray*
> *Wid my burden, I couldn't hear nobody pray*

The ancestors are the link to "the power without beginning." They are not only omniscient, they are great thinkers. They pondered the riddles of existence. Questions such as, where did we come from? Who cares whether we live or die? On whom may we depend for health, shelter, land, liberation? These questions are important to the ancestors.

Creation Stories

In Yoruba land (Nigeria), the ancestors said that in the beginning was Olodumare. Olodumare, the supreme deity, lived in the heavens with many divinities. Among them were Orisanala, the deputy in charge of ordering the created world; Orunmila, the deputy in charge of knowledge; and Esu, the deputy in charge of rituals. The ancestors would tell of a watery marsh far below the heavens and there the god of the sea Olokun was in charge. Although the deputies had specific responsibilities, occasionally the divinities who resided in the heavens would visit the wild marshes to hunt.

According to the ancestors, one day Olodumare looked down on the watery marshes and pondered what to do with it. Should he leave it as it was or should he transform it into a meaningful and purposeful place? Should the supreme deity of the heavens people this watery marsh with divinities and other living beings? A plan formed in his mind and he purposed to form the watery marsh into earth. But a further question emerged. Did he need to go himself or should he send deputies? Olodumare summoned his deputy Orisanla, gave him a leaf with loose earth, a white hen and pigeon to spread the earth, with instructions to create earth. Orisanla followed the instructions closely. He visited the marshy waste, scattered the earth and placed birds where he placed the earth. The birds scattered the earth, and wherever the earth fell it became dry land. Because the birds did not scatter the earth evenly, there emerged hills, valleys, and mountains.

At the completion of phase one, Orisanla was asked to prepare the earth for human beings. The birds were to be multiplied and trees were to be planted for the benefit of human beings. The first human being, Oreluere, along with others—who were created in heaven by Olodumare—made their way from heaven to earth. The supreme deity is the creator of human beings, and because of this special relationship between human beings and Olodumare, human beings became the center of the earth. Animals, plants, and the natural environment are provided for humanity, and they establish a relationship with the natural order as they deem fit. It is instructive to note that the African doctrine of creation has an anthropological point of departure, in that humanity is the center of the created world. The world was created for humanity and the high creator-God seeks to meet the needs of humanity. This means that with human beings at the center of the created world, the sun and moon have someone for whom to shine, the wind provides life and energy for man and woman, and every living thing is created to support and enhance their well-being. This does not negate the interconnectedness of the created order or the chronological priority of the high creator God and the lesser deities, but it means that the universe is at the service of humanity and the point of departure for talk about the created order is humanity.

Human beings who were made in heaven traveled to earth. Soon there were so many human beings that there was a scarcity of water. In his response to Orisanla's plea for more water Olodumare sent rains from the heavens. Orisanla was further commissioned to mold physical forms from the dust of the earth. He was free to use his imagination and create forms as he deemed wise. He could make the forms white or black, perfect or imperfect. However, it was the task of Olodumare to make the physical form a living being by placing life in this form. It was clear that the lesser divinities could make the physical forms but they could not give life.

On one occasion, Orisanala spied on Olodumare in order to discover the secret of making lifeless forms living beings. Olodumare discovered the plan and placed Orisanla in a deep sleep. When he awoke he discovered that all the forms had become living beings.

The ancestors were good at storytelling. They pointed out that from the start there was a good relationship, an uninterrupted harmony between human beings and the spiritual world. In one story that depicted the relationship between earth and heaven people were seen as very close to heaven. People were even allowed to go to heaven to request what they needed. In other stories the deities would teach people how to cultivate crops, how to cook, and in some cases how to make beer. God provided for their physical and spiritual needs. In some stories God lived among the people; in other stories God was a frequent visitor. The relationship with God was like that of a family in which God was the parent and all their needs derived from their relationship with God. Other stories tell of how God created the earth so that the sun would have someone for whom to shine.[1]

Most stories of the creation of the world in Africa regard the supreme deity as creator. All life comes directly through divine creation. In his text, *Creative Evangelism,* Harry Sawyer supports this view and points out that all over Africa it is believed that God is the source of life, animate and inanimate, and, as Supreme Being, is omnipotent. While it is true that the Supreme Being delegates tasks and responsibilities to lesser divinities, life in all its forms comes from God. Because of this reality, human beings must not take the life of another, because life which comes from God belongs to God. Because persons belong to God, if one is angry and plans to harm another, that person must first seek permission from God. "So the Mende of Sierra Leone always invoke the Name of God before uttering a curse on anybody. Again, if anyone wishes to secure power to achieve some gain by accredited means, it is assumed that he has to use certain other elements of creation. But he, too, must seek permission of God before presuming to use any element of creation."[2] This principle of first receiving permission from God whether one would do harm or good to another became of first importance for ancestors as they translated African practices to the New World. The doer of both evil and good must first seek permission from God, because both good and evil are from God. There are times when one will be heard pleading with God to remove from the back of the person, that is, stop protecting him or her in order that that person may become vulnerable. God has his back, that is, God is protecting him.

Stories of Providence and Sin

The bottom line is that all persons, enemies or friends, are under the protection of God and no harm may befall one without the will of the supreme deity. As long as a person has divine protection, that one is safe from all harm.

> The notion of God as man's protector extends over all kinds of action. When a man is successful in life it is thought among the Mende of Sierra Leone that God supports his activities by defending him from evil. So they say, "God is at his back." So too, one escapes serious danger because God defends and protects one. Again, one commits a crime and is not caught because God is defending and protecting one. So the offended party is heard to exclaim, "O God, come away from his back!" i.e., "O God do not go on defending and protecting him!" When he is caught one hears the comment, "God has come away from his back," i.e., God has ceased to defend and protect him."[3]

Sin is punished, but this punishment is meted out by the lesser deities. Although good and evil come from God, God and the ancestors are especially intolerant of lies. God is regarded as just and will requite wrongdoing. "It is significant that persons accused of a crime among the Mende never adopt a lie as a measure of self protection when brought before cultic or other spirits assumed to reside in a 'medicine.' Similarly, lies are not tolerated when addressing the ancestors. The spirits are vengeful because they are regarded as akin to human beings. The ancestors, from experience during their life time, do not accommodate lies."[4] A necessary consequence for lying to the ancestors or a medicine man is often death. Both the medicine man and the ancestors are regarded as being able to see beyond the world of appearances; hence, one needs to be scrupulous in doing and telling truth.

In African mythologies it is often pointed out that the supreme deity who knows the truth about human beings cares what happens to human beings. Much time and thought is not given to philosophical questions of divine existence; the emphasis is on an explication of what it means to affirm absence or presence of God in human life. Good health is a sign that God is with you. The converse is true; sickness and death are signs that God has left one, or has removed from one's back, that is, has ceased protecting one. "So to the question, 'How are you?' or 'How stands your tone of health?' the usual reply is 'There is no fault in God,' i.e., 'I am quite well, thank you!' The Yoruba reply to the question, 'How are you?' is 'I thank God.' God as the strong one bestows upon man good health. Sickness is, therefore, apparently due to a failure on God's part to maintain His power to maintain the health of the individual. But on closer examination the origin of sickness and death is only indirectly attributed to God."[5]

There are communities throughout West Africa who contend that sickness is often an expression of divine resolve for an individual to consider joining the community of the ancestors. Sickness is often purveyed as a divine messenger to prepare one to join the company of the ancestors. Both sickness and death are seen as agents of the divine. There is the profound sense that everything happens for a reason, whether good or bad, and God who creates everything is able to use them all for his purposes. Nothing happens outside the divine prerogative.

> The Temme say that once God use to send down His messenger to recall man to himself when he had finished his allotted span of life. But one man who was rich, vigorous and wicked, resisted the messenger. God then sent other messengers whom the man beat up. Two years after wards, however, God sent sickness to soften him up. So he lay down and could not rise from his bed again. Later God sent Death, who then took the man away. The Mende of Sierra Leone talk of illness as "that which softens up an adult who is supposed to be full of vigor."[6]

The Akan of Ghana, from whom many Africans in the diaspora hail, and who regard their king as sacred, seek to protect him from contacts with death and from women during their menses for fear that as women lose blood, it could become infectious. "A menstrual woman is supposed among the Akan to destroy the spirit which produces gold so she is not allowed near a gold-mine. Mende men believe they would die if they happened to be present at the birth of a child. The operative notion is that the loss of power by the king's vital energy, or of the power latent in gold, or of male energy through the influence of some other agency. . . . So the Mende of Sierra Leone and the Bantu of the Lower Congo say they are 'dead' of hunger or fatigue, or that the least obstacle or illness is 'killing' them."[7] It is clear that one of the concerns here is the need to be aware and careful of external forces that may eviscerate or dissipate one's power.

But the relationship was breached between heaven and earth. Some stories claim that people with dirty hands touched the face of heaven. Other stories portray human beings as greedy and self-indulgent, which caused heaven to recede from earth.

African Views of Time

During my stay I was constantly reminded of the African traditional view of time. Both college students and community leaders pointed out the limits of the Western view of time, that moves in a linear frame from past to present and then to the future. One young community leader argued that envisioning a long future was not helpful to the community if people were being asked to sacrifice the present for an uncertain future. In the African traditional view of time, people lack interest in a long future and notions of a life in the great beyond, which is another way of talking about a distant future. Time is proffered as a composition of events which have occurred, those which are taking place now, and those which are about to occur. Africans, influenced by the Kenyan philosopher and theologian John Mbiti, contend that there was a sense of time having a long past, a present, and a short future. This conception of time was to be differentiated from the Western view in which there is a long past, a present, and a long future. In African thought the future which is not about to happen is considered potential time and not actual time. Actual time includes both past and present. In African thought, time moves backward from the present to the past. The Swahili words, "Sasa" and "Zamani" are used to refer to the phenomenon of time moving from the present to the past. The ancestors, it is claimed, live in the Zamani period and when one dies one leaves the Sasa period for the Zamani. John Mbiti elucidates the understanding of time extant in the community:

Sasa has the sense of immediacy, nearness, and "newness"; and is the period of immediate concern for the people, since that is "where" or "when" they exist. What would be "future" is extremely brief. This has to be so because any meaningful event in the future must be so immediate and certain that people have almost experienced it. Therefore, if the event is remote, say beyond two years from now, then it cannot be conceived, it cannot be spoken of, and the languages themselves have no verb tenses to cover that distant "future" dimension of time. When an event is far in the future, its reality is completely beyond or outside the horizon of the Sasa period. . . . But before events become incorporated into the Zamani they have to become realized or actualized within the Sasa dimension. When this has taken place, then the events "move" backwards from the Sasa into the Zamani. So Zamani becomes the period beyond which nothing can go.[8]

Mbiti's characterization of the Sasa and Zamani periods as Micro-Time and Macro-Time is most illuminating, especially as he points out that both periods overlap. It is in the Sasa period that people live and from which they project themselves into the past and to some degree into the future. The Sasa, which includes its own present, past, and future, is referred to by Mbiti as Micro-Time. It is helpful to note that the future in Micro-Time is so immediate that it is almost accessible, it has almost occurred and slipped into the past. To live into this future is to have become one with it; it is to be drawn into the future by one's imagination. In the Sasa period, events that are several years away are seldom spoken of. "Furthermore, research into a number of East African languages has shown that these languages do not possess a vocabulary which can directly express concepts of a distant future, and if one makes a circumlocutory attempt to describe something in the distant future, the expression becomes vague or conveys little meaning, if anything. Events in the Sasa must be about to occur, in the process of actualization, or they must have been recently actualized or experienced."[9]

On the other hand, Mbiti refers to the Zamani period as Macro-Time. Like the Sasa period it has its own past, present, and future, and intersects with the Sasa period. As one would expect in order for events to become actualized in the Zamani period, they have to occur in the Sasa period. The movement from the Sasa to the Zamani period is "backward" in which everything ends. Mbiti speaks of the Zamani period as the vast storehouse of everything that happens. "It is a storehouse for all phenomena and events, a vast ocean of Time where everything gets absorbed into an aspect of reality which is neither after nor before."[10]

According to Mbiti, human life follows a rhythm of nature rather than any understanding of chronological time. Life follows the rituals of birth, puberty, initiation, marriage, procreation, old age, death, and joining the company of the ancestors. Complementing this rhythm is that of seasons, years, days, nights, months. "This two-fold rhythm of Nature is "everlasting": as it happened in the past, it is happening now and it will do so forever. There is no 'end' to this continuous rhythm and cycle, and there is no 'world to come' . . . Time has no end."[11] Because there is no concept of "world to come" there are no myths concerning the end time, nor concerning a primordial state. John Mbiti points out that he has been able to identify one tribe in Tanzania that has myths concerning an eschatological end of the world. "In their eschatological myth it is held that when the end of the world draws near the sun will turn into darkness (evidently from a thick cloud of dust, a swarm of bees and a flock of birds), then two suns will rise (one from the east and the other from the west) and when they meet in the middle the world will end."[12]

It is believed all over Africa that human beings were originally intended for immortality. Death was occasioned by a number of factors, among them, discourtesy to messengers of immortality, disobedience, witchcraft, departed spirits, and at times God's will. But the reality of death does not erase the hope in immortality. Mbiti points out that throughout the continent of Africa, belief in the existence of life after death continues, albeit at different levels. Death destroys the body, but the spirit lives on, because it was intended for immortality. An important key in understanding one's existence after death is its memory by friends and relatives. Before death, one lives in the Sasa period prior to entering the Zamani period. As long as one is remembered by friends and family one continues to live in the Sasa period and this may last for several generations. "People continue to recall his words, his personal traits, and in many societies libations are poured and food-offerings are made. If he appears, it is to his own family, especially to the other members, and he is recognized by *name* as so and so. . . . So long as he is remembered by name he is not really dead: he is alive, and such a person we would call the *living-dead*."[13] As long as there is someone to remember the departed, he is dead only in body but not in spirit and therefore enters the state of the living-dead. The living-dead also live on in their progenies and they are remembered in their character traits. Life after death in many respects depends on the way the dead are remembered by the living. This means among other things that life after death continues as it did prior to death, no less no more. Nothing new happens, life, albeit spirit life, continues as a cycle. There is no such notion as a new future, or some notion of resurrection. If you were a good person then you will be a good spirit, a good ancestor, if you were obstinate and mean, then that existence continues in the spirit world. "Life in the hereafter is a carbon copy of the present; it inspires neither hope nor longing. There is no 'Golden Age,' no 'paradise,' and no 'resurrection,' upon which to anchor one's hope. The afterlife is simply a mechanical, inevitable continuation of life, generally neither better nor worse than life in the present world. There are, generally speaking, neither rewards nor punishments awaiting individuals after death. Punishments and rewards come in this life."[14] And yet because of the inevitability of physical death, there is a sense of a thin veil between the spirit world and this world. One important reason for religion is to investigate the mystery and relationship of these two worlds. In the spirit world are the *living-dead*, some of whom serve as intermediaries between both worlds, and between God and the living.

What Makes Human Life Human?

In *Aspects of Religion and Life in Africa*, the noted West African theologian Kwesi Dickson writes in support and in question of some of the claims of the East African theologian John Mbiti. Dickson points out that the claims he makes are centered around the life of the Akan people but have pertinence and relevance regarding most peoples of Africa. He poses as a central question for African peoples, what is the element that really makes life human? And he claims that across the board, the answer is relationship with the Supreme Being and with others.

> There is the Akan belief, which has its counterpart among many African peoples, that the element that really makes one a human being emanates from the Supreme Being—he it is who gives a person an *okra* or soul, and it is the *okra* which really makes one a human being; it is in connection with the question of the relation between God and man that the concept of Destiny comes up for consideration.[15]

According to Dickson, to be human in an African context is to live in the tension between a destiny that is imposed by the Supreme Being and one that is chosen by the individual. He uses two Akan words to illustrate his point, *nkrabea* and *hyebea*. While both words point to fate or destiny, *nkrabea* points to a destiny imposed on the individual by the Supreme Being. On the other hand, *hyebea* points to a self-chosen destiny. "To the Akan, God outlines what is to be the individual's mode of life on earth, similar views are held by the Nupe, the Nuer and other peoples. The almost continent-wide evidence of the prevalence of this view is well documented."[16] According to Dickson, most Africans believe that God has the final word, the ultimate responsibility regarding human affairs. When misfortune befalls one, people often say, it is his destiny. People are often quiet regarding their assessment of what is the case when something good happens. Dickson finds it interesting that although God has the final authority regarding what occurs in human affairs, there is no equivocation concerning the nature or character of God when bad things happen to people over which they seem to have no control.

On the other side of the equation, human beings are responsible for their destiny. "To the Tallensi, for example, it is man who speaks his Destiny before birth. This is the prenatal Destiny which might be evil or good. . . . [The] Tallensi conception in detail, notes that there are two values attaching to this belief: to hold that man is responsible for his life is to relieve society at large of responsibility for the individual's life. . . . At any rate, the main idea to which attention is being drawn here is that of man being accountable for what happens to him."[17] Dickson casts his argument in terms of an African paradox, since on the one hand God is in charge and responsible for what happens in the lives of Africans, yet on the other hand there is human accountability. Dickson becomes concerned that the God-human responsibility/accountability is complex, and so as a good theologian Dickson tries to make it neat and tidy rather than allow the paradox to remain. He suggests four possible responses to the seeming conflict between *nkrabea* and *hyebea*. The tension between *nkrabea* as God's supreme rule in the affairs of people, and *hyebea* as self-chosen Destiny, especially when life has careened out of control, is an attempt to affirm that the divine appointed destiny does not obviate human responsibility. These claims make one wonder how Dickson makes sense of New World slavery that consigned the lives of twelve million Africans to a fate of chattel slavery? He states, "The pervasiveness of the idea of God's primacy should have made it unnecessary to insist on human accountability, were the latter not considered such a cardinal concept. Indeed, a person's *nkrabea* may be modified for the worse through evil living, hence the Yoruba belief that 'a good destiny unsupported by character is worthless.' "[18]

Dickson's second reflection on the paradox of the role of divine and human responsibility for destiny among Africans is that it is possible to alter one's *nkrabea* should the outcome seem to be heading to a bad end. It is widely believed that through traditional preparations made possible by priests and medicine practitioners, one is able to alter the circumstances for the better.

The Yoruba act in the belief that given certain conditions, a person's destiny may be altered. They therefore take steps to see that a happy destiny is not spoilt and that an unhappy one is rectified. On the whole, the Yoruba teach caution and patience as one goes on in life. They desire long life and pray for it as they feel that it is seldom that the morning really shows the day with regard to the working out of destiny. Thus, they would consider of no lasting importance whatever misfortune or prosperity attends a person's early life.[19]

There is then a sense that Africans are active in taking responsibility for their destiny, with the confidence and belief that they are able to change their lot in life. The third response to the seeming conflict between *nkrabea* and *hyebea* is that when one's destiny seems to be dictated by illness and misfortune, the traditional response is to resist through medicines. Illness and misfortune are not considered natural and normal, hence the need to resist them, "to the extent that the gods might be threatened with dire consequences should they fail to ensure the well being of members of the society."[20] It is of first importance that the well-being of members of society should be maintained, since their well-being ensures the equilibrium of the society. The well-being of the individual contributes to the well-being of the society. The final response is that members of the society do all they can to avert misfortune, as it does not have an essential place in the order of things in the world. It is considered an aberration.

> When danger threatened, the Central Luo did all they could to avert it, and to rid the homestead of it. The beliefs and practices I have described and certain knowledge of medicines were used to diagnose, explain, interpret the individual causes of misfortune and ill health, and they also provided the means and ways of coping with the individual situations of anxiety and stress. But when all these have failed, when the game of ritually acting out their deeply felt needs and desires and hopes had produced no satisfactory results, at this level, the Central Luo became skeptical and irreligious, and preferred to face the facts of life coolly and realistically. When your son died you wept but amid the tears, you declared, "Wi-lobo"; "This is the way of the world."[21]

Professor Dickson helps us to understand that whether in East or West Africa when misfortune comes, one recognizes that, as is said in East Africa, "This is the way of the world" or in West Africa among the Akan, "This is in accordance with what God has arranged." But the main point here is that one only knows that it is the way of the world or the way of God after everything has been done to cancel or avert it. Misfortune as such does not have any ontological status in this life. It is natural and normal for good things to happen to members of the society. This, Dickson claims, is one reason that when good things happen, no one bothers to say it is the will of God, or the will of the world. The good, so to speak, is part of the natural order.

What then of time? Dickson agrees that talk about destiny leads to talk about time. He mentions, rather jovially, that time in Africa is divided into European and African time. African time moves at a slower pace, in part because time is often understood as events. But Dickson is careful to mention that he believes John Mbiti overstates the case in regard to his view of how African people understand the future. Dickson states:

> In my own experience African peoples express the future in various ways: in the premium placed on large families, much to the dismay of family planning specialists; in the acquisition of land, and in the need for a proper burial. And I could have mentioned other characteristic ideas which are premised on there being a future, a future which, admittedly, is not given detailed chronological specification, but a future all the same. . . . It is true that many African peoples believe in reincarnation.[22]

Dickson admits that Mbiti does not discount the place of a future in Africans' understanding of time. The difference between their understanding of a future concerns the duration of the future. While Mbiti argues for a shorter view of a future, Dickson proffers a longer one. While Dickson argues that time and destiny are conjoined in the celebrations of festivals which on the one hand look back to recount a historical journey and on the other hand to the hope and promise of renewal, he does not tell us whether his articulation of destiny belongs to the past, future, or present. The point to note, however, is that at the reenactment of festivals, the past is recounted and remembered so that it may be at the service of the future. This means that at a certain level Dickson's understanding of how the past functions in African understanding of society is radically different from that of Mbiti. For Dickson, the past is the servant of the future and is not an end in itself as such. "The facts relating to the past are there, but these are recalled in order to ensure future stability. The need to recreate society is enacted in many different ways at festivals, but basically the enactment consists of certain symbolic actions and the verbalization of certain patterns; the intention is, as it were, to bring into being a new society, a society without discord and without evil and disease and all that may destroy society's equilibrium."[23] The festivals are really about the emphases one attributes to time as, on the one hand, festivals point to an ideal time in the past when society was at its best and an emphasis on renewal at the festival to ensure a happier and better future. The festivals help re-create the future and highlight the ideal past. A prayer cited at the festival bring past, present, and future together as time and destiny are conjoined:

> I invoke you all, all the ancestors; You who trekked from far away Hodge; You who came and founded the State of Anlo; You who bore many fruits; I make an offering, asking for guidance; We always call on you. We plead for peace, perfect peace; Make evil fly over our heads, and goodness come to all. We ask for peace, let there be rain; Let there be rain that peace may reign. And all our chiefs, the little innocent ones, all our men, all women, every child of the soil, Bless them with unity, let their thoughts and words be one. Let the State be one, make it stand as one. Drive off evil to the desert beyond River Danyi, Drive it off to the deserts beyond the sea, To the deserts beyond the lagoon, drive it far away; Rest the State in peace, yes in peace, perfect peace.[24]

The prayer makes clear that peace, and guidance and well-being for all African people, are a part of the natural order seen as people's destiny. The ancestors to whom prayers are offered, in this instance, are asked to allow evil to fly far away and the reign of peace to fall on all the members of the society. This is their natural destiny. In this prayer Kwesi Dickson reminds us that worship among African peoples is a way of life and worship is addressed to the divinities. "West African peoples do not usually have temples dedicated to the Supreme Being. This is due to the fact that He is not localized in the thought of the people. For example, the Yoruba describe God *as A te rere kaye* 'He Who spreads over the extent of the earth.' This means that to them, Deity is so great, so undimensional and so majestic that He cannot be confined within space. . . . the Nupe song 'God is in front; He is at the back' shows that God is omnipresent, transcendent and, at the same time, immanent."[25] And yet in African thinking worship points to the mystery of the Supreme Being, as if on the one hand, there are usually no temples built for the veneration of God; on the other hand, there are altars built for his direct worship. This is so because all worship is indirectly aimed at the Supreme Being as the divinities who are worshipped are intermediaries between people and the Supreme Being. These divinities have no authority or existence apart from that of the Supreme Being, who appointed and authorized them for a specific purpose. "That is why every act of worship or ritual has an ultimate reference to the Supreme God who must sanction it. The Yoruba will say 'A se' at the end of each petition to God or any of the divinities. 'A se' means 'may it be sanctioned by God' or, 'may it receive approval.' "[26]

In his book, *An Essay on African Philosophical Thought*, Kwame Gyekye answers Kwesi Dickson's earlier question, "what is the element that makes one human from an African perspective," by pointing out that the basis for thought about destiny and freedom is based on reflection on the experiences of individuals. "It is your destiny (*nkrabea*) that makes you you, and my destiny that makes me me. . . . *Nkrabea* therefore literally means, the manner of the message . . . given by the Supreme Being to the individual soul, which (message) was to determine the manner in which the individual was to live in the world."[27] For Gyekye the concept of destiny is many-faceted; it involves status, occupation, as well as the time of death when the human soul is to depart this world. However, his analysis differs from that of Dickson and Mbiti in regard to their view of time. According to Gyekye, one's destiny as assigned by the Supreme Being does not have two distinct messages—one for the temporal world and the other for the nontemporal. He thinks that the attempt of scholars to set up a dichotomy between *nkrabea* and *hyebea* is misleading.

> All these confusions stem from holding that the words *nkrabea* and *hyebea* refer to different concepts. . . . There is no evidence in the sources that leads one to believe that two different "messages," that is, scrolls of destiny, are borne by the individual into the world. The message, whether determined by the individual's own soul or given to it by the Supreme Being, is a single message, but its content is many-faceted. *Nkrabea* (or *hyebea*) therefore expresses a concept of destiny that is totalistic, encompassing all aspects, temporal and non-temporal, though not in detail, of an individual's mundane existence.[28]

Gyekye makes it clear that he subscribes to some notion of an all-inclusive destiny, a destiny given by the Supreme Being. After fieldwork among the Akan regarding the soul in the appropriation of that destiny, he argues that the Akan people do not differentiate between the destiny given to them by the Supreme Being and that chosen by them. Individuals do not choose their destiny; the Supreme Being has already decided the contours and context of that destiny.

Gyekye and Dickson are closer than it may seem. While Dickson seems to have more of an opening for the relationship of *nkrabea* and *hyebea*, which I translate in broad strokes as destiny and human freedom, Gyekye in a discussion of "the general nature of destiny" indicates that the destiny given by the omniscient represents the broad outline of a person's life and not the details of that life. "That is, the message (*nkra*) borne by the soul is said to be comprehensive; it determines only the broad outlines of an individual's mundane life, not the specific details. It follows that not every action a person performs or every event that occurs in one's life comes within the ambit of his destiny."[29] He points out that his discussants in his research were emphatic in their claim that there are areas in which the content of one's destiny is set, as in the time of death. A minority of the people observed that even one's station and rank in life are also determined beforehand by the Supreme Being. This means, then, that the contour and context of destiny remain vague. However, all the people interviewed observed that "the inexplicable events in one's life, the unalterable and persistently habitual traits of character, the persistent actions and behavior patterns of an individual are all traceable to destiny."[30] It is of first importance to note that this turn to the all-inclusive notion of the content of one's destiny given by the Supreme Being is tapped into only after all other explanations fail. In this sense, then, the Akan, according to Gykeye, are not with the answer which is equated with *nkrabea* but with the question equated with *hybea*. One turns to one's destiny given by the Supreme Being in order to understand the riddles and paradoxes of life after everything fails. Destiny remains the general outline for explaining the mystery and ambiguity of life. This means then that the Akan do not attribute everything to destiny.

In dealing with the knotty problem of whether one can alter or change one's destiny, Gykeye pointed out that there were basically two responses. There were some who claimed that one's destiny may be changed by magic or religious means, while others claimed it was unalterable. He sided with the latter, as he argues that the majority of persons interviewed understood one's destiny as one's basic attributes. "Moreover, if, as I have argued destiny is determined by the *omnipotent* Supreme Being, it obviously cannot be changed. Hence, the insistence of the proverbs I have seen that God's destiny cannot be avoided or changed is logical."[31] What, then, if one has inherited or received a bad destiny? If it is the Supreme Being who assigns one's destiny, is there such a thing as a bad destiny? This question does not arise, according to Gykeye, because what is at stake in the asking of this question is the Akan's understanding of the nature of the Supreme Being. In Akan thought, the Supreme Being is considered good. "Goodness is the prime characteristic of God. The hawk says: 'Whatever God does is good.' "[32] Because of this one's destiny is good and anything that contradicts this is not essential in terms of being human, the stuff that contradicts the essential goodness and wholeness are temporary and can be changed through magic or religious means.

There is the making of a theology of hope in Gykeye's portrayal of the Akan's view of destiny and freedom. Although Gykeye does not use the word "freedom," which is implicit in *hybea* as Kwesi Dickson makes clear, he nonetheless ends up arguing against a sense of resignation and passivity which seems to be the end point of a thesis that is heavy on destiny, which is given by the omnipotent Supreme Being and light on notions of human freedom. His thesis on the destiny given by the Supreme Being as equivalent to one's basic attributes is an attempt to compensate for the low anthropology expressed by an assigned destiny. Because of the confidence in the goodness of the Supreme Being it is clear that the Supreme Being would not assign an inferior destiny, and this opens the door for change of any destiny that is inferior and assigned by society or others, or even by oneself. This means, then, that hidden in destiny, assigned by the Supreme Being, is freedom to change any attribute or characteristic that is not for the uplift of the individual or the community since a good God summons the individual to be good. Both Gykeye and Dickson point out the way forward in talk about the human response to destiny and the goodness of the Supreme Being who created everything good. Even if the content of one's destiny equals one's basic attributes, the ultimate responsibility to decide what those attributes are belongs to each individual. For the Akan, it is the individual who is certain of the content of his destiny. Others may not speak of that destiny with confidence, because they were not there when that destiny was assigned by the Supreme Being.

A World Peopled by Spirits

It is believed throughout Africa that the Supreme Being has created lesser deities that serve as his agents. There are many such spirits who are charged with specific functions in relation to people and their societies. Many of these spirits are revered within homes and villages. "The most universal of these household gods, and that which is given first rank, is the Ikenga, and no house may be without one. It is the first god sought by a young man at the beginning of his career, and it is the one to which he looks for good luck in all his enterprises."[33] Stephen N. Ezeanya points out in his article, "God, Spirits and the World,"[34] that although spirits are agents of the Supreme Being, this seems to be the case more in theory than in fact. The reality is that spirits do not have to receive gifts from the Supreme Being in order to distribute them to people. The spirits are often very self-sufficient and often seem to have their own minds as they act independently from the Supreme Being. The relationship of spirits to the Supreme Being is like this:

> God created these spirits and assigned them their special responsibilities and areas of jurisdiction. They have their resources and have full powers to act without consulting God or asking for permission. They,

unlike the Supreme God, can sometimes disappoint man; this is why both success and failures are attributed to them. Like the Greek gods of old, they have some of the limitations of man. They can be hungry, angry, jealous and revengeful. In view of this man must always seek to be on best terms with them.[35]

The spirits are both male and female and it is important to offer sacrifices to them. Although spirits may be associated with a stream, tree, or animal, Africans are clear that they are not revering the material form, but the spirit that indwells that reality. It is clear that the material thing of itself does not have spiritual power, the power comes from the spirit. Additionally, it is believed in several African cultures that, at birth, each human receives a spiritual double known as *chi* that is always with him or her from the time of conception and is charged with the responsibility to ensure that the individual's destiny is achieved. The *chi* as protecting spirit often has a shrine built for its veneration, at which sacrifices for assistance are offered. The faith in a protecting spirit is found in many cultures in Africa. Ezeanya points out that for Africans there are four types of spirits; the Supreme Being, lesser divinities, ancestral spirits and evil spirits. There is a mutuality between the spirit and the human worlds, they depend on each other. "The world of men and the world of spirits are not two independent worlds; for one has no meaning without the other— they are complimentary. Man has need of the spirit-world, while the minor spirits have need of men to gladden their hearts, to feed them with fat things."[36] But mutuality does not mean equality; it is clear that spirits are senior partners and will often punish human beings for failure to venerate them or to maintain the equilibrium.

We noted earlier that spirits are agents of the Supreme Being and often act as intermediaries between people and the Supreme Being. This is especially the case with the ancestors. "West African peoples believe that only those who live a good life, live to a ripe old age, die good death, and are accorded full burial rites can become ancestors."[37] Here we note the interdependence between ancestors and people. There are shrines in homes for the veneration of ancestors who are regarded as members of the family. The relationship between the ancestors and the family help to create an indivisible link between the unseen and the seen worlds. "There is no rigid distinction of influence between members of the community still here on earth, and those that are in the world beyond. When here on earth, they were elders of their families. Now that they have been veiled from us, they are still elders in the world of the spirits. They do not cease to interest themselves in the general welfare of their families."[38] Although there is an interdependence between the ancestors and

the human family, in death, the ancestors' powers are enhanced. Their poten-
tialities and dignity are enlarged, and there is considerable power for harm or
for good. Although no longer visible, their powers are enormous as they help
the community with issues of sickness or health, prosperity or adversity, and
they are influential in the general well-being of the family.

An analogy may help here to illustrate how the concept of ancestorship has
continued in the Caribbean. My biological mother died when I was eight
months old, and because there were no cameras in my village, I have never
seen a portrait of my mother. Desiring to see what mother looked like, I enquired of my elder sister Cherry if she would be willing to describe mother to
a painter or artist who would offer a rendering of her. My request made my
sister impatient, and she asked, "What have you done for mother lately"?
"What do you mean?" I asked, "mother has been dead for over sixty years?"
My sister's response was that it was my turn to plant a garden for mother,
rather than to be thinking about myself. Mother needs your love, she added,
and if you really want to see mother, look at the children in the family, look in
their eyes—you will see mother.

According to my sister, mother needed my love and my gifts, she who had
already given life to me was now in need of love. My sister taught me how to
share food, pour libation—Jamaican rum—and to always eat and leave something on my plate for the ancestors who may be around. There was also the
sense in the community that the ancestors were always near to protect one
from harm and to keep one safe. Additionally, the ancestors are the guardians
of family morality

> Belief in ancestor supplies strong sanctions for public morality. They
> are the guardians of traditional morality. They, therefore, demand a
> high sense of respect for the traditional law and custom. The living
> must live as they have lived. It is believed that just as the living parents
> have power to punish disobedience in the youth or dereliction of filial
> duties, so also the neglected or offended ancestors can punish their
> offspring for moral offences, and they can bring disaster on the whole
> family. Thus murder, sorcery, witchcraft, stealing, adultery, bearing
> false witness, taking false oath, hatred, incest, and other evils are all
> condemned and punished by the ancestors.[39]

Awolalu and Dopamu in *West African Traditional Religion* help us draw some
practical conclusions from the West African understanding of ancestors. Ancestors provide a basis for cohesion in the society and remind the community
that earthly existence is finite and that death is the necessary door through

which everyone must pass. Death is the door through which one passes from physical to spiritual existence. This means that death is not necessarily negative, as it is in the case of the death of a young person who has not fulfilled her destiny, in contradistinction to a good death when an older person dies. The death of a young person is considered an occasion for mourning, while the death of an older person who has realized her destiny constitutes a time of rejoicing. Death signals a time when the deceased goes on a journey and must have articles for the journey, often carrying messages for those who have gone on before. Often the good person returns in the life of a child, while the bad person is excluded from the happy life. Ancestors continue to be interested in the daily life of the family, remaining in close contact with immediate members of the family, and they expect to be consulted in matters of importance to the family. Awolalu and Dopamu sum up the importance of ancestors:

> They can punish people for offences; they can extend their blessing to their descendants for fulfilling their obligations. They are, therefore, the custodians of public morality. . . . Offerings are made to them from time to time; libations are poured to them; and festivals are held in their honor. . . . They serve as intermediaries between men and divinities, and between men and God.[40]

Although there seems to be a mutuality of purpose between the living-dead and the living, it is clear that the living-dead, or the ancestors, have more authority and power than the living in relation to the existence of the family. The truth is that because of their power, the ancestors are to be loved but also to be feared because they can use their power to punish or to advance the material or spiritual health of the family. "In all ceremonies of any significance, on the occasion of birth, marriage, death, funerals, or investiture, it is the ancestors who preside, and their will yields only to that of the creator. . . . The same blood, the same life participated in by all and received from the first ancestor, the founder of the clan, circulates in everyone's veins."[41] African life is characterized by life in community in which ancestors form an indispensable link. According to Mulago, we dare not forget that it is their blood that runs in our veins and their life that pulsates in our hearts. Life exists in a vital union with all members of the community, and the expression of community is made possible by the ancestors, who define its identity and parameters. The bottom line is that the dead are not really dead, and so it is appropriate to refer to them as living-dead, who continue to be invested in the living. It is a beautiful thought that parents who have gone on before continue to protect the family, especially when its existence is threatened, and in cases punish members of the family who need correction. Ancestors are guardians of the values and traditions of the family.

Although it is widely believed that the Supreme Being lives in the sky and therefore is inaccessible to the human family, in many tribes because of the immediacy of the ancestors and their constant presence when remembered by the living, God has come to be regarded as "the Great Ancestor." "More significant in this context is the notion that God is the Great Ancestor and, like the human ancestors, He is always present with man. So the Kono of Sierra Leone call him *Yataa*, 'He is the one you meet everywhere.' The Temme title, *Kurumasaba*, probably means 'The God whose image we are.' . . . Thus God, for the African, is both the Great Ancestor who, perhaps because of the range of human existence and their activities on earth, comes to be attributed with ubiquity and omniscience."[42]

Looking Toward Black Churches

It is clear that there is much to learn from the philosophy and theology of the ancestors. John Mbiti in his dissertation for Cambridge University, *New Testament Eschatology in an African Background*,[43] pursues the claim that Africans are not naturally oriented toward a long future and understand the future in terms of the past. According to Mbiti, to join the ancestors who have died, one does not go to a heaven in the future but one moves from the Sasa period to the Zamani period where the ancestors dwell. It is precisely at this point that Mbiti claims that the revolutionary contribution of Christianity to African Traditional Religion is in the concept of heaven, which offers a long future that has implications for life in the present. This concept makes it possible for time that has not yet happened, potential time, to provide a horizon for the future. One has to wonder how this new future would function in African cosmology. Would it clash with the Zamani period, or would it provide psychic and mythic space for dreams? I believe John Mbiti overstates his case in claiming that Africans do not conceptualize a long future, otherwise Africans would not plant trees for children. The maturation of the tree points to a future which encompasses a great deal of time ahead. The tree represents a sign of faith in a future many years ahead.

But Mbiti's thesis seems to provide an opening for the insertion of Christian claims that the Great Ancestor will, in His time, offer a new heaven and a new earth, that old things will pass away and the new future will transform both the Zamani and the Sasa period. Mbiti shows that the way forward, even for African Traditional Religion, is to tap into possibilities made possible by a new future. For example, Mbiti points out that he is unable to find in stories of the ancestors any hope of repairing the breach between heaven and earth. The stories indicate that there was a time when heaven and earth were close, but human error caused a distance to develop between them. According to Mbiti, there are no stories of the return of harmony and closeness between earth and heaven. It is precisely at this point that Mbiti believes the new future that Christianity proffers brings hope and possibilities for healing the rift between heaven and earth. "It is remarkable that out of these many myths concerning the primeval man and the loss of his original state, there is not a single myth to my knowledge which even attempts to suggest a solution or reversal of this great loss."[44]

In *Theology in Africa* Kwesi Dickson mentions how Africans make a ready connection between their way of life and that of people in the Old Testament.

> I am often struck with astonishment, when I hear F. reading to those people Old Testament stories, at the resemblance between the manners of the Israelites and other primitive nations and the Basutos. Could you have watched their faces the other day as they listened to the story of Abraham, Eleazar, and Rebekah; every word seemed so telling; she, though so rich, at the well drawing water; indeed every detail comes home here with a force which dwellers in cities can never know.[45]

Dickson points out that although there are exceptions to this rule, for the most part a majority of Africans are partial in regard to the Old Testament. There is a sense among the people that the Old Testament speaks to the underprivileged and dispossessed and therefore speaks to their situation. "The story of the exodus, with its oppression-salvation motif, has in America inspired sermon and song for three centuries. It should occasion no surprise that Africans in South Africa were not long in discovering this appeal. In a country where racial laws relegate them to the backyards of society, the story of a slave people who triumphed against great odds is bound to have special appeal."[46] According to Dickson, it was not only in South Africa that the Bible was found as an instrument of liberation but also in colonial Africa where the call to self-awareness and freedom were clear. The colonial situation of oppression made the Bible attractive as a tool for liberation, but over and beyond that is the pervasiveness of religion and life.

> Birth, puberty and marriage, death: these are events which are held to be full of meaning because of their sacred associations; not only do these life-stages involve, as it is believed, the working of invisible and irresistible forces, but they also remind society constantly of its

obligations to the spirit powers—God, the divinities, the ancestors, etc. Agricultural pursuits bring the African face to face not only with God who gives rain and sunshine, but also with the Goddess of the earth. . . . Similarly, in ancient Israel religion was not divorced from life.[47]

Africans find the atmosphere of the Old Testament like the one they breathe. Their agricultural lifestyle, their frank talk about children and the extended family, the love of genealogy and the concrete ways in which they talk about God and people, all these realities make the Old Testament important for African self-awareness and liberation.

In his book *The Slave Community,* John Blassingame gives us some clues concerning the acculturation and adaptation of Africans in the American South and the Caribbean. He helps us understand why African retentions survived in the Caribbean and Latin America to a much greater extent than in the United States of America. He agrees with W.E.B. Du Bois's classic text *The Negro Church* that the new that confronted Africans in the New World was life on the plantation, and that for better or for worse, the Christian church—and in this case the master's church—had an invaluable role to play in their domestication and to some extent in their liberation. Blassingame points out that although the Christian church saw itself as the protector of the Indians and took many steps for the amelioration and alleviation of the harsh conditions of oppression meted out to them, the church, beginning with Bartolome De Las Casas, did not have an equal interest or commitment for the freedom of African slaves. He puts it this way:

By royal decree and philosophical commitment, the major focus of the Latin American Catholic Church's missionary activity and interest in promoting social welfare was the Indian. Beginning with De Las Casas's successful plea for the humane treatment of Indians and the substitution of black bondsmen for red ones, the Catholic Church was preoccupied with freeing those Indians who had been enslaved, and Christianizing them. . . . Never did the Catholic Church anywhere in Latin America manifest the same apostolic fervor, offer the same protection, or devote the same resources to blacks as it did to Indians. At the same time the clergy men were trying to prevent the exploitation of Indians, they were joining the crews of Portuguese and Spanish slave ships bound for Africa. Not only did the priests bless the enterprises, they also baptized the slaves on the shores of Africa in a Latin ceremony understood neither by the whites nor the blacks.[48]

The church seemed to have had some success in Christianizing enslaved persons as long as the numbers were small, but as slavery became an economic institution and the church itself began to hold mortgages for slave owners and was among the large slave owners, the balance of power tilted in the direction of the planter class. The interest in sugar, coffee, and tobacco took precedence over that of enslaved Africans. "The more the slaveholders complained about the interference of priests, or expressed their fear that religious instruction would lead slaves to feel first that they were equal to whites and later encourage them to rebel, the more the Portuguese and Spanish monarchs turned a deaf ear to the Church. By the nineteenth century, Catholic humanism had lost its battle with colonial materialism."[49] The Catholic Church was overcome by materialism, and as Orlando Patterson points out, this was also true of the Anglican Church in English-speaking colonies throughout the Caribbean.[50] Both Patterson and Blassingame point out that from the eighteenth century on, the Catholic and Anglican churches in the Caribbean and throughout Latin America gave in to the demands of the planter class and it would not be unusual for enslaved persons to hear sermons commanding "slaves [to] be obedient to your masters as unto God, for this is the will of God." It is quite clear here that from the eighteenth century on the Catholic and Anglican churches in the Caribbean took sides: they sided with the master class against the enslaved population. Enslaved persons were taught that their masters were their fathers to whom they owed respect, obedience, and love. This was true in Virginia as it was in the Caribbean.

Although enslaved persons in the United States and the Caribbean heard the same types of sermons and received the same kinds of religious instruction, there were important distinctions in both contexts. Enslaved persons in the Caribbean did not have as close contact with clergy and the planter class as in the United States. On the one hand, many owners of plantations throughout the Caribbean resided in Europe. There was absentee ownership; the plantation was run by overseers and managers, most of whom resented being in the Caribbean and therefore allowed enslaved persons much freedom to grow their own gardens, practice their own religion, and shape their own worldviews. This was in distinction to enslaved persons on the US mainland, who lived in close proximity to their masters and were often under the direct supervision of the owner. Frederick Douglass tells of masters hiding in the bushes to spy on enslaved persons to make sure they worked from sunup until sundown. Often masters themselves would punish slaves for perceived infractions. But the situation was quite different in the Caribbean both in the material and spiritual worlds. For example: "Cuba presents a perfect illustration of the problem the Church faced. In 1860 there were only 779 clergy men in Cuba to serve the religious needs of 1,199,429 inhabitants, or one clergy-man for every 1,539 inhabitants. Even if the white population had been ex-cluded from the clergy's charges, there were too few priests, outside of the urban centers, to give much pastoral care to bondsmen. Cuba's clergymen were concentrated in the cities, with 401, or 51 percent, of them in Havana. While in Havana there was one clergyman for every 80 slaves, the other 378 clergymen had to serve 343,950 slaves in the other provinces or an average of one clergyman for every 907 slaves."[51] This relative freedom that enslaved persons experienced in Cuba was the case throughout the Caribbean as Afro-Caribbean people were able to adapt their religious and cultural styles to the new environment, especially in burials, birth and puberty rites and rituals, marriage, and the community approach to work. It must also be kept in mind that Afro-Caribbean persons who were members of established churches were nominal members, as they continued African religious practices, beliefs, languages, and customs. And these practices have carried over to the present day. Many Caribbean people will keep membership in established churches as a symbol of social mobility in the wider culture but belong to churches that are steeped in African practices. During the colonial administration of these countries, drumming was forbidden in the majority of Christian churches, whether Protestant or Roman Catholic. Afro-Caribbean people would attend the established churches at 11 A.M. then go to indigenous churches where they would chant and dance to drumming all night long. Sometimes the all-night drumming carried over into the following day. The truth is that continuing well into the twentieth century, large numbers of African Americans and Afro-Caribbean people believed in the religion of their African parents.

> Because creation stories, Supreme Beings, spirits, priest-healers, and elaborate moral and ethical systems were central in African religions, the native Africans enslaved in America found it relatively easy to un-derstand similar features in Christianity. Many Africans were initially attracted to Christianity because they believed the "life after death" concept the white ministers emphasized meant that they would even-tually join their ancestors in Africa. For others, the attraction of Chris-tianity was that it appeared "that white people could make the book *talk*" when they read the Bible. A Baptist missionary to the Yoruba de-scribed some of the congruencies between Christianity and African religion in an 1853 report: "besides their knowledge of the one and only God, the Yoruba have words to express sin, guilt, sacrifice, interces-sion, repentance, faith, pardon, adoption. . . . They believe . . . there is a heaven and a hell, and some very soon learn to desire the great salva-tion when they hear the gospel.[52]

Africans did not abandon their religious worldviews but sought to blend them and make them relevant to Christian practices. Pocket crosses their masters would wear were understood as charms that would keep evil spirits at bay. Jesus was a healer similar to the medicine man back home in Africa and the Bible was a story book not unlike many of the stories they were familiar with of a woman going to the well to draw water, or a chief having many wives and owning much land, and the importance of circumcision and sacrifices and burnt offerings. The missionaries "attacked concubinage, drumming, dancing, the Christmas festival and Sabbath breaking. This practically covered the field of Negro amusements and immoral behavior in one of these respects and was grounds for expulsion from church. The establishment was especially strict in respect to marriage and discouraged baptism of illegitimate children. This meant in practice that at least 70 percent of the population was barred from the church. In spite of decades of missionary training, Jamaicans would not get married. Young women felt that marriage was a form of slavery."[53]

In 1740, and especially after 1760, enslaved persons in Virginia and throughout the American South were exposed to the Great Awakening, in which a number of Methodist, Baptist, and Presbyterian preachers offered the Christian gospel to enslaved persons. Through the fiery preaching of the Great Awakening several African Americans were allowed admission to these evangelical churches through baptism and sought to interpret Christianity through the prism of African religion and culture. Commenting on the admission of African Americans to the Christian church during the early years of 1790s, the Baptist chronicler John Leland states:

They seem in general to put more confidence in their own color, than they do in whites; when they attempt to preach, they seldom fail of being very zealous; their language is broken, but they understand each other, and the whites may gain their ideas. A few of them have undertaken to administer baptism, but it generally ends in confusion; they commonly are more noisy in time of preaching than the whites, and are more subject to bodily exercise, and if they meet in any encouragement in these things, they grow extravagant.[54]

It should not be inferred that the majority of African Americans were participants in the Great Awakening. In fact, the converse was true as the majority of enslaved Blacks in Virginia were in rural areas and as such did not have easy access to camp meetings. Additionally, many masters did not trust the openness of these revival meetings and were unsure what enslaved persons would make of the teachings of the Christian church. John Leland notes, "Many masters and overseers will whip and torture the poor creature for going to meeting, even at night, when the labor of the day is done."[55] In his published dissertation for the University of Virginia in 1914, Joseph B. Earnest Jr. captures the thinking of Whites regarding African Americans' view of religion during the Great Awakening: "It is certain that the Negro came to America with his mind reeking with gross superstitions, depravity, and ignorance so profound, that he clung to these while facing the inevitable, with an enthusiasm worthy of a zealot. Their barbarous natures, moral degradation and fantastic beliefs were already deeply chiseled into the tables of their hearts."[56] Joseph Earnest concludes that it was impossible to inscribe on the hearts and minds of African Americans authentic Christianity as preached by the evangelicals, not only because of their superstitions but because many missionaries and masters alike did not regard them as human. It is worth noting that one of the foremost Black intellectuals writing at the same time as Joseph Earnest Jr.—W.E.B. Du Bois—writes of the religious expression of Africans in the Americas as superstition. "It was not at first by any means a Christian Church, but a mere adaptation of those heathen rites which we roughly designate by the term Obe Worship, or 'Voodoism.' "[57] According to Du Bois, African religious beliefs, coupled with the presence of the African priest on plantations who interpreted Christianity from an African framework, made it impossible in the first two centuries of slavery for the Black church to be anything besides a blending of African and Christian beliefs. In Black churches that were formed and administered by persons of African descent, the bias was toward African ways of thinking, especially a reliance on the centrality of spirit. The African worldview was essentially one in which spirits peopled the universe. Worship was always the worship of spirit mediated by spirit. "At first the system was undoubtedly African and part of some more or less general religious system. It finally degenerated into mere imposture. There would seem to be some traces of blood sacrifice and worship of the moon, but unfortunately those who have written on the subject have not been serious students of a curious human phenomenon, but rather persons apparently unable to understand why a transplanted slave should cling to heathen rites."[58] With Du Bois, we must investigate how much of what he terms heathen rites shaped the religious worldviews of Africans in the New World.

Looking Back—Looking Forward

Although the worldview of the African is religious, the African identity that emerged was not shaped by Christianity. The Christian witness on the continent may be traced to the fourth century, yet outside of Egypt and Ethiopia, it is difficult to document any attempt to Christianize Africa prior to the twentieth century. In his book *Toward an Indigenous Church,* Professor Bolaji Idowu comments on the failure of the Christian church to shape the African ethos:

> There was a church in North Africa. That church was the mother of those great makers of church history—Augustine, Tertullian, Cyril, Athanasius, to name a few. She is no longer in existence today; she perished long ago. And why? It is basically because she remained a foreigner and never belonged to the environment in which she lived. Was that not partly the reason for the death of the church founded in Nigeria in the fifteenth century through the activities of the Portuguese and Spanish missionaries?[59]

According to Idowu, the God presented by Portuguese and Spanish missionaries was a foreigner who did not know the African traditions and culture and seems to have had no interest in them. With these claims in mind, we sum up the main traditions in African religions. Most Africans attribute the creation of the universe to God. God is the creator of human beings and their world. Professor J. K. Agbete describes the central tenets of God in African Traditional Religions which non-Christians and non-Moslems attribute to their supreme deity. These attributes may be classified under two categories:

a. The external and intrinsic attributes of God
1. God is almighty: The world is wide but God is the master
2. God is omnipresent: If you want to tell God something tell the wind
3. God is omniscient: A great being whose vision nothing can escape
4. God is transcendent: Once upon a time there lived an old woman whose favorite dish was fufu. Every time she pounded fufu the pestle went against the sky which was then very near to the earth. On one occasion the sky felt so much disturbed by the old woman's pestle that it receded to its present distance from the earth. (The point is that God lives in the sky or is the sky)
b. The moral attributes of God
1. God is a good creator. The hawk says, everything created by God is good
2. God is a God of order. God does not like disorder, therefore God has given a name to everything
3. God is gracious. God pounds the fufu for the armless person[60]

God is portrayed as the source of all life, and as Supreme Being, God has all power. Humanity in all its manifestations comes from God and constitutes the point of departure for talk about cosmology and theology. To raise the epistemological question concerning the nature and being of God presupposes an understanding of the nature and being of people. "Everything created by God is good." People and their God in history is the theme of African Traditional Religion. In this worldview, God does not exist for God-self, but for people. Human beings are at the center of this cosmology. The natural order, plants, animals provide resources for human beings as they navigate the mystery of life. It is appropriate to mention that in African Traditional Religion people are not born ill. There is no notion of original sin that we find in St. Augustine and in certain portions of the Bible. According to St. Augustine it is not possible not to sin and one of the central depictions of human beings is that they are sinners. Theologians of the Christian church along with several passages in the Bible indicate that human beings are pathologically ill. Human beings are born in sin and iniquity and the central reality of human life is that we are sinners. In African Traditional Religions everyone is born whole, everyone is born sinless. This means, among other things, that everyone has equal access to the tree of life. When sin occurs it is dealt with; this may mean shedding the blood of a rooster or a goat for the offense and one moves on with one's life. In African Traditional Religions, it is not sin that is original; it is wholeness, it is wellness. Sin is an intrusion and has no ontological status in relation to human beings. Sin is parasitic and is not constitutive of what it means to be human. To be human is to receive one's life as a gift with all heaven and earth in the service of sustaining and supporting wholeness and wellness.

3

Black Church Experience South
of the Border

IT HAS BEEN noted, in a variety of contexts, that over eleven million Africans survived the Middle Passage and were forced to work on plantations in the New World. Of this number about 450,000 arrived in the United States. "All the rest arrived in places south of our border. . . . So, in one sense, the major 'African American experience,' as it were, unfolded not in the United States, as those of us caught in the embrace of what we might think of as 'African American Exceptionalism' might have thought, but throughout the Caribbean and South America, if we are thinking of this phenomenon in terms of sheer numbers alone."[1] This no doubt explains, in part, the numerical advantage Black people in the Caribbean have had over their counterparts in the United States. This is an advantage that provides a measure of leisure, confidence in protest, and the luxury of majority thinking—the result of many Caribbean nations having populations of more than 90 percent of Afro-Caribbean people. The Caribbean sociologist Barry Chevannes writes of growing up in Jamaica and taking it for granted that he was a member of a rural plantation community, never having occasion to question who he was as a member of a Black majority. This changed for him when he became a student in a Jesuit seminary in the Berkshire Mountains in New England, the only Black person among 200 seminarians and faculty.

> Then one Sunday afternoon, the Boston College Glee Club put on a concert for the seminary community, and there as the curtain opened was a black face, the only one among 60 choristers. My heart leapt and I was disturbed. What difference should a black face make? Why should I find in his presence there such special and evidently personal

significance as to create within me this new and troubling emotion? I had never before known such feelings of affinity, and it seemed to me as unnatural as it was spontaneous. In the reception afterwards I resisted the pull for as long as I could, but it turned out that I too was not unnoticed by him, and so we met, the beginning of a life long and fruitful friendship, which was to usher me into the world of being black, into civil rights, Martin Luther King, and the black Boston ghetto of Roxbury. This kind of magnetic pull was and still is to some extent, quite normal in the United States. . . . However, it is quite foreign to Jamaica, where being black is the condition of the overwhelming majority.[2]

It was noted in earlier chapters that because of the numerical advantage of enslaved Africans on plantations in the Caribbean, enslaved persons were able to preserve their stories and traditions. The memory of Africa lingers and is manifest in culture, especially at points where religion and culture meet. An added advantage, of course, was the reality of absentee ownership of plantations as many owners resided in Europe and this provided Black sacred space for the creation and practice of Black churches. It is also widely recognized that many enslaved persons were acculturated in the Caribbean prior to being auctioned off to colonies in North America for work on plantations. Winston James in *Holding Aloft the Banner of Ethiopia* points out that there was an enduring relationship between the Caribbean and the American South, particularly between Barbados and South Carolina. "Barbadian slaves had been taken by their British owners colonizing South Carolina during the seventeenth century, and earlier in the same century slaves from Barbados constituted an important portion of the population of Virginia. South Carolina was in fact developed by and in subservience to Barbadian interests, supplying beef, pork, and lumber products to the island in exchange for sugar. . . . In the eighteenth century South Carolina extended and deepened its trading relations with other Caribbean colonies, Jamaica surpassing Barbados as a market for its products. Up to 1700, it is safe to assume that all the slaves in South Carolina came from the Caribbean and Barbados in particular."[3] James further indicates that fair estimates of the Black population in South Carolina during the eighteenth century point to 15 to 20 percent of enslaved persons in South Carolina as being from the Caribbean. The same may be said of the Black population in Boston during the eighteenth century. The population of Caribbean people in the United States was very small during the nineteenth century but exploded after the Civil War. "Indeed, the foreign-born black population, which was almost wholly Caribbean in origin, increased fivefold between 1850 and 1900, from 4,067 to 20,236, and distinguished Caribbean migrants populate the annals of nineteenth-century Afro-America."[4]

As early as the 1600s, Barbados, Jamaica, and later Saint Domingue displaced Brazil as the leading sugar producer in the Americas. In part because of the American Revolution in 1776 until the end of the century, sugar exports from the Caribbean were disrupted, creating opportunities for Brazil and Spanish colonies to enhance production. "Those opportunities increased further in the 1790s, when the slaves of Saint Domingue rose up in an epoch-making revolution that by 1804 had abolished slavery—the first New World nation to do so—and created the independent republic of Haiti. By ending slavery, the revolution also put an end to the richest plantation economy in the world. In 1791 Saint Domingue had exported over 80,000 tons of sugar; in 1804, about 24,000; in 1818, less than a thousand; and in 1825, only one."[5] In a profound sense, we may acknowledge that the only successful slave revolt in the Americas was the Haitian revolution. Many of the elites in Haiti fled to Cuba and Puerto Rico as the fear of slave uprising spread even to Brazil. "In 1814 a group of merchants and planters from the Bahian capital of Salvador wrote to the king to express their fears about the rising state of rebelliousness among the slave population. After cataloguing incidents of assault, crime, and 'insolence' by slaves, they concluded that, unless harsh measures were taken, 'nobody with good sense can doubt that the fate of this captaincy will be the same as that of the island of Saint Domingue. . . . [The slaves] know about and discuss the disastrous occurrences that took place on the island of Saint Domingue, and one hears mutinous claims that by St. John's Day there will not be one white or mulatto alive.' "[6] The spark of freedom was ignited, and the flame burned brightly as enslaved persons on the US mainland, and the Caribbean islands agitated for freedom.

> In 1806 Spain banned the entry into Cuba and Puerto Rico of all people of color arriving on ships from Haiti. The governor of Puerto Rico added to this measure by ordering a listing of slaves in every municipality of the island and a report on "where they gather." Despite these measures, major slave conspiracies were uncovered on both islands in 1812. . . . Authorities in Puerto Rico uncovered the slaves' plans before they came to fruition; in Cuba, free black conspirators (several of them Afro-Dominican veterans of the Haitian Revolution) managed to coordinate uprisings of plantations slaves in the province of Havana. . . . The principal Cuban conspirator, free black carpenter and militiaman

Jose Antonio Aponte, was arrested and put to death. Among the incriminating evidence found in his house were portraits of Haitian independence commanders Toussaint L'Ouverture and Henri Christophe gracing his parlor.[7]

Slavery and the plantation economy thrived during much of the 1800s in Cuba, Puerto Rico, and Brazil. In Cuba, sugar exports increased tenfold and by even a larger ratio in Puerto Rico. Cuba became the world's largest exporter of sugar in the Western hemisphere. Refusing to abolish slavery until 1886, just two years ahead of Brazil. "Between 1800 and 1850 Brazil received 1.7 million Africans, as many as during the entire 1700s. Cuba received 560,000 (and an additional 150,000 between 1850 and 1867), and Puerto Rico some 50,000."[8]

African Faith and Christian Teaching

The ethos of slave society was permanently altered throughout the Caribbean; African culture was enhanced as visible expressions of Africa were seen in music, dance, and religion. Africans who took their religion with them to the fields, to markets, and certainly to the forests combined African ways of worship with tenets and teaching of Christianity. "During the second half of the 1700s, the church had tried to convert the cabildos [African congregations] into Catholic religious brotherhoods, assigning each of them a patron saint and instructing their members in Catholic doctrine and observance. As elsewhere in Latin America, African worshippers were receptive to Christianity, but insisted on retaining African gods and rites as well; and the cabildos were the setting within which these gods were worshipped and preserved."[9] It is worth noting that it was the combining of their African faith with Catholic teaching that created Santeria on Cuban soil. Similar claims may be made of Haiti's Vodou and Brazil's Candomble. "Santeria, like Brazil's Candomble and Haiti's Vodou, as we have seen, was a religion born of the slave trade. Cuban slaves combined their Yoruba faith with Catholicism in a mix that is unique to the island, its population, and its culture. Once again, the Yoruba orixas and Catholic saints worked together to help slaves bear their bondage with faith and dignity. Santeria is sometimes even called the way of the saints."[10] However, the key to understanding the role of African religion in the New World has to do with the role of the spirit of the ancestors combined with spiritual and supernatural forces in nature. One role of the priest is to safeguard the sacred mysteries enshrined in these traditions. Another role is to use their access to these mysteries through the ancestors, to alleviate the plight of their clients in offering them protection against the enemy and in divining possibilities of the future. Through Santeria the priest is able to intervene in daily affairs, on the one hand, and on the other, to divine the future which includes a description of one's relationship to the orishas. "But in reading the relationship between the orishas and their followers, the santeros 'did things' as well. The purpose of the divination was to identify the spiritual forces determining one's path, through life, and to help individuals avert danger and misfortune on that path by harmonizing their relationship with the gods."[11] "In the Catholic countries of Brazil, Haiti and Cuba, slaves were permitted to form ethnic associations ('governments,' 'nations' *cabildos*, religious fraternities) where African languages, dances and religious beliefs could be perpetuated."[12] This helps to explain the survival of African retentions in much of Latin America and the Caribbean. However, it must be kept in mind that the Haitian revolution did circumscribe African retentions to a degree as plantation owners feared that if they did not curtail the freedoms of Black people, what happened in Haiti would also happen in their countries. There were other variables. "Plantations in the Caribbean were larger than in the United States. At the end of the eighteenth century, the average sugar plantation was staffed with 180 slaves; in Virginia and Maryland the average plantation had less than 13 slaves. Because of the smaller percentage of whites living in the Caribbean islands and because of the size of the typical sugar plantation, blacks there had less contact with European culture. Westernization was a much slower process. Also, through the end of the eighteenth century and the beginning of the nineteenth century, the large majority of the slave populations of the British and French islands were African-born."[13] Further, in the North American colonies, slaves born in Africa comprised only 20 percent of the Black population at the end of the American Revolution and by 1860 almost 100 percent of slaves in the United States were native-born. For numbers of these slaves the memory of Africa had begun to fade as many were fifth-generation Americans. These persons had not had any personal contact with Africa, and most of them had no acquaintance with those who did have such contact.[14] The fading of the memory of Africa for African Americans opened the door for Christianity to begin to shape the ethos of Black life in American colonies in a way that was not yet possible in the Caribbean.

Christian Churches and Slavery

It is worth remembering that the church during the sixteenth and seventeenth centuries did not challenge the system of slavery as it was practiced in the New World. Indeed, the church benefited from slavery as in the case of Barbados where the Anglican Church owned the large Codrington plantation and was responsible for administering a plantation larger than 700 acres and 300 slaves, with the burden of turning a profit. We are told that Christopher Codrington, one of the wealthiest plantation owners in the Caribbean, bequeathed his estate to the Society for the Propagation of the Gospel (SPG) in 1710. Commenting on the opportunity to Christianize slaves on the Codrington plantation, Bishop William Fleetwood of England explains:

> If all the Slaves throughout America, and every Island in those seas, were to continue infidels forever, *yet ours alone must needs be Christians.* We must instruct them in the Faith of Christ, bring them to Baptism, and put them in the way that leads to everlasting Life. This will be preaching by *Example,* the most effectual way of recommending Doctrines, to a hard and unbelieving World, blinded by Interests, and other Prepossessions.[15]

Caribbean theologian Kingsley Lewis points out that the bishop of the Christian church was wrong in seeking to make Christianity compatible with slavery. "In fact, the SPG proceeded on its assumption that in a humane regime the Negro could become a Christian, educated and skilled, and yet remain by the law of the colony, in a state of slavery. The SPG therefore found itself in the position of trying to make money out of its plantations to finance its altruistic experiment, but in so doing, being subject to the same laws of production as the rest of the plantocracy."[16] The Society for the Propagation of the Gospel visited the age-old question, "Can one be a slave and Christian at the same time?" and with Bishop Fleetwood and church practice answered in a resounding yes. The SPG saw their experiment as an opportunity to make peace with the planting class by demonstrating that the best slave is a Christian slave, one who could be civilized, Westernized, educated, and could prove to all that the values of Christianity were consonant with those of plantation life. If one could be slave and Christian at the same time, it opened the door, on the one hand, for the preaching of the Christian gospel to enslaved persons, which included salvation for the souls of the enslaved, and on the other hand, it provided a rationale for Christians and churches to own slaves. The truth is the church's approach and commitment to religious instruction did not threaten slavery as an institution; rather, the peculiar institution was supported and upheld.

In the United States the situation was similar as many clergy owned slaves, among them the preacher of the Great Awakening, George Whitfield, who kept slaves at his Bethsaida plantation in Georgia. This was also true of the first priest to be ordained in the New World:

The case of Bartolome de Las Casas is well known: . . . he recommended, in a letter to the Crown, that a certain number of slaves be put at the colonists' disposal, with the object of preserving the remaining Indians of La Espanola. Las Casas at the time did not consider the cruelty of the transatlantic slave trade. Nearly all the representatives of the church thought and acted in like manner. In 1521, Alonso Manso, the first bishop of Puerto Rico, requested twenty black slaves as compensation for the Indians assigned to him. Ten years later, the bishop of Santo Domingo, Sebastian Ramirez de Fuenleal, spoke in favor of free slave importation (sin licencia). . . . The blacks would guarantee the growth of the island and would increase the extraction of gold.[17]

The church sought to change the souls of enslaved persons but did not understand the body as a site for liberation. If the soul belonged to God, the body belonged to the master and salvation of the soul was in the next life. The church's theology of the body taught that the appropriate posture of the Black body was in serving and honoring the master as one honored God. The Reverend Charles Colcock Jones, one of the great southern preachers in a *Catechism* written for enslaved persons writes:

Q: What are the Servants to count their Masters worthy of?
A: All honor.
Q: How are they to try to please their Masters?
A: Please them in all things, not answering again.
Q: Is it right for a Servant when commanded to do anything to be sullen and slow, and answering his master again?
A: No.
Q: But suppose the master is hard to please, and threatens and punishes more than he ought, what is the Servant supposed to do?
A: Do his best to please him.
Q: Are Servants at liberty to tell lies and deceive their Master?
A: No.
Q: If servants will faithfully do their duty and Serve God in their stations as Servants, will they be respected of men, and blessed and honored of God, as well as others?
A: Yes.[18]

The religious teaching offered here was self-serving as the Reverend Mr. Jones owned three plantations with about 100 slaves.

It was in the church's interest to make plantation life amenable for enslaved people as more humane working conditions would contribute to the humanizing of the master; if the slave worked diligently, the master would not have a need to brutalize the slave. Further, there would be more of an understanding between master and missionary if as a result of the church's instruction slaves would run away less and be more industrious. The church accepted the social arrangement in which enslaved people were at the bottom of the society and treated as property rather than persons with dignity and responsibilities as they allowed the church to make peace with the planter class. It was clear that the primary concerns of the master class were forced labor and the idolatry of money in which the profit motive seemed to be everything, and not the liberation of enslaved persons. Even if touched by the horror of slavery, the missionaries did not seek to overthrow the system of slavery. The church, whether Catholic or Protestant, sided with the planter class against the enslaved African foreigner, and this was the case on both sides of the Atlantic.

Body as Site of Liberation

But Black people would fight back not only through revolts, running away, and insurrections but also by calling on their ancestors. Enslaved people remembered Africa, and Africa became a controlling metaphor of liberation. "In Puerto Rico, some black women were imprisoned for practicing witchcraft and spiritualism under the government of Gabriel de Roxas (1608–14). Archbishop Cristobal Rodriguez y Suarez reported yet another case. Witchcraft and other types of black magic had been observed and punished since 1610 by the court of inquisition of Cartagena de Indias."[19] Churches made it clear that their primary concern was with saving the souls of the enslaved person and not disrupting plantation life. Even when the church baptized the bodies of enslaved persons, it was a way of receiving them into a community that sacralized the system and structure of slavery with the hope that baptism would make enslaved people more obedient and diligent to the demands of the planter. The miracle was that "despite those persecution measures, the African slaves succeeded in keeping their own religious world. Uprooted from their homeland, they maintained some of their identity and so filled the vacuum to which the church only paid attention in an inadequate way."[20] Frederick Douglass summed up the way a majority of enslaved persons viewed Christianity—with suspicion—as a religion of the oppressors. Although they gave it nominal attention and saw in the Bible and its liturgy elements of freedom, they were willing to mix Christianity with the veneration of the ancestors and the spirit they encountered in the natural world, be it in the forest, in animals, or in streams. This begins to explain why it was that enslaved persons placed more faith in an African interpretation of Christianity than in the missionaries' articulation of Christianity. The bottom line was that for African peoples, the test regarding the political efficacy of religion was whether it resulted in freedom or in bondage. The great American abolitionist Frederick Douglass states these issues succinctly.

> But the church of this country is not only indifferent to the wrongs of the slave, it actually takes sides with the oppressor. It has made itself the bulwark of American slavery, and the shield of American slavehunters. Many of its eloquent Divines, who stand as the very lights of the church, have shamelessly given the sanction of religion and the Bible to the whole slave system. They have taught that man may, properly, be a slave; that the relation of master and slave is ordained of God; that to send back an escaped bondman to his master is clearly the duty of all the followers of the Lord Jesus Christ; and this horrible blasphemy is palmed off on upon the world for Christianity. . . . They strip the love of God of its beauty and leave the throne of religion a huge, horrible, horrible repulsive form. It is a religion for oppressors, tyrants, man-stealers, and *thugs.*"[21]

From the beginning of their sojourn in the New World, enslaved Africans saw through the hypocrisy of Christianity that one justification for their enslavement was their conversion to Christ. And yet plantation ethics as it was practiced by the master and missionary were conflicted in that possible conversion of Africans to Christianity did not result in their physical freedom nor in the dismantling of the "house of bondage." The argument often given by missionaries and masters for the justification of enslaved Africans was that it was an act of divine providence that the Africans of heathen Africa would be brought within the pale of the Christian church through the instrumentality of slavery. One dilemma concerned the meaning of conversion and baptism for an enslaved person. At one level there was concern as to whether Christians could be enslaved or the state was required to free the enslaved once he or she became a Christian. But there was a deeper issue, and that concerned the very identity of the African. Could the African really become Christian and share this special identity reserved for Europeans? There is another way of expressing this dilemma: was it really possible to translate the Christian message into African culture without Christianity losing its essence, and if this experiment succeeded would this elevate the African to an equal status with the European? If the Christian gospel were translated into the culture of the enslaved, would the Gospel's power to save be lessened? At the heart of the debate was a religion and culture split for Europeans that did not exist for enslaved Africans. Slaves who did not experience this split between religion and culture were eager to be baptized and hopefully share in the equality before God that the church's book seemed to promise.

In the end, as Frederick Douglass suggests, there were more pressing and pragmatic considerations that master and missionary had to take into account. On the one hand, there was the fear that to Christianize the slave and offer baptism was at the same time to extend the hand of fellowship and an invitation to shed Africanness and become Christian and European. What if baptism and church membership made slaves forget their place ? What if it made them uppity, and what of the "unwritten law that a Christian could not be made a slave"? Many masters were not comfortable in exposing enslaved persons to the teachings of the Bible for fear that the equality the Bible claims all people share before God might be transposed to the expectation of a relationship between slave and master. This was one reason for the suspicion often expressed by the master in relation to the slave's introduction to Christianity, the fear that there was a liberation motif hidden in the teachings of the Bible which enslaved persons who read the Bible for themselves might have discovered. This was an understandable fear associated with allowing enslaved persons to preach and handle the dangerous book, the Bible.

Harriet Jacobs, a slave on a plantation in Virginia, recalls a typical sermon from the Anglican priest, the Reverend Mr. Pike, which was aimed at reminding the enslaved of his or her place in plantation society.

When the Rev. Mr. Pike came, there were some twenty persons present. The reverend gentleman knelt in prayer, then seated himself, and requested all present, who could read, to open their books, while he gave out the portions he wished them to repeat and respond to. His text was, "Servants, be obedient to them that are your masters according to the flesh, with fear and trembling, in singleness of your heart, as unto Christ." Pious Mr. Pike brushed up his hair till it stood upright, and, in deep, solemn tones, began: "hearken, ye servants! Give strict heed unto my words. You are rebellious sinners. Your hearts are filled with all manner of evil. 'Tis the devil who tempts you. God is angry with you, if you don't forsake your wicked ways. . . . Instead of serving your masters faithfully, which is pleasing in the sight of your heavenly Master, you are idle, and shirk your work. God sees you. You tell lies. God hears you. . . . Your master may not find you out, but God sees you, and will punish you. O' the depravity of your hearts. You must forsake your sinful ways, and be faithful servants."[22]

Harriet Jacobs points out that enslaved people understood that the organized church was in the service and often employ of the plantation and that the Anglican Church represented the interests of the master. According to Harriet, the Reverend Mr. Pike continued, "Obey your old master and your young master—your old mistress and your young mistress. If you disobey your earthly master, you offend your heavenly Master."[23] Harriet points out that they went home highly amused determined that they would return to hear him again. Enslaved persons were not surprised that the preacher equated their earthly master with God. They understood intuitively that the preacher had an agenda to keep them in their place and to exploit all means that they "would serve their earthly master as they serve God." And yet they would critique the teachings of the White preacher by not only finding humor in his obvious political agenda but by using the master's language against him. Not only would they humor the master when he suggested that in pleasing the earthly master they were at the same time pleasing the heavenly master but they at the same time implied that the heavenly master had all power on earth and in heaven. Enslaved persons were able to use the received missionary's theology against him and the master class to suggest that the master did not have all the power. This is illustrated in an answer and question session between an enslaved candidate for baptism and a missionary that represented both the church and the status quo:

> *Minister:* Well, Thomas, do you know who Jesus Christ is? *Candidate:* Him de son of god, Minister. *Minister:* What did Jesus come into the world to do? *Candidate:* Him come to save poor sinners. *Minister:* Do you think he is able to save sinners? *Candidate:* Me know him able. *Minister:* How can you know that he is able? *Candidate:* Because him make de world: and if him make de world, him able to do all Tings: and minister no tell we often-time dis make him left him fader Trone, and come into dis sinful world. *Minister:* What makes you wish to be baptized? *Candidate:* Because Jesus Christ, put under water, rise up again and we wish to pattern after him. *Minister:* Perhaps you think the water will wash away your sin? *Candidate:* No, no; water no wash away me sin; nothing but the precious Massa Jesus blood wash away me sin.[24]

Enslaved persons discovered through their own reasoning and were able to confirm their claim through their own reading of the Bible that there was another "Massa" who had all power and could do all things because this was demonstrated in God's creation of the world and in the suffering of Jesus. The God who created the world had given evidence beyond dispute that this God was on the side of victims, and that this God who allowed his son Jesus to suffer and to die for poor sinners such as enslaved Thomas, this God had to be a precious Massa, unlike the earthly Massa. With confidence in this precious Massa, Caribbean people would sing, "Do Lord, Oh do Lord, Oh do remember me, way beyond the blue." They had confidence that this precious Massa would remember them in their suffering.

Harriet Jacobs tells us that enslaved people would make up their songs. One went like this:

> *Old Satan is one busy ole man;*
> *He rolls dem blocks all in my way;*
> *But Jesus is my bosom friend;*
> *He rolls dem blocks away*

Harriet shares what it was like for her as a slave to attend a Methodist class meeting in Virginia. "I went with a burdened spirit, and happened to sit next to a poor, bereaved mother, whose heart was still heavier than mine. The class leader was the town constable—a man who bought and sold slaves, who whipped his brethren and sisters of the church at the public whipping post, in jail or out of jail. He was ready to perform that Christian office anywhere for fifty cents."[25] The class leader turned to the woman who sat next to Harriet and said, "Sister, can't you tell us how the Lord deals with your soul? Do you love him as you did formerly?" She rose to her feet, and said in piteous tones, "My Lord and Master, help me! My load is more than I can bear. God has hid himself from me and I am left in darkness and misery." Then striking her breast, she continued, "I can't tell you what is in here! They've got all my children. Last week they took the last one. God only knows where they have sold her. They let me have her sixteen years, and then—O! O! Pray for her brothers and sisters! I've got nothing to live for now. God make my time short."[26]

Harriet does not share with us the name of her enslaved sister. This sister called on her enslaved peers to join her in prayer for her children who were sold away from her. She asked that prayers be offered to the God who hides and allows her to be engulfed in darkness and misery. She pleaded with her brothers and sisters to accompany her in "the valley of deepest darkness" where she needed to hear them cry out to the God who hides in darkness.

With the memory of Africa and African notions of community fresh in their hearts enslaved persons would often pray, "way down yonder by myself, I couldn't hear anybody pray." The loss of community, the loss of family, to have one's children sold away, to be married until you are sold, made her pray that God would make her time short in this vale of tears and deepest darkness. Harriet tells us that the response of the community was to break out spontaneously for over an hour in singing. The people sang as though they were free:

> *Ole Satan thought he had a mighty aim;*
> *He missed my soul, and caught my sins*
> *Cry Amen, cry Amen. Cry Amen to God*
> *He took my sins upon his back;*
> *Went muttering and grumbling down to hell.*
> *Cry Amen, cry Amen, cry Amen to God.*
> *Ole Satan's church is here below*
> *Up to God's free church I hope to go*
> *Cry Amen, cry Amen, cry Amen to God.*[27]

They accepted the planter's church for what it was, "Ole Satan church is here below" but there was hope in "God's free church." The planter's church was the church in which the constable who whipped them was the preacher who asked them to testify to what God had done for them. This was the church in which the preacher told them to serve their earthly master with the same devotion they gave to God.

Enslaved persons' "hermeneutic of suspicion" was turned into a hope for liberation, as they knew intuitively that the Bible was about earthly freedom. Enslaved persons began to decouple the Bible from missionary teaching and refused to regard it as a book for oppressors, or experts, but a book for their community. When they were able to read it for themselves, they allowed their faith in ancestors, and their God, to direct them as through its teaching they called into question the oppressive history of slavery.

But we may ask, if on the one hand enslaved persons saw through the hypocrisy of the master and missionary who hid the teachings of divine justice and equality in the Bible from them, why did they continue with Christianity? Could it be that as they joined the faith of their ancestors and God with history they began to understand as Frederick Douglass taught, that the God of the Bible was not on the side of oppressors?

In a poignant chapter in his book, *The History of the Negro Church*, the noted historian Carter G. Woodson speaks of this joining of faith and history as "The Dawn of the New Day." What may we enquire constitutes the dawn of a new day in the encounter of people of African ancestry with Christianity? Did Woodson's understanding of the new dawn posit a discontinuity engendered by African faith with the house of bondage as this was experienced in 200 years of slavery?

The Dawn of a New Day

According to Carter G. Woodson, something new happened in the revival movement that swept the American colonies in the 1740s onward. There was a break with the old attitude toward the enslaved:

> Although the attitude of the Catholic pioneers was not altogether encouraging to the movement for the evangelization of the Negroes, still less assistance came from the Protestants settling the English colonies. Few, if any, of the pioneers from Great Britain had the missionary spirit of the Latins. As the English were primarily interested in founding new homes in America, they thought of the Negroes not as objects of Christian philanthropy but rather as tools with which they might reach that end. It is not surprising then that with the introduction of slavery as an economic factor in the development of the English colonies little care was taken of their spiritual needs and especially so when they were confronted with the unwritten law that a Christian could not be held a slave.[28]

Woodson mentions that there were exceptions to this rule by organizations such as the Society for the Propagation of the Gospel which was formed by the Anglican Church in 1701 for the express purpose of preaching the Christian gospel to Indians and Negroes who were considered infidels and heathens. But the hope of being transformative was compromised as the SPG in 1710 accepted the Codrington plantation in Barbados with 300 slaves and spent much time administering the plantation rather than preaching a gospel of liberation. But even with good intentions to evangelize enslaved persons, many churches along with organizations like the SPG had to deal with concerns and questions of productivity, whether religious instruction would mitigate against the central purpose of their enslavement, to work on plantations in the New World and thereby make a profit for the master. Issues of race and capitalism took precedence over evangelization and the saving of the soul of the slave. Masters needed to be persuaded that Christianity would serve as a tool of social control and perhaps be more useful than the whip. Would the formal introduction and instruction of Christianity to Black people mean that they would be patient and humble, less prone to run away, and willing to work harder and even serve the master the way they were instructed to serve God? Would the plantation preacher make the case that the master is God's representative on earth, and the duty of the enslaved is to serve as if they were serving God? Woodson frames the issue for us:

> During the latter part of the seventeenth century and throughout the eighteenth, there were rising to power in the United States two sects, which, because of their evangelical appeal to the untutored mind, made such inroads upon the Negro population as to take over in a few years thereafter the direction of the spiritual development of most of the Negroes throughout the United States. These were the Methodists and Baptists.[29]

Woodson reminds us that a change of heart occurred among the Baptists and Methodists as they had a long record of disinterest in evangelizing Black people. "Whitefield in Georgia advocated the introduction of slaves and rum for the economic improvement of the colony. He even owned slaves himself, although Wesley, Coke and Asbury opposed the institution and advocated emancipation as a means to thorough evangelization. The work of the Methodists in behalf of the Negroes, moreover, was still less directed toward their liberation in the West Indies than on the continent."[30] But if we bracket the zeal of Whitfield to use enslaved persons to increase the economic standing of Georgia, Woodson would wager that Methodists like Freeborn Garretson, and Bishop Asbury were traveling evangelists like the apostles of old in their mission and ministry to the master in the interest of enslaved Blacks. Bishop Asbury referred to slaveholders as sons of oppression who were inexcusable before God for holding and keeping fellow human beings in bondage. Freeborn Garretson called on slave masters to let the oppressed go free and spoke of slavery as a sin. Further, in 1784 the Methodist Conference declared "slavery as contrary to the laws of God, man and nature, and hurtful to society." Slaveholding members of the church were given a year in which they were expected to release their slaves. "Much agitation had been caused by this discussion in the State of Virginia and in 1785 there came several petitions asking for suspension of the resolution passed in 1884 and it was so ordered in 1785 in the words: 'It is recommended to all our brethren to suspend the execution of the minute on slavery *till the deliberations of a future conference*; and that an equal space of time be allowed to all our members for consideration when the minute shall be put in force.'"[31] The Conference pledged to work for the destruction of slavery and pointed out that traveling preachers would forfeit

ministerial privileges if they became slave owners. The passion for revival and
the fervor generated by the Great Awakening were not enough to dismantle
the house of bondage so skillfully constructed by slave society. Slavery as an
economic necessity proved too much for Christianity, and in the meantime,
both enslaved and free lived with the ameliorative and palliative effect of
Christianity. The Great Awakening had the effect of highlighting the importance of religious instruction for enslaved persons which was seen by many
within the church as a religious duty that would enhance master-slave relationships and at the same time increase productivity on plantations. It was a
win-win situation for both the church and the master. The truth is, slavery
emerged as a Christian institution. The church's outreach to the enslaved sati-
ated the consciences of the oppressor class and it comforted the enslaved and
gave them an otherworldly hope of life beyond the sky. Masters became persuaded that the best slaves were those who were baptized, as baptism would
neutralize the passion to run away and challenge the master's authority. This
form of reasoning provided an incentive for the master to encourage the
Christianizing and therefore Westernizing of the enslaved. Carter G. Woodson leads us to one of the unintended consequences of the Great Awakening,
that several Black persons who became members of the Christian church
were licensed to preach and had the responsibility of interpreting the Good
Book to their constituencies. Woodson heralds the dawn of a new day:

> In those cases in which Negroes were permitted to preach, they found
> themselves confronting not only the opposition of the more aristocratic
> sects but violating laws of long standing, prohibiting Negro ministers
> from exercising their gifts. When their ministrations were of a local
> order, and they did not stir up their fellow men to oppose the establish
> order of things, not so much attention was paid to their operations.
> When, however, these Negroes of unusual power preached with such
> force as to excite not only the blacks but the whites, steps were gener-
> ally taken to silence these speakers heralding the coming of a new day.
> This opposition on the part of the whites apparently grew more strenu-
> ous upon the attainment of independence. As British subjects, they
> had more toleration for the rise of the Negro in the church than they
> had after the colonies became independent. While struggling for lib-
> erty themselves, even for religious freedom, these Americans were not
> willing to grant others what they themselves desired.[32]

Preachers such as Richard Allen saw the importance of founding a church
and tailoring the gospel not to support the house of bondage, but to dismantle

it. For example, there would be few if any White preachers who would preach on Moses leading an exodus of slaves from Egypt to freedom in some promised land. White preachers did not see the body as a site of freedom; the freedom they advocated was of the soul before God, which was another way of talking about otherworldly freedom. Charles Joyner frames the issue for us in relation to one of the outstanding preachers of the Great Awakening, the Reverend Charles Colcock Jones. "The Reverend Jones was not only pastor of Savannah's First Presbyterian Church but also master of three rice plantations and more than one hundred slaves in Liberty County, Georgia. While he seemed genuinely concerned for the salvation of his slaves' souls, there is no question that he consciously and deliberately used religion as an instrument of discipline and control."[33] It was the exception rather than the rule to find a White preacher who was invested in the liberation, in physical and socioeconomic terms, of enslaved Black people.

Richard Allen who founded the first independent Black church was the most famous of Black preachers. Born a slave of Benjamin Chew in Philadelphia, he was sold with his family to a planter in Delaware and came to hear the preaching of Freeborn Garretson. Allen was converted in 1777 and three years later began his career as a preacher.

> Struck with the genuineness of his piety, his master permitted him to conduct prayers and to preach in his house. The master was one of the first converts of this zealous man. Feeling after his conversion that slavery was wrong, Allen's master permitted his bondmen to obtain their freedom. Allen and his brother purchased themselves for $2,000. . . .
> Richard Allen then engaged himself at such menial labor as a Negro could find. He cut and hauled wood while preaching at his leisure. . . .
> Bishop Asbury frequently gave him assignments to preach.[34]

Albert Raboteau suggests that the new reality that the Great Awakening brought was conversion of enslaved persons and a new ethos in which master and slaves worshipped as the emphasis on the New Gospel Order opened the door for Black persons to participate actively in the religious culture as preachers, exhorters, founders of mutual aid societies, and churches. Christian churches under the aegis of the Great Awakening preached that the White church had a responsibility to proclaim spiritual liberty to a captive and enslaved people. The problem that the White church sought to address was sin as a spiritual and moral force that kept Black people in their blindness, and the moral responsibility of the master class to provide for the spiritual and physical needs of the enslaved within the context of slavery. "Increasingly, slavery was not only accepted as an economic fact of life, but defended as a positive good, sanctioned by Scripture and capable of producing a Christian social order based on the observance of mutual duty, slave to master and master to slave. It was the ideal of the antebellum plantation mission to create such a rule of gospel order by convincing slaves and masters that their salvation depended on it."[35] Although many slaves were exposed to Christianity during the closing decades of the eighteenth and early years of the nineteenth century, Raboteau further cautions us not to get too naive concerning the impact of Christian churches on the majority of enslaved persons as those who lived in rural areas did not have ready access to Christian missions or independent Black churches during this time. The impact of Baptist and Methodist witness among enslaved persons was primarily in relation to urban areas. The great majority of enslaved persons in rural areas were still outside the pale of the institutional church. Raboteau cites the concern of the Reverend Charles Colcock Jones:

> It is true they [slaves] have access to the house of God on the Sabbath; but it is also true that where the privilege is within their reach, a minority only, (and frequently a very small one) embrace it. There are multitude of districts in the South and Southwest, in which the churches cannot contain one tenth of the Negro population; besides others in which there are no churches at all. It must be remembered also that in many of those churches there is preaching only once a fortnight, or once a month, and then perhaps only one sermon. To say that they fare as well as their masters does not settle the point; for great numbers of masters have very few or no religious privileges at all.[36]

The Emergence of Plantation Missions

It was not enough to encourage enslaved persons to attend the institutional church when the church was not within easy reach, many slaves felt unwelcome, and much preaching they heard was irrelevant. Therefore, clergy persons such as Colcock Jones pressed the issue of taking the church to the slaves by creating on several plantations missions to the slaves. Competing with plantation missions in the mind of the master class was the abolitionist movement, which pressed for the freeing of the slaves in southern states. The master class had to be convinced that a plantation mission was not another iteration of the abolitionist movement, or a convenient opportunity for slave preachers to misguide the enslaved population. The truth is that the closer the plantocracy was historically to the memory of a slave revolt, the more assurance the plantation mission preachers had to provide the master that they would guarantee that the baptized slave would be a humble and dutiful worker. It is here that the hard work of plantation missions lay—to convince masters that the mission was not a threat to the plantation economy and ethos, as its focus and "mission" was in saving the soul and not freeing the body.

With the anti-literacy and abolitionist injunctions in mind, plantation missions were able to arrive at a set of guidelines for the instructions of enslaved persons by the clergy. These guidelines had in mind the peculiar need for plantation missions in the southern states to keep intact the plantation ethics and economy. As plantation missions received blessing from master and missionary, it was agreed that there should be a sermon by a preacher on the Sabbath with an understanding that there would be occasions during the week for a lecture or meetings a couple of evenings to facilitate visiting or resident clergy. It was also highly recommended that the master and his family attend plantation worship to set a good example for the slaves. Further, there should be much emphasis on the training of children, with Sabbath schools which adults were expected to attend. Underlying these approaches to instruction offered at plantation missions was the requirement that instruction should be oral. "The oral method required that the teacher first pose the questions, state the answers, and then ask the class to repeat question and answer until both were memorized. After that, the teacher would ask each pupil in turn to answer a question."[37] The Presbyterian Colcock Jones sums up the goal of the oral method as it is expressed in his Catechism:

> To count their Masters "worthy of all honour," and those whom God has placed over them in this world; "*with all fear*," they are to be "*subject to them*" and obey them in all *things*, possible and lawful, with good will and endeavor to *please them well* . . . and let Servants serve their masters as faithfully behind their backs as before their faces. God is present to see, if their masters are not.[38]

In a cogently argued article, "Community Regulation and Cultural Specialization in Gullah Folk Religion," Margaret Washington examines the role of the plantation mission in the Gullah community in South Carolina. According to Washington, the role of the plantation mission was to bind an oppressed community to the religion of the oppressor class in which Christianity would serve as a tool of control and plantation management. The plantation mission was a subtle way of inserting Christianity into plantation culture with the aim of domination through religious influence. And this on the part of the master class was ingenious as enslaved Africans were most vulnerable in the area of religion and were least likely to suspect foul play.

> Once frenzy over the Vesey Conspiracy had waned somewhat, the South Carolina Methodist Conference, supported by a few influential planters, led the way in advocating openly the religious instruction of slaves and engaging actively in instituting plantation missions. The movement began in 1829 and concentrated mainly in the low country, where Methodists insisted that thousands were living and dying without ever hearing the gospel and consequently were "as destitute as if they were not inhabitants of the Christian land."[39]

The problem as slave masters saw it in relation to the church was that in the Vesey Conspiracy, class leaders of the church were involved and Vesey himself cited scriptural warrants to support his plans for revolt. It is precisely at this point that church leaders of the Methodist Church convinced the planter class that the answer was proper instruction from clergy of the church in place of the misteaching from Black preachers who were not under White supervision. "While denying an association with the black strike for freedom, the Methodist hierarchy [believes] that offering slaves 'true' religion would secure the public safety while fulfilling spiritual obligation. The 1822 plotters, Methodists argued, had been beguiled by black leaders preaching a false Christianity mixed with African superstitions."[40] We must not lose sight of the fact that plantation ethos was always suspicious of Christian teaching and fearful of the implications of the Bible in the hands of enslaved persons. One reason for making it unlawful for Blacks to learn to read and write was the stated and unstated implication of Blacks stumbling on the egalitarian implications of the Bible. Black people who could read and write were considered dangerous as in keeping with a Protestant ethic they would interpret that dangerous book for themselves. The revolts and revolution in Haiti, the Carolinas, and Virginia only made the danger more palpable.

Another approach to ensure that the revolutionary implication of the Bible was hidden from the oppressed was to teach a false eschatology that this world was a vale of tears and although life was hard for enslaved people, if they obeyed their masters and worked faithfully to please them they would inherit heaven beyond the sky when they died. However, in this context masters needed to be assured that there would be segregation in heaven as slave and master could not inherit and inhabit the same heaven. Black people were taught that there was a wall between master and slave in heaven but there were holes in the wall that would allow the slave to peek through and watch her mistress as she goes by.

> You slaves will go to heaven if you are good, but don't ever think that you will be close to your mistress and master. No! No! there will be a wall between you; but there will be holes in it that will permit you to look out and see your mistress when she passes by. If you want to sit behind this wall, you must do the language of the text "Obey your masters."[41]

We are reminded that these were often the kinds of sermons at plantation missions for the consumption of enslaved persons. Christianity as proclaimed and practiced by the missionary class had a political agenda, to provide control and be a tool for plantation management. Several scholars point out that the first Great Awakening in Virginia did not galvanize Black people to join churches in masses, since most Black people lived on plantations in rural areas and were not exposed to revivalists who were primarily in urban centers. However, the revival that began with Shubal Stearns in 1755 provided a basis for the first all-Black congregation. "Missionaries Philip Mulkey and William Murphey gathered a black slave congregation on the plantation of William Byrd III on the Bluestone River at a point which is now called Mecklenburg, Virginia. The slaves' names and experiences were not preserved, but they entered the Baptist folklore as true and lasting Christians, even when they were sold away from this plantation. . . . In 1772, another black church was constituted there, and its congregants later served as the nucleus for the Petersburg Baptist congregation of 1820."[42]

The Silver Bluff Church

This in part explains what happened at Silver Bluff, South Carolina, in the founding of the first Independent Black Baptist Church about 1773–75 on the plantation of George Galphin. Galphin was considered a kind and generous master. "The spirit of justice and kindness, it appears, was manifest in all his dealings with the peoples of the weaker races, who were daily about him. The red man and the black man alike saw him a man of kindly soul. David George, who was ever a British subject, described his former master as an 'anti-loyalist.' N. W. Jones, speaking as an American, pronounced him a 'patriot.' Neither spoke of him except to praise."[43] But as culturally sensitive as he was in relation to both Indian and African culture he had to give permission and did in fact grant permission for one ElderPalmer (Wait Palmer, pastor of First

Baptist Church of Stonington, Connecticut), a White Baptist Pastor to gather a mission church on his plantation where enslaved persons could congregate for worship. It is of interest to note that the founding of Bethel A.M.E. Church by Richard Allen was in 1794, much later than the founding of Silver Bluff. Certainly, it was in 1787 that Allen and Absalom Jones and other Black members walked out as a group and founded the Free African Society of Philadelphia. The A.M.E. Zion Church was founded in 1796 in New York City while the first church founded by Black Episcopalians, the St. Thomas Church, was also started by Bishop William White in 1794 in Philadelphia and the Lombard Street Presbyterian Church was begun in 1807. This calls attention to the historical priority of the Silver Bluff Church.

> There were Negro Baptist churches in the South for more than a quarter of a century before they began to be constituted in the North, and about half a century before the first church of the kind was planted in the West. When in 1805, moreover, the first African Baptist Church was organized at Boston, Massachusetts, it was not only the first Negro Baptist church in North, but it was also the only independent Negro church except St. Thomas Episcopal Church of Philadelphia which had a Negro rector. The Boston African Baptist Church had for its pastor a Negro, The Rev. Thomas Paul, a man of such intelligence and piety, such commanding presence and pleasing address, that pulpits everywhere in Massachusetts and his native State of New Hampshire, were open to him.[44]

David George a childhood friend of George Liele, who also had roots in Virginia and was for all intents and purposes an early pastor of this plantation mission, tells of the roots of the founding of the first Black Baptist Church in Silver Bluff, South Carolina, in his letter to John Rippon, a founder of the British Baptist Missionary Society, and editor of the *The Baptist Annual Register 1790–1793*:

> Brother Palmer, who was pastor at some distance from Silver Bluff, came and preached to a large congregation at a mill of Mr. Galpin's; he was a very powerful preacher. . . . Brother Palmer came again and wished us to beg Master to let him preach to us; and he came frequently. . . . There were eight of us now, who had found the great blessing and mercy from the lord, and my wife was one of them, and Brother Jesse Galphin. . . . Brother Palmer appointed Saturday evening to hear what the lord had done for us, and next day he baptized us in the mill

stream. . . . Brother Palmer formed us into a church, and gave us the Lord's Supper at Silver Bluff. . . . Then I began to exhort in the Church, and learned to sing hymns. . . . Afterwards the church advised with Brother Palmer about my speaking to them, and keeping them together. . . . So I was appointed to the office of an elder, and received instruction from Brother Palmer how to conduct myself. I proceeded in this way till the American war was coming on, when the Ministers were not allowed to come amongst us, lest they should furnish us with too much knowledge. . . . I continued preaching at Silver Bluff, till the church, constituted with eight, increased to thirty more, and 'till the British came to the city of Savannah and took it.[45]

It is clear that David George served as pastor of this fledging congregation during the Revolutionary War as there was fear among the planter class that Palmer and Liele would offer too much knowledge about the war to the slave membership of this early Black Baptist church in the United States.

And yet with all the excesses and abuses of relating Christianity to enslaved people, they not only saw through the caricature of Christianity, but as they claimed it, they adapted it to their needs and situation and it flourished in their hands. This seems to be what happened at Silver Bluff and in the phenomenal story of a number of enslaved persons from plantations along the Savannah River who were introduced to the Christian faith, made it their own, transformed what was handed to them, and in an extraordinary way spanned the distance between the Caribbean and the North American colonies, and later Africa.

Alfred Pugh in *Pioneer Preachers in Paradise* states:

There is an invisible but undeniable religious-cultural gospel thread of Christianity that has for more than two centuries connected the descendants of African people living in the United States with the descendants of African people of Jamaica, the Bahama Islands, Haiti, and the Greater Caribbean Basin. The thread began with a slave preacher whose name was George Liele (a.k.a. Lisle) [who] was born about 1750 or 1751 in the English colony of Virginia.[46]

The story centers around the first ordained Black Baptist minister in the United States and the Caribbean, George Liele, along with fellow colleagues, David George, Jesse Peters, and Brother Amos, all disciples of Liele. John Parmer Gates narrates the story of Liele's contribution to Black church history:

About two years prior to the American War of Independence a Negro slave by the name of George Liele was converted under the preaching of Matthew Moore, a white Baptist minister in Brooke County, Georgia. This was to mark the beginning of a preaching career destined to be one of the most colorful in early Negro history. For it was after several years of preaching on plantations in the vicinity that Liele cast his lot with the British who occupied Savannah in 1778, and in the months following was able to plant the seeds of a Negro Baptist church. When, at the close of the war in 1782, the British evacuated Savannah he went with them to Jamaica where he eventually established the first Baptist work on that island. Indeed, the claim has been made for Liele that he was the first American Baptist foreign missionary, preceding even the work of Carey by fifteen years.[47]

Liele was born of slave parents on a plantation in Virginia about 1750. In his letter from Jamaica to John Rippon *of The Baptist Annual Register* Liele speaks of his father as devoutly religious and that he had learned from both White and Black persons that his father was the only spiritual person in that county. It is believed that Liele suggested that his father was the only Black person who had been affected by the religious awakening in the county. We noted earlier that enslaved persons in rural counties were not likely to have been affected by the Great Awakening in the same way as persons in urban centers. "Now George Liele, although not a runaway slave, appears to have had some liking for the Tybee River, as a place of abode, and it is probable that when he could no longer visit Silver Bluff, and was both in camp with Henry Sharp (who had not only given him his freedom, but also taken up arms against the revolutionists), he reported to Tybee island to preach to the refugees there assembled. At any rate, when Liele appears in Savannah, Georgia, as a preacher of the Gospel . . . he came up to the city of Savannah from Tybee River."[48] Although Liele had received freedom from his master to travel for the cause of preaching, his presence in Tybee Island, where enslaved persons who had cast their lot with the British sought refuge, suggests that his primary commitment was to be in solidarity with his people who were oppressed. The presence of enslaved persons who sided with the British assembling in vast numbers on Tybee Island could be one reason for the harsh persecution that people of African descent had to bear in the Savannah region after the war. The leaders of congregations who remained in the region after the war and were visible as pastors of their flock were especially susceptible to persecution from patriots.

The pastor of Big Buckhead Baptist Church in Burke County, colonial Georgia, the Reverend Matthew Moore, was the brother of Mildred Moore Sharp, wife of Henry Sharp, George Liele's master. It should not unduly surprise us, then, that George Liele attended a church of which his master's brother-in-law served as pastor, and quite early became a member and was licensed to preach. We are told that this church was in the tradition of Separate Baptists. Charles Walker explains: "So many of Whitefield's converts became Baptists that he is reported to have remarked, 'my chickens have turned to ducks.' These converts were soon called 'New Lights' and when they withdrew from the old established churches became known as 'Separate Baptists.'"[49] Over against the Separatists are Regular or Particular Baptists who tended more toward a Calvinistic viewpoint and were very conservative in worship, evangelism, and doctrine. Separate Baptists were zealous in making confessions of sin and believed in the guidance of the Holy Spirit and the authority of the Bible. "They insisted upon an 'Experience of Grace' which was to be publicly confessed before a person was received into the church and baptized. They were much freer in accepting a man's profession of a call to preach than were the Regular Baptists. Yet, they examined him closely and were careful to have a presbytery of ministers for his ordination. They exerted discipline in the churches and in the association over the churches. Their preachers preached with 'the holy twang' and enthusiasm."[50] This sets the context for the Silver Bluff Baptist Church which was inspired by the polity and ecclesiology of Separate Baptists, and the life and ministry of George Liele and his colleagues. Liele was a member of the Big Buckhead Baptist Church. This church was also a separate Baptist church, and since Liele was a frequent preacher at Silver Bluff, it should not surprise us that the general ethos of the separate Baptists would prevail there as well. George Liele was about twenty-three years old when he was converted to Christianity through the preaching of Matthew Moore. Speaking of his conversion Liele states: "This state I labored under for the space of six months. . . . I felt such love and joy as my tongue was not able to express. After this I declared before the congregation of believers the work which God had done for my soul, and the same minister, the Rev. Matthew Moore, baptized me, and I continued in this church about four years, till the [e]vacuation."[51] After his conversion Liele acknowledged his call to preach. The plantation minister Matthew Moore arranged for Liele to preach a trial sermon before the congregation and in 1775 ordained Liele. "He was given permission, to preach, evangelize and baptize slaves on the Sharpe plantation and surrounding plantations on both sides of the Savannah River. The Galphin Plantation on the Province of South Carolina side of the river was included in his evangelizing area. . . . His ministry would follow the pattern of others who had been impacted by the Great Awakening. From the onset, he preached to black and white men, women, and children; challenging them to confess Jesus Christ as Lord and master as the prerequisite for faith by baptism by immersion."[52]

Liele's owner Henry Sharp released him from slavery and allowed him to practice his preaching gifts at plantations along the Savannah River. He was able to boat along the Savannah River for about four years, visiting plantations as far north as Silver Bluff in South Carolina. It was there that Liele reconnected with a childhood acquaintance David George, one of the leaders of the nascent church on Galphin's plantation. "Under Liele's guidance, George, who taught himself to read, began to preach. With Mr. Galphin's approval, Palmer, assisted by George Liele, organized a plantation church for slave worship. Its first pastor was Reverend Palmer. Liele also preached for the slave congregation with whites present as required by colonial law."[53] It was under Liele's preaching that David George was converted and later, appointed by Palmer, became an elder and preacher at the Silver Bluff Church. "When British troops occupied Savannah during the Revolutionary War, George and his family, and other members of the Silver Bluff church left the Galphin Plantation to live near Savannah under British protection. In 1782, they were among the first group of slaves (with about five hundred whites who supported the King of England) permitted to migrate to Nova Scotia on British ships. In 1784, he organized a church of about sixty members; a racially mixed congregation. . . . Ten years later, to escape cold weather . . . twelve thousand people of color left Nova Scotia to settle in Sierra Leone, West Africa."[54]

Another member of the Silver Bluff Church, which dates back to 1773, is Jesse Peters who along with David George joined the underground church during the Revolutionary War in the Savannah area. He also came under the influence of the preaching of George Liele. Unlike David George who fled to Nova Scotia and George Liele who left for Jamaica, Jesse Peters voluntarily remained in Georgia and assumed the leadership of "the remnants of the Silver Bluff Baptist Church."

> Soon afterwards, Peters led a group of members to Augusta where, in 1791, a church was formally constituted as the Springfield African Baptist Church (later renamed Springfield Baptist Church). . . . Seventy-six years later, in 1867, Augusta Institute, a school for the primary purpose of preparing black men for the ministry and teaching, was founded by a Baptist minister and cabinet maker, the Reverend William J. White. It was located in the basement of the Springfield Baptist Church.

Augusta Institute, later renamed Morehouse College, is presently located in Atlanta, Georgia, its student body composed of mostly black males. The Reverend Dr. Martin Luther King, Jr. was one of its most renowned graduates.[55]

It is of interest that the person who is responsible for resurrecting the work in Silver Bluff was Jesse Peters who chose not to migrate to other shores like David George and George Liele. Instead, he remained in bondage in Georgia and South Carolina, and through his instrumentality the church found a new home; and in a tradition that Liele took with him to Jamaica, it coupled church and education.

> The man who was instrumental in resuscitating the work at Silver Bluff was Jesse Peters. . . . Having been connected with the Silver Bluff Church from the very first, and only separated from it during the Revolutionary War . . . Jesse Peters was eminently fitted, at least in one particular, to take up the work at Silver Bluff which David George had abandoned in the year 1778. He knew the place and he loved the people. . . . Why this young man, who had obtained his freedom by going to the British at the fall of Savannah, in 1778, remained in America to resume the condition of slave . . . is not known.[56]

African American Mission in the Caribbean

In his letter to Rippon, writing from Jamaica, Liele mentions that Jesse Peters officiated with Abraham Marshall in the ordination of Andrew Bryan, one of the last persons Liele baptized in Savannah prior to leaving for Jamaica. Andrew Bryan was successor to Liele in serving as pastor of First African Baptist Church in Savannah. The work of Andrew Bryan was pivotal in the further establishment of the Black church in Georgia and Bryan faced what seemed at times like insurmountable persecution from opposition by the White establishment to his work.

> From Liele's departure, in 1782, to the time of Andrew Bryan's ordination, in 1788, the little flock at Savannah, Georgia, was bitterly persecuted, but its work for resuscitation, and progress was wonderful— wonderful because of the moral heroism which characterized it. It is reasonable to suppose, however, that much of the opposition to the church at Savannah from 1782 to 1787 was due to the circumstances in

which it had come into being, and not to any real antipathy to the cause of Christ. For it must be borne in mind that it was a creature of the Revolutionary War, and of British origin, having been planted when the rightful people of Savannah were languishing in exile. . . . Bryan and his associates were beaten unmercifully for their persistency in holding on to the work, but they were prepared to yield their lives to martyrdom sooner than relinquish what George Liele had instituted. So it lived—lived amid the fires of persecution.[57]

George Liele who went to Jamaica in 1783 and founded the Ethiopian Baptist Church in Kingston, the capital city of Jamaica, speaks of one Brother Amos who planted a church in Providence, Nassau, in the Bahamas. Walter Brooks the historian tells us that Brother Amos came under the preaching of George Liele both at Silver Bluff and during the Revolutionary War in the Savannah area. "He arrived in New Providence (Nassau) in 1788 to establish a direct link between the church in Savannah, Georgia and the first group of Baptists in the Bahamas. . . . [It is] said that the land on which the original church was constructed was bequeathed to Prince Williams by one Amos Williams, a man of color from the English colony of South Carolina."[58] It is interesting to note the way an African ethos suffused the approach to preaching of these men who left Silver Bluff, South Carolina, and Savannah, Georgia, for the Caribbean and in their own way told the story of Christianity to natives there. Concerning Jamaica, we are told that George Liele began his ministry at the race course, which was the name of a large park in Kingston, Jamaica. He would seek to preach in what Jamaicans would later call "in the open air." Many evening services were in the open air, sometimes under trees. This was also true of Brother Amos, in the Bahamas. "The first Baptist preacher, Brother Amos, was another educated free black man, who came to the Bahamas in 1783 and preached the Afro-Baptist faith under a large spreading tree in the Eastern District of Nassau. . . . In 1791 he wrote to George Liele in Jamaica to the effect that he had 300 members and by 1812 it was reported that the church in New Providence had 850 members. This may have been the church that became the Bethel Baptist Church under Samba Scriven, Prince Williams and Sharper Morris. If so this church was formed in 1801 when Prince Williams spearheaded a move to buy a lot on what is now Meeting Street."[59] Another leader of the church in the Bahamas was Shadrach Kerr. Shadrach, who was born in New Providence in the Bahamas, in 1832 tells of an experience of his youth that described life in the Caribbean and the trauma of enslaved Africans brought from mother Africa to work on plantations in the Caribbean.

As a young boy growing up, Shadrach witnessed from Fort Fincastle an event that he remembered vividly for the rest of his life. HM Schooner *Hornet* had captured two Portugese slavers in Nassau Harbour laden with Africans; one contained 680; the other 750, all chained side by side and stowed away between decks. Men, women, and children, who were intended to be sold as slaves in Cuba, but now in British waters were declared free. These Africans were landed, taken to a place called "The Tea House" and distributed to all the leading families in the city for civilization. To his father [were] given two men, one young woman, and three boys. Great curiosity was aroused when they were brought to his home, with a simple bit of rag bound across of their bodies. They had glistened skin, as though they were greased and they were half starved, though their limbs were stalwart.[60]

Shadrach reminds us that slavery in Cuba continued until 1886 and in Brazil until 1888. A similar story is told in Jamaica of a ship with slaves from Abeokuta, Nigeria, that was captured under similar circumstances in Westmoreland, Western Jamaica, and the slaves were settled in a village that they called "Beokuta" to remember their village in Africa. When I served churches in Westmoreland, Jamaica, in the 1960s there were several persons from this village who attended my church.

The worldviews that African American preachers confronted in the Caribbean at the turn of the eighteenth and early decades of the nineteenth centuries reflect communities in which the memory of Africa was very strong and Africa served as a controlling metaphor. Ernest Payne culling from letters that George Liele wrote to John Rippon of the British Missionary Society in 1791–93, describes life in Kingston: "The godlessness of the place filled him [Liele] with concern, and he began boldly preaching on the Kingston racecourse, forming, with a handful of other American refugees, a little Baptist Church. Almost at once he was imprisoned on a charge of teaching sedition, but when the day of the trial came no accusers appeared, and he was released. There was much opposition to be met. The life of Kingston was in general wild and dissolute."[61] What the British theologian refers to as life in the Caribbean that was "wild and dissolute" was the presence and practices of the African church. Du Bois reminded us in his *Negro Church* that the African church was not at first a Christian church. According to Du Bois, it was throughout the Caribbean in the first 200 years the practice of Vodou, Obeah, and Myal. What confronted Liele and his compatriots throughout the Caribbean was the practice of Obeah and Myal. It must have been a curious sight for enslaved people in the Caribbean to see African Americans in Trinidad, Bahamas, and in

Jamaica preaching their version of Christianity. Prior to the arrival of these African American missionaries to the Caribbean, enslaved persons there adapted the religions they had brought from Africa to the Caribbean context. In earlier chapters I have alluded to the practice of Vodou in Haiti, Santeria in Cuba, and Orisha worship in Trinidad. I would like now to highlight two forms of African religion that confronted George Liele in Jamaica: Obeah and Myalism.

The Native Baptist Church

In Ashanti, the word for wizard is *Obayifo* and throughout the Caribbean this became Obeah. Caribbean people believed that the Obeah man or woman had the power to fly, to leave his or her body, and to inflict harm on the enemy. Obeah flourished in Caribbean society not only because the society had lost its equilibrium and was in a state of disorientation but also because there was a void for a religious practitioner. The traditional African priest had lost his power in an alien society, but as he joined forces with the Obeah practitioner they became a formidable force to reckon with in slave society.

Leonard Barrett calls attention to the Maroon rebellion of 1760 by the Ashanti warrior Tacky. Led by Obeah man Tacky, the warriors prepared for war by mixing rum with gun powder and grave dirt. Blood drawn from the arm of each participant was added and then the mixture was drunk in turn by each warrior. The drinking of this mixture meant that the covenant to fight until death was sealed by each participant. After this rebellion the fear of an Obeah man was so pervasive that the government of Jamaica passed laws against him. The sum of the law was that anyone convicted of practicing Obeah would face the possibility of being sentenced to death. This did not solve the master's problems as Afro-Caribbean people believed "Massa can't kill Obeah man."[62]

In West Africa, the worship of gods was organized in cult groups, often esoteric, which used drums, dancing, dreams, and spirit-seizure as part of organized worship. An aspect of this survived in Jamaica through a ritual referred to as *Myal*. Perhaps the real difference between Obeah and Myal is that whereas the Obeah man is usually a private practitioner, hired by a client for a specific purpose, the Myal practitioner is a leader of a group, devoted to an organized religious life. But, as was illustrated in the scenes of Tacky calling on warriors to blend rum, blood, and grave dirt together and then drink it in establishing a covenant, the lines between Obeah and Myal are often blurred.

Winston Lawson informs us that Myalism embodied African-derived cosmology and is the first documented religion cast in the African mold on

Jamaican soil. At the heart of the rituals that highlight Myal is the Myal dance. The Myal dance observed was in honor of the minor deities or ancestors who were feared. An important feature of this dance was spirit-possession. It was widely believed by participants in Myal that the dance gave them the ability to elude capture when they escaped and made them invincible to bullets.[63]

Philip Curtin argues that a number of the African Americans who migrated to Jamaica with George Liele merged their Baptist faith with Jamaican Myal and created the Native Baptist Church. The loose structure of the Baptist church allowed them to include African traditional practices such as drumming, dancing, and spirit-seizure—in short, the practices of Myal. One of the key leaders of the Native Baptist Church who migrated from the United States with George Liele was George Lewis, who rejected the missionary version of Christianity in favor of his own, more African, style. Lewis "had been born in Africa and taken to Virginia as a slave. After the American Revolution he was brought to Kingston, where his mistress let him work as a peddler in return for a monthly fee. He mixed peddling with preaching along his route in the parishes of Manchester and St. Elizabeth and spread his doctrine through the southwest part of the island."[64] Other African American leaders in the tradition of George Lewis were George Gibb and Moses Baker. According to church historian W. J. Gardner, for four years (1783–87) Baker "lived in utter disregard of religion."[65] Of course, by religion Gardner meant the Christian religion. Philip Curtin provides clues of the organizational structure of native Baptist churches:

> The organizational basis . . . was the "leader system," an adaptation of the English Wesleyan practice of dividing the church members into classes for teaching. Possibly, the Native Baptists picked it up from the few White missionaries who were already at work in Jamaica, but more likely it was their American training. In any case the leader system underwent some strange transformations. The class-leaders became something more than just a teacher of new converts. They were real spiritual guides, taking a position equivalent to leadership of a Myal cult group, and their power over the classes was authoritarian to the point of tyranny.[66]

Native Baptists adopted a doctrinal position that elevated "the spirit" and neglected the written word. "The followers of Baker and Gibb were required to be possessed of the 'the spirit' before baptism was administered. This meant the spirit had to descend on the applicant in a dream, which was then described to the leader. . . . There evolved a regular technique and ceremonial for bringing on spirit-possession, which included a fast according to a set canon followed by a trip into the bush alone at night to wait for the spirit to descend."[67] A theology of spirit provided an openness for Native Baptists to make the theological connection they saw necessary. In this church, John the Baptist had the priority over Jesus Christ, since he baptized and accepted Jesus into his church, so to speak. Jesus was one of the prophets and was not equal with God. Therefore, it should not surprise us that Alexander Bedward, following in the tradition of the Native Baptists, could change his title from "Shepherd" to the "Incarnation of Christ" with a promise that on December 31, 1920, he would ascend to heaven, thereby destroying the rule of White people and establish the kingdom of Bedwardism on earth. Bedward could equate himself with Jesus who had power to heal, prophesy, and change the oppressive order that was killing Black people. The Native Baptists who merged Jamaican Mayalism with an Afro-American faith changed the theological culture in amaica and proffered another religion over against Christianity and African religion. It was more than an amalgamation of African and Christian worldviews; it was an attempt to create a religion that was in the service of liberation. This came to the fore in 1831 when a class-leader Sam (Daddy) Sharp of the Native Baptists signaled the beginning of the end of slavery in Jamaica in a revolt that was called the Baptist War. The focus of this war was Afro-Jamaicans organizing to withdraw their labor. The focus was on the institution of the plantation. A total of 120 buildings on the estate were torched as Afro-Jamaicans insisted that they were human beings who had a right to freedom and to withdraw their labor from institutions that held them in slavery.

Edward Hylton, one of Daddy Sharp's followers, tells of a time he was in the hills and received a message from Daddy Sharp to attend a meeting at Johnson's house on Retrieve plantation in St. James. The gathering took the form of a prayer meeting.

> After a while Sharp spoke to them in a low, soft tone so that his voice would not be heard outside. According to Hylton, he kept them spellbound while he spoke of the evils and injustices of slavery, asserted the right of all human beings to freedom and declared on the authority of the Bible, that the White man had no more right to hold Blacks in bondage than Blacks had to enslave Whites.[68]

The meeting went late into the night as they agreed on a strategy to overturn slavery. They covenanted not to work on Christmas holidays but to seize their right to freedom in faithfulness to each other. "If backra [master] would pay them, they would work as before. If any attempt was made to force them to work as slaves, they would fight for freedom. They took the oath and kissed the Bible."[69] What Daddy Sharp intended was a nonviolent protest, which would be expressed as a labor strike. The plan was that the day after Christmas holiday an overseer or a driver would go to "busha"[overseer] on each plantation and inform him that enslaved people would not work until the owner agreed to pay wages. The bushas were to be kept on the plantation until they agreed to pay wages for work. The leadership of the Native Baptist had organized themselves into a trade union arm of the Native Baptist Church, advocating and negotiating wages for enslaved people. Philip Curtin suggests that what in fact was happening was that the native Baptists had skillfully taken the Baptist missionary organization from White missionaries and were using the Baptist organization as a European trade union leader might use the bargaining power of workers.[70]

This seems to be the case as later developments attest.

On 27 December William Knibb, visiting Moses Baker's chapel at Crooked Spring, now Salter's Hill, tried to persuade the slaves that rumors about freedom having been granted were untrue, but his words were received with evident dissatisfaction by many of the slaves present, several of whom left the chapel offended: "The man . . . must be mad to tell us such things."[71]

Further, missionary Knibb stated:

I am pained—pained to the soul, at being told that many of you have agreed not to work any more for your owners, and I fear this is too true. I learned some wicked person has persuaded you that the King of England has made you free. Hear me! I love your souls and I would not tell you a lie for the world; I assure you this is false, false as hell can make it. I entreat you not to believe it, but go to work as formerly. If you have any love for Jesus Christ, to religion, to your ministers, or to those kind friends of England who have helped you build this chapel, and who are sending a minister for you, do not be led away. God commands you to be obedient.[72]

Fired by the spirit of the Native Baptists, Daddy Sharp responded:

We have worked enough already, we will work no more; the life we live is too bad, it is the life of a dog, we won't be slaves no more, we won't lift hoe no more, we won't take flogging anymore.[73]

Sharp and his freedom fighters interpreted the message of liberation through the hermeneutic of freedom. They understood the body as the site of freedom. It is reported that when Daddy Sharp was apprehended he said that he "had rather die than be a slave." The price paid by Daddy Sharp and his people for freedom was very high. In the aftermath of the Native Baptist War, 600 Afro-Jamaicans were killed by British forces. In their defense, they killed fourteen Whites. But the seeds for the destruction of slavery were sown. On August 1, 1834, a partial freedom was granted to British colonies throughout the Caribbean with the abolition of slavery August 1, 1838.

It is quite clear that the Baptist movement that George Liele initiated in Jamaica went in directions he could not have imagined. A central distinction between the position that Liele advocated and which was practiced by the Native Baptists had to do with perspective. While Liele benefited from being a member of a Christian community in Georgia and earlier Virginia, he was able to interpret the world, slavery, and African religions from an African frame of reference. For example, one of the first sermons he preached while in Jamaica was from Romans 10:1: "brethren, my heart's desire and prayer for Israel is that they might be saved." In this sermon he compared the plight of Afro-Jamaicans with that of the children of Israel in Egypt. The sermon was regarded by the authorities as incendiary, and as a consequence he was imprisoned. The laws of Jamaica made it extremely difficult for Liele to practice his version of Christianity, making the claim that Afro-Jamaicans like the children of Israel needed to experience exodus. In 1802 a law was passed stating that if a free Black person was found guilty of preaching sermons advocating freedom of enslaved persons he would be committed to prison and kept at hard labor. If the preacher were a slave, he should be put to hard labor for the first offense.[74] Liele made peace with the planter class by agreeing to work within a system dictated by the laws of Jamaica. On the other hand, the converse was the case for Native Baptists who while committed to Baptist organization and freedom opted to work outside the system engineered by the plantocracy. The Native Baptists interpreted the world and Christianity from an African frame of reference inspired by Myal religion, as was the case with Daddy Sharp who challenged both the Christian church and the state in the quest for freedom. Liele introduced Afro-Jamaicans to a radical version of Christianity which they interpreted through Afro-centric lenses. In a context of slavery, two forms of Baptist expressions of faith emerged: Baptist orthodoxy, which seemed very important to Liele, and Native Baptist, which departed from Liele's teaching—at critical points choosing a hermeneutic of freedom and liberation. Without Liele neither would have emerged.

4

The Plantation Church

AT THE TURN of the twentieth century, W.E.B. Du Bois made the claim that the new reality that confronted enslaved Africans in the Americas was the plantation. According to Du Bois, it was religion, carried by Africans from their homes in Africa, that engendered their survival in a strange land, and in their new environment—plantations in the Americas. Africans "stolen from the homeland" and brought across the Atlantic as human cargo to plantations in the Americas carried their religion with them and this allowed the Black church "to be the sole surviving social institution of the African Father-land."[1] The Black church, which was at first an African church, was the center of hope as it provided the means of socialization, education, and entertainment for Black people stranded on plantations in the Americas far away from their homes in Africa. According to Du Bois, the traditions of the Black church are in religious customs and practices carried over from Africa, and the blending of these practices and customs became an integral part of Black Christianity. The roots of the Black church are in Africa and this church functions at the center of social life for Africans in the Americas. Perhaps the most important key in understanding the capacity and ability of African religion to survive in its new expression as the Black church, and to provide the means of liberation for enslaved persons on plantations, is the African priest. According to Du Bois, it was through the leadership and ingenuity of the African priest that the Black church emerged, survived, and became the means of liberation for enslaved persons.

> The power of religion was represented by the priest and medicine man. Aided by an unfaltering faith, natural sharpness and some rude knowledge of medicine, and supported by the vague sanctions of a half-seen world peopled by spirits, good and evil, the African priest wielded a power second only to that of the chief, and often superior to it.[2]

There is a direct link between the founding and maintenance of the Black church, the African priest, and the medicine man. Du Bois suggests that plantation life was so harsh and cruel that without the Black church and the leadership provided by the African priest it is questionable whether enslaved Black persons would have survived.

Du Bois reminds us that enslaved Africans first encountered the plantation in the Caribbean. It is worth noting, as was mentioned in Chapter 1, that life for enslaved Africans on plantations in the New World began as early as 1502 in the Caribbean, compared to the beginning of the migration of Africans to Virginia in 1619. The change that confronted Blacks in the New World was quite traumatic, according to Du Bois, because life was not ordered by an African chief in the context of the clan or the tribe but was now dictated by the White master on a plantation in the Caribbean and later in the American colonies. Life in the clan, or tribe, had intimacy marked by bloodlines, with rules and customs that gave priority to a sense of community. This was lost on the plantation when life was reduced to an aggregation of individuals in a common space, with rules and directives enforced by a master. The hallmark of this existence was exploitation in both sexual and economic terms.

According to Du Bois, a mark of the new reality that confronted enslaved Africans in the context of the plantation was, in many instances, having to work from sunup until sundown and sometimes by the light of the moon. This he calls a new polygamy—a new family life against the resistance of Africans but enforced by the master class. "Gradually, however, superior force and organized methods prevailed, and the plantation became the unit of a new development. . . . The vast and overshadowing change that the plantation system introduced was the change in the status of women—the new polygamy. The new polygamy had all the evils and not one of the safeguards of the African prototype. The African system was a complete protection for girls and a strong protection for wives."[3] One of the evils of the plantation culture was that enslaved persons were not introduced to any concept of voluntary labor. Usually, work was enforced and the circumstances of slavery made labor demeaning. Worse than the attitude toward work was the lack of respect for women on plantations. Du Bois admits that it all depended on the temperament and character of the master. "Where the master was himself lewd and avaricious the degradation of women was complete. Where, on the other hand, the plantation system reached its best development, as in Virginia, there was a fair approximation of a monogamic marriage system among the slaves; and yet even here, on the best conducted plantations, the protection of Negro women was but imperfect; the seduction of girls was frequent."[4]

Plantation as Context

One may concur with Du Bois that the new reality that confronted Black people in the Americas was the plantation, so I would like to look at the plantation as a framework for understanding the expectations of the master class in relation to enslaved persons. Before we look at the world that enslaved persons carved out for themselves using religion as a cultural and theological tool, we will look at the sociopolitical context of their oppression—the plantation. It is safe to infer that there were some expectations that confronted enslaved persons in the workplace. At one level, the master class expected enslaved persons to internalize notions of the self as inferior. The end result was for the enslaved person to become "a perfect servant." This included a child-like respect and affection for the master and his family. This commitment to the plantation took precedence over all things.

In his classic text, *Deep like the Rivers,* Thomas L. Webber suggests that on many plantations throughout the American colonies, proper etiquette on the plantations insisted that Black people be kept ignorant. This was especially true in the instance of fieldhands. "With regard to field hands in particular, many plantation authorities apparently believed that the more ignorant the black person, the better the slave. The basic means of nurturing this ignorance was to close off any avenue of access to knowledge of the larger world."[5] Plantation etiquette insisted that, as much as possible, especially in the case of fieldhands, all their needs be provided for on the plantation. This was true even in the case of marriage. Webber opines that most plantation owners preferred enslaved persons to marry persons on their plantation, and if an enslaved person married someone from another plantation, the master usually took steps to buy that spouse. "It was better for a master to buy husbands or wives for his bondsmen when necessary. Otherwise, 'if they cannot be suited at home,' it should be a settled principle that they must live singly."[6] It cannot be overstated that marriage was temporary, as enslaved persons understood that they were married until they were sold. Further, in many cases, marriage did not render the wife off limits from the master. The master owned both husband and wife and was free to dispose of them as he saw fit. They were his property.

There were strict rules about social intercourse, as slaves were required to limit social meetings and exchanges to folks on their own plantation. There was a nervousness among the master class that slaves would become restless, "believing the grass to be greener in the other plantation." The goal, then, was for each plantation to be self-enclosed, providing for the needs of its inhabitants. White preachers were brought to plantations to provide for the spiritual needs of Black people. The same was true of musicians and medical staff in an attempt to prevent Blacks from traveling off plantations. "Slaves," recalls Bill Sims, who had been a slave himself in Missouri, "were never allowed to talk with white people other than their masters or someone their masters knew, as they were afraid the white man might have the slave run away. The masters aimed to keep their slaves in ignorance."[7] There are reports that there were masters on plantations in the American colonies who especially did not want their slaves to meet poor Whites for fear that enslaved persons would conclude that there were others who were in a worse position than they were. It seems that one of the worst fears which masters had of enslaved persons gaining knowledge of other owners' plantations was the dread of any comparative analysis—the dread that they might discover, through comparison, that there were other slaves on plantations who were better off than they were. "A slave, . . . was not to preach, except to his master's own slaves on his master's premises in the presence of whites. A gathering of more than a few slaves (usually five) away from home, unattended by a white, was an 'unlawful assembly' regardless of its purpose or orderly decorum."[8]

The limiting of slave knowledge extended to books or other forms of written material. It was the law in all slave states, except Kentucky, for anyone including the master to teach an enslaved person to read and write. The master class feared that enslaved persons who were able to read or write would forge passes for themselves and their family and become agitated through reading inflammatory materials.

"Is there any great moral reason," asked the editors of the *Presbyterian Herald*, "why we should incur the tremendous risk of having our wives slaughtered in consequence of our slaves being taught to read incendiary publications?" Speaking before the Virginia House of Delegates after that legislature had passed a bill prohibiting the "education" of blacks, one delegate declared: "We have as far as possible closed every avenue by which light may enter their minds. If we could extinguish the capacity to see light, our work would be completed."[9]

Plantation etiquette was enforced by laws and patrols paid by masters. Black people who were caught off their plantations without a pass received thirty-nine stripes on the back. Enslaved persons who were found to be able to read or write were sold or segregated from the general population, and this was also the case of Black people who were found to have knowledge of the outside world. There were severe penalties for those who were discovered learning to read or write. In several cases a finger was cut off or a cheek branded, as a warning to others who might be so inclined. The penalty was even worse for those who attempted to teach an enslaved person to read or write. "Jamie Parker's grandfather, and fellow slave, Scipio, was put to death for attempting to teach Jamie to read and spell from the Bible."[10]

There was an incipient paternalism that was emblematic of life on most plantations. The master provided for all the needs of the Black family. It was his task to provide for material and spiritual needs of the enslaved family and to protect and safeguard them. The truth is that the relationship of the master to the enslaved person was not just one of the powerful in relation to the powerless, but of one who made decisions in matters of life and death in relation to enslaved families. "The life of free blacks in the South was presented as one of hardship, insecurity, and poverty. Without the care of a rich and powerful white master, these deprived blacks were unable to provide for their own nourishment and medical care and were constantly exposed to thievery and unrestrained harassment of the poor white population. . . . Numerous stories were told about slaves of 'free coloreds' begging to be made slaves and to be taken under the protective wing of a sympathetic master."[11]

In order to institutionalize plantation ethics and etiquette, many masters devised and developed ways to ensure that enslaved persons internalized their own inferiority in relation to their beliefs in the superiority of their masters. One could argue that the cardinal doctrine, or belief, on every plantation was the assumed inferiority of the enslaved in relation to the master class. It was understood that slaves at all times obeyed their masters and submitted to their will. "The condition of the slave being merely a passive one, his subordination to his master and to all who represent him is not susceptible of modification or restriction. . . . [H]e owes to his master, and to all his family a respect without bounds, and an absolute obedience, and he is consequently to execute all orders which he receives from him, his said master, or from them."[12] Although the language for consumption indicates that the master expected slaves to be passive, it is quite clear that the reality was different, as laws enacted throughout the American South and Caribbean islands made it illegal for enslaved persons to strike a White person, except in cases where they were protecting their masters. Further, as was mentioned earlier, slaves could not leave the plantation without a pass, use abusive language to a White person, or talk back to a member of the master class, beat drums, dance, sing African songs, speak in their native languages, get married, or own property without the blessing of White folks. Slaves could be sold or traded, depending on the will of the master. The bottom line: slaves were not fully human; they were chattel and treated as property that the master owned. "Whatever his name, 'every man slave is called boy until he is very old, then the more respectable slaveholders call him uncle. The women are all girls until they are aged, then they are called aunts.' Any other honorific titles were discouraged, as attested to by escaped slave, William Grimes of Virginia, who was whipped for referring to a slave woman as 'miss.' "[13] This is not just an interpretation of the worst epoch in world history, nor the subjugation of a possible twelve million Africans, over a period of 400 years, in which they were forcibly taken from their ancestral homes in Africa to work on plantations in the Caribbean and the United States, and in which their lives were regulated by the master class, but something far worse—the denuding of the power of the enslaved person rendering him or her powerless. It is precisely in this relation of domination that the master class owned the time, work, family, and body of the enslaved person. And this is what took plantation slavery to another level of exploitation and domination, the level in which to own an enslaved person was to reduce him or her to the status of a thing. The master class could not relate to the enslaved person as person, but had to make him or her into something less than human. This reality of the master owning not only the production and skills of the enslaved person but the person as well is illustrated in the Caribbean. An eye-witness account originated from a Quaker meeting in the British colony of Tortola in which Charles F. Jenkins, himself a Quaker, pointed to the anomaly of John Pickering, the governor of Tortola, a Quaker, who owned 500 slaves and another Quaker, who owned 1,000 slaves. Jenkins pointed out that in the eighteenth century there were some 12,000 enslaved persons on the island compared to about 900 Whites. He questioned whether it were possible, in the eighteenth century, for one to be slaveholder and a Quaker in the islands. Commenting on notes in the minutes of a Quaker meeting on the island he wrote: "There is little information as to the treatment of slaves in Tortola. The minutes of the Meeting mention them but once. While Dr. Lettson was on the Island, he was sent for by a hardhearted master to cut off the leg of a Negro, who had run away and been recaptured. It is needless to say how greatly he was shocked. . . . In 1802, . . . there were 155 vessels engaged in the slave trade, capable of carrying 40,000 blacks, four-fifths of whom went to the British West Indies. In 1803, a ship load of slaves arrived in Tortola and was publicly auctioned off to the planters."[14] We already noted that throughout the Caribbean and in American colonies, enslaved persons had no legal rights to marriage, parenthood, personal security, and property.

The Struggle for Personhood in Virginia and Cuba

The claims of the master over his slave in the colony of Virginia were so complete that the master's power to take the slave's life was never challenged. "So thoroughgoing was the right of possession of the slave's person and the consequent loss to the latter of even the right to personal security, that under Virginia law, killing of a slave by his master was not considered a felony for, as the code logically reasoned, 'it cannot be presumed that prepensed malice, (which alone makes murder felony) should induce a man to destroy his own estate).'"[15] As Du Bois pointed out earlier, this was indeed part of the new reality that confronted Black people in their lives on the plantation.

According to Herbert Klein the erasure of the legal personality of the enslaved person, where the enslaved person was never the subject of human rights but always its object, was not the case in Cuba. And this, according to Klein, calls attention to the difference between the legal codes as they pertain to legal personalities in both colonies. In Cuba, the legal codes highlighted the personality of the Black person; in Virginia the Black person was reduced to chattel. This is an interesting delineation that Klein suggests between Spanish colonies in the Caribbean and British colonies on the American mainland. It is clear then that in chattel slavery, enslaved persons were reduced to a level below the ranks of human beings—they were things to be manipulated, and if the master so chose, destroyed; "not only were these two slave codes of an entirely different structure, . . . they sprang from entirely different sources of authority, a fact that had much to do with their subsequent development. In Virginia, chattel slavery was created entirely by the customary, judicial, and statutory decision of colonial origin, whereas in Cuba, the source of the slave code was fundamentally royal enactments and prior metropolitan law."[16] It could then be one of the consequences of settler colonialism, which we find in British colonies on the American mainland, that local legislatures, or self-governments, had the final word on the slave code whereas in the Caribbean, in which local life was directed by a metropolitan power, or royal decree, word had to come from outside—from a distant power, not under the immediate influence of local governments. This is an important point to keep in mind as we look at both realities that confronted enslaved persons in the Caribbean and colonies on the mainland. It was the use of slave religion and culture in defying and ultimately breaking the resolve and power of White control as weapon against Black humanity. Klein points out that the rights that applied to Englishmen were specified in the original charter. These natural rights did not apply to relations and rights of aliens such as Africans and Indians, which means that the powers to effect these relations were divided between the imperial and colonial governments. The colonial powers had the right to establish the obligations and duties implied in these relations as they related to internal affairs and the imperial government as they applied to international relations and commerce. "As there existed no precedent for Negro slavery in English common law, the Virginians, through their customary, judicial, and statutory practices and decisions, thus created their own slave regime. Although the English crown did have undisputed right of review on all colonial statutory codes, it never exercised this right in regard to the creation of the Virginia slave codes."[17] It is no surprise then that when the first twenty Black people landed in Jamestown, Virginia, in 1619 they were treated as servants and not slaves, as there were no slave codes on the books. "Coming from the Spanish West Indies and therefore being Christians, the majority of these first Negroes were treated in the matter of labor and rights much as their fellow white servants, some receiving an education, and most being granted their freedom dues after their period of labor."[18] Edward Long, in his classic text *The History of Jamaica,* points out that it was customary for White people from Europe to be sent to the West Indian colonies to work as servants in the eighteenth century, as was the case in colonial Virginia. Long puts it this way:

> Great numbers used formerly to be brought from Scotland, where they were actually kidnapped by some man traders, in or near Glasgow, and shipped for this island, to be sold for four or five years term of service. On their arrival, they used to be ranged in a line, like new Negroes, for the planters to pick and choose. . . . Many of these menial servants, who are retained for the sake of saving a deficiency, are the very dregs of the three kingdoms. They have commonly more vices, and much fewer good qualities, than the slaves over whom they are set in authority; the better sort of which heartily despise them, perceiving little or no difference from themselves, except in skin, and blacker depravity.[19]

Both in Virginia and many Islands in the Caribbean, Black and White people worked on plantations as servants. This was the case in Virginia in the eighteenth century, and certainly much earlier in the Caribbean. With the absentee owners residing in Europe, most of the White servants from Europe served as overseers in the Caribbean. In Virginia, they had a definite advantage because of their color, and so, for better or for worse, race began to play a critical role as "after 1640, the colored population of Virginia began to be increasingly divided between servants and slaves, with the majority who came after the fourth decade being immediately reduced by the planters who bought them to servitude 'for life.' It also became increasingly difficult for the Negro servant to prove his right to freedom, and the class dwindled rapidly. For the colonial leaders early recognized that they could possess the labor of the Negro for his lifetime with little opposition from any outside power."[20] In the second half of the seventeenth century, indentured servants were phased out in Virginia, and Black people and their progeny were servants for life. The children of White servants were born free while the progeny of Black people were born slaves. The Black child was owned by the master, even in his mother's womb. This is a sense in which we may speak of "natal alienation," as not only were children slaves—working on plantations at the tender age of six—but they could and in many cases were sold away from siblings and parents without any discussion with them or their families. The master displayed absolute power over enslaved Africans as the African was owned absolutely by the master from inception to the grave. This was not the case with White servants, who were indentured servants but were never slaves. This pattern points to the racial factor in plantation slavery:

> That racial prejudice was one of the factors, aside from economic considerations, that may have influenced the enslavement of the Negro and the development of the legal institution of slavery is seen in the curious documents on the early reaction to the miscegenation between the races. In September of 1630, it was ordered by the governor and council that "Hugh Davis be soundly whipped, before an assembly of Negroes and others for abusing himself to the dishonor of God and shame of Christians, by defiling his body in lying with a Negro." In 1640 Robert Sweet was also convicted of dishonoring himself with a Negro, and this time the Negress was whipped. And in 1662 those found "fornicating with a Negro" were to be fined double the amount meted out for such offence.[21]

Klein suggests that as early as 1630 race was a problem in Virginia for both the White colonial class and Black people. As early as 1630 there were questions of a superior and an inferior race, which undoubtedly, framed a racial argument for the enslavement of a race of people. Klein opines that this was not the case in Cuba, as Castillian Cuban and Afro-Cuban expressed no antipathy toward each other. It was the nomadic temperament of the Indians, coupled with arguments of their unsuitability for plantation work, that saved them from White domination on plantations. However, there was no question that the Virginia planter was the first to arrogate the Black person to the status of "slave for life." "Although the legislative or statutory structure of Negro slavery was not begun until 1662, there already appeared as early as 1640 county court cases recognizing the institution as it was being created in practice. In that year, John Punch, a Negro, was made to serve for life as punishment for running away, whereas the two whites with him had but four additional years added to their time."[22] If the Virginia planter class was the first to reduce Black people to slave for life, it is fair to say that this was ratified by the Virginia General Assembly.

> Although the conscious construction of the status of the Negro in the statutory codes was not until 1662, there were references to the condition of slavery in prior acts of the Assembly. The first use of the word "slave" occurred in an act dated 1655, which declared that "if Indians shall bring in any children as gages of their good and quiet intention to us and amity with us . . . the country by us their representative do engage that we will not use them as slaves." The first use of the phrase "Negro slave," however, did not occur until March 30, 1660. On that date appeared an act that was designed to encourage the importation of Negroes, especially by the Dutch. It provided "that if the said Dutch or other foreigners shall import any Negro slaves . . . they were to be granted reductions on the duty for the tobacco they received as payment for the said Negroes."[23]

As early as 1661, it was agreed that any Englishmen who brought Indians for trading would not sell them as slaves but as servants who would serve no longer than Englishmen. When questions arose concerning the status of children born to an enslaved woman and an Englishman, the legislature ruled that the child assumes the status of the mother. If both parents were slaves and Black, the progeny belonged to the master. The Virginia Assembly regarded it as important to clarify the status of newly imported slaves in relation to their country of origin and religion. Because of this on October 3, 1670, it was stated, "'all servants not being Christians imported into this country by shipping shall be slaves for life.' The act was careful to exclude Indians from this definition, and they were not enslaved in the colony until after 1676."[24] This injunction was overturned in 1682 to include Indians and all Blacks who were imported as slaves irrespective of their religion. The badge of skin color was definitive in terms of one's destiny as a slave. Later, there was a logical connection between being African and slave. Africa seemed to provide an inexhaustible source of labor for work on plantations. To be Black and slave were synonymous. The burden of proof was on the African, whether mulatto or Black, to prove otherwise. As the Virginia slave codes emerged it began slowly but surely to strip away the rights of Black people, assigning them to the status of chattel. It began to take root in the culture that enslaved persons had no rights, were not entitled to justice. The bottom line was that the slave had no right to freedom. It was a forgone conclusion that the slave was not considered in law as human. As early as 1662, it was made legal for a master to kill any slave who tried to run away and in the process offered resistance. Further, the Virginia Assembly stipulated in 1705 that if any "'white man or woman, being free shall intermarry with a Negro or mulatto man or woman, being bond or free, [that person] shall be . . . committed to prison' and the minister marrying them severely punished."[25]

The free Black person was under the same restrictions as those in bondage. It was not uncommon for free Blacks to be kidnapped by slave masters and the burden of proof was on the Black person to prove he was not the slave of the White person making the charge. It was extremely difficult for the African to win his freedom as it was a forgone conclusion that he was inferior and his word could not be trusted to stand against the claim of the master. An exception to this was the case of Richard Allen, who was well known in Philadelphia.

> On most plantations slaves were not allowed to sing African songs, dance African dances, or speak African languages. The practice of conjuration was universally outlawed. The very word "African" was meant to invoke the image of ignorant savagery and the words "black" and "dark" (as in darkey) carried connotations of evil, immorality, and ugliness. Blacks were taught that their skin was ugly, that their lips and noses were unaesthetic and malformed, and that they carried a natural smell that was offensive. Like sheep, Negroes did not have hair but wool. . . . When they died, slaves were buried in a separate graveyard set apart from the white burial grounds.[26]

The bottom line pointed to the inferiority of African culture and the superiority of the European way of life. The separation between the races that was lived out on the plantations in the colonies extended even to the grave.

Enslaved persons were required to wear a happy countenance at all times on the plantations. Plantation ethics required outer expressions of happiness and laughter. Africans in the New World trapped on plantations were obligated to obey and perform their duties cheerfully. There was a theological basis for the master's insistence that Blacks should work cheerfully even under the most oppressive circumstances. A part of the reasoning was that it was a privilege to work as a slave, hence a slave should display at all times a happy countenance. Further, the master was God's representative on earth, who knew what was best for the slave and a smiling slave gave expression to the kindness of the master and would, in fact, produce a more humane master as long as the slave was industrious and cheerful. Failure to work hard and be cheerful would cause the master to brutalize the slave. "Henry Banks, who was born a slave in 1835, remembers that he 'was whipped once because the overseer said I looked mad: "Come here, you d – d selfish son of a b – h, I'll please you by the time I've done with you." Then he whipped me, so that I couldn't hollow.'"[27] Enslaved persons were expected to be cheerful and singing, displaying signs of happiness at all times. Frederick Douglass mentions this ethos that characterized life on plantations both in the Caribbean and the American colonies.

> Does a slave look dissatisfied? It is said, he has the devil in him, and it must be whipped out. Does he speak loudly when spoken to by his master? Then he is getting high-minded, and should be taken down a button-hole lower. Does he forget to pull off his hat at the approach of a white person? Then he is wanting in reverence, and should be whipped for it. Does he venture to vindicate his conduct when censured for it? Then he is guilty of impudence,—one of the greatest crimes of which a slave can be guilty. Does he ever venture to suggest a different mode of doing things from that pointed out by his master? He is indeed presumptuous, and getting above himself; and nothing less than flogging will do for him.[28]

These rules of etiquette were expected and required at all times and failing to comply meant a violent response from the master. It was understood by enslaved persons that the will of the master applied to every aspect of plantation life. Slaves understood that the master had the right to whip, sell, or trade members of the family whenever and for whatever reason. The bottom line was that slaves were chattel property whose will was always subordinate to that of the master class. And yet the peculiar requirement in the face of the master's abuse is that slaves were expected to regard them as gracious, kind, and having the best interest of the enslaved. One way in which the master class advanced this ethos of ultimate control "was to divide and conquer." "Planters also promoted a separating status hierarchy among their slaves. Obedient fieldhands were taught they were better than the 'bad nigger'—the malcontent or runaway. Drivers were taught they were better than common fieldhands; domestics, that they were better than any fieldhand; skilled tradesmen, that they were better than the average house servant. This hierarchy was reinforced by the granting of special material comforts to those higher on the scale."[29] In another way to keep enslaved persons off balance in relation with each other, many masters took care to ensure that slaves came from different regions in Africa, with different language patterns and as much as possible were hostile toward each other. This of course would lessen the possibility of enslaved persons coming together for insurrections. Fernando Ortiz, in *Cuban Counterpoint: Tobacco and Sugar,* captures for us the sense of difference among Africans and their sense of dislocation and displacement on plantations in the New World:

> The Negroes brought with their bodies their souls, but not their institutions nor their implements. They were of different regions, races, languages, cultures, classes, ages and sexes . . . socially equalized by the same system of slavery. They arrived deracinated, wounded, shattered, like the cane of the fields. . . . No other human element had to suffer such a profound and repeated change of surroundings, cultures, class and conscience. . . . The Indians suffered their fate in their native land, believing that when they died they passed over to the invisible regions of their own Cuban world. The fate of the Negroes was far more cruel; they crossed the ocean in agony, believing that even after death they would have to re-cross it to be resurrected in Africa with their lost ancestors. . . . The Indians and the Spaniards had the support and comfort of their families, their kinsfolk, their leaders, and their places of worship in their sufferings; the Negroes found none of this. They, the most uprooted of all, were herded together like animals in a pen, always in a state of impotent rage, always filled with a longing for flight, freedom, change, and always having to adopt a defensive attitude of submission, pretense, and acculturation to a new world. Under these conditions of mutilation and social amputation, thousands and thousands of human beings were brought to Cuba year after year . . . from continents beyond the sea.[30]

The plight of enslaved persons alluded to by Ortiz represents the situation on plantations throughout the colonies in the Caribbean and the American mainland. Uprooted, rejected, and confronted with a life of social dislocation and death, they somehow sought to carve out redemptive space for healing and wholeness. Ortiz refers to the "impotent rage" of enslaved persons always poised for flight or a defensive attitude for submission.

Orlando Patterson, in "The Constituent Elements of Slavery," points out that one of the underlying issues in plantation slavery was the imbalance of power, relations of inequality, or domination in which the world of the master as it intersected that of the enslaved person was one in which the master class exercised total control and power over the enslaved person. "Slavery is one of the most extreme forms of the relation of domination, approaching the limits of total power from the viewpoint of the master, and of total powerlessness from the viewpoint of the slave."[31] Patterson problematizes the relation of domination between master and slave and suggests that the master's total control or domination of the slave might result in his dependence on the slave and the powerlessness of the slave might also result in an attempt of the slave to control the master. Patterson argues that it is difficult if not impossible to sustain slavery without violence on the part of the master class in part because the enslaved person has not bought into the master's need for surplus in order to make the capitalist experiment work.

> In one of the liveliest passages of the *Grundrisse*, Karl Marx, while dis-
> cussing the attitudes of former masters and slaves in post-emancipation
> Jamaica, not only shows clearly that he understood slavery to be first
> and foremost "a relation of domination" . . . but identifies the peculiar
> role of violence in creating and maintaining that domination. Com-
> menting on the fact that the Jamaican ex-slaves refused to work beyond
> what was necessary for their own subsistence, he notes: "They have
> ceased to be slaves, . . . not in order to become wage laborers, but, in-
> stead, self-sustaining peasants working for their own consumption. As
> far as they are concerned, capital does not exist as capital, because au-
> tonomous wealth as such can exist only either on the basis of *direct*
> forced labor, slavery, or *indirect* forced labor, wage labor. Wealth con-
> fronts direct forced labor not as capital, but rather as *relation of domina-
> tion*." . . . Indeed, the comment was provoked by a November 1857 letter
> to the *Times* of London from a West Indian planter who, in what Marx
> calls, "an utterly delightful cry of outrage," was advocating the re-impo-
> sition of slavery in Jamaica as the only means of getting the Jamaicans
> to generate surplus in a capitalistic manner once again.[32]

According to Patterson, the master-slave relation was based on violence and would not survive without violence. The dilemma was that when a worker was fired, that person would seek another job because he is a worker. The case was different with the enslaved person, as he was no longer interested in forced labor but was now free to choose his or her future, which usually was one without the master. While the enslaved person could do without the relation of domination in which the master forced and coerced labor, the master had to await the shipment of new slaves to begin the relation of domination all over. He was stuck in that relation of domination and could not move on unless he wished to abandon the capitalist system of profit. Profit was the goal of the master class, and violence was the means by which he exacted and extracted labor to keep the mills of industry operating. There was no plantation, however generous the master, in which the whip (violence) did not at least serve as a threat.

The Master and the Will of the Enslaved

Patterson points out that if violence was an indispensable instrument of the plantation, another inviolable condition was the will of the enslaved person being an extension of the master's. The master class required an effacement of the ego and will of the enslaved, as the master lived in a constant place of fear—fear that the enslaved person would awake and claim her space and place as human, requiring justice and freedom. The master wanted to believe that the enslaved person had no ideas, no thoughts but those of his master. The slave was socialized into plantation life through the aegis of the master and his life was to do and fulfill the master's will. "In his powerlessness the slave became the extension of his master's power. He was a human surrogate, recreated by his master with god-like power in his behalf. . . . Without the master the slave does not exist and he is socializable only through the master."[33] The master was father to the enslaved person as he gave him his name. He was his provider and protector for him and his family. The master was often the source of his being. Certainly, if the master believed the soul of the enslaved person belonged to God, it was clear to all and enforced by law, that the body belonged to the master, who often made no connection between the missionary preaching to the soul of the enslaved person and his brutalizing the body in order to make a profit.

The next element of plantation life that Patterson underlines is that of natal alienation—the loss of family both extended and immediate. "Alienated from all 'rights' or claims of birth, he ceased to belong in his own right to any legitimate social order. All slaves experienced, at the very least, a secular excommunication. . . . Slaves differed from other human beings in that they were not allowed freely to integrate the experience of their ancestors into their lives, to inform their understanding of social reality with the inherited meanings of their natural forebears, or to anchor the living present in any conscious community of memory."[34] The plantation sought to destroy the memory of Africa and, in fact, denied Black people their heritage. I believe that Patterson got it right when he insists that the plantation did not and could not deny Black people their history, but, in fact, denied them their heritage in its attempt to erase the memory of Africa and to effect a distance between them and the home land. They were denied a history with siblings, parents, children, and ancestors; the slave became "a genealogical isolate," with no sense of belonging to family or any right or claim to love. It is in this sense that Patterson advances his thesis that plantation life was the instrument of social death.

> The refusal formally to recognize the social relations of the slave had profound emotional and social implications. In all slave holding societies slave couples could be and were forcibly separated and the consensual "wives" of slaves were obliged to submit sexually to their masters; slaves had no custodial claims or powers over their children, and children inherited no claims or obligations to their parents. And the master had the power to remove a slave from the local community in which he or she was brought up. . . . Nothing comes across more dramatically from the hundreds of interviews with American ex-slaves than the fear of separation.[35]

A consequence of natal alienation was that of the master asserting all rights over the enslaved, claiming powers of life and death—and he seemed to have the symbols to make this stick. For example, slaves were branded often on their cheeks to show to whom they belonged. Then they were forbidden to use African names and had to assume names assigned to them by the master, often the master's name. These symbols were to encourage the myth that the African was without a past, and as Patterson explains, even when this is disproved, the genealogical pool seems rather thin. The question is raised, how far back, genealogically, can Africans who were transported across the Atlantic to plantations in the new World go in fashioning their identity?

I must confess that as a great-grandson of slaves in the Caribbean, I have visited Africa several times in attempts to trace the roots of my genealogical tree and have been surprised at how shallow these roots are. The language barrier has been a great obstacle, as it excludes me from customs and rituals and practices that would be helpful in identifying streams of knowledge that would be useful. The shameful truth is that I could not locate my roots, and I feel ashamed to settle with a strange name that does not honor my parents and ancestors. It was even difficult to identify my own community to honor those roots, which would help me honor the name of my parents and ancestors.

Patterson indicates that one of the travesties of the enslaved condition was that of the slave having to honor the name of his master/oppressor and unable to defend the name of his own parents/ancestors. The slave had no power to honor and defend the name of his parents, and to pass on that name to his children

The counterpart of the master's sense of honor is the slave's experience of loss. The so-called servile personality is merely the outward expression of this loss of honor. "I was called up on one of her [Miss Ada's] birthdays, and Master Bob sorta looked out de corner of his eyes, first at me and then at Miss Ada, and then he made a little speech. He took my hand, put it in Miss Ada's hand, and say: 'Dis your birthday present, darlin.' I make a curtsy and Miss Ada's eyes twinkle like a star and she take me in her room and took on powerful over me."[36]

It is quite clear that in many instances the context of the plantation in slavery threatened and often destroyed the humanity of enslaved persons in the New World. On the one hand the plantation represented the world that confronted Black people, whether in the Caribbean or in the United States. From the perspective of the planter class, Black people were not supposed to survive. The organization of slavery aimed toward the obliteration not just of their culture but of their identity as Africans and any sense that they were human beings, made in the image of God—a people who were created for equality and dignity.

In the New World the process by which the Negro was stripped of his social heritage and thereby, in a sense dehumanized was completed. There was first the size of the plantation, which had a significant influence upon the extent and nature of the contacts between the slaves and the whites. On the large sugar and cotton plantations in the Southern States there was, as in Brazil and the West Indies, little contact between whites and the Negro slaves. Under such conditions there was some opportunity for the slaves to undertake to re-establish their old ways. As a matter of fact, however, the majority of slaves in the United States were on small plantations. In some of the upland cotton regions of Alabama, Mississippi, Louisiana, and Arkansas the median number of slaves per holding did not reach twenty; while in the regions of general agriculture based mainly upon slave labor in Kentucky, Maryland, Missouri, North Carolina, South Carolina and Tennessee the median number of holding was even smaller.[37]

The World Black People Made

These important reminders by E. Franklin Frazier not only put in perspective for us the context that confronted enslaved Africans on plantations in the New World, but give us a sense of resources that were available to them

in their attempt to fight acculturation and accommodation as they sought to
carve out their world and affirm their humanity. Frazier's claim that in the
West Indies slaves had more freedom to retain their African culture is true,
as the proportion of slaves to Whites was quite sizable in many instances.
For example, "In the year of the great rebellion there were five people of
African descent—the great majority of them enslaved—for every European
in the Danish colonies. On St. Thomas, blacks outnumbered whites by
3,741 to about 650, and on St. John 1,087 to 208. To control this captive
population, planters staged an elaborate choreography of terror."[38] It is quite
clear that the sheer numbers of Blacks in relation to Whites on plantations
gave them some advantage over Blacks in the United States in terms of retaining African culture and religious practices. Coupled with this was the
reality that unlike their peers in the United States, Caribbean Blacks did not
have the close scrutiny that settler colonialism engendered. For example, in
North American colonies, plantations were much smaller in size with the
master-owner always in close proximity and often personally invested in the
daily routine-life of enslaved persons. Because in the Caribbean there was
often absentee ownership of plantations, overseers and drivers were not as
committed to pressuring the enslaved population in the regular running of
the plantation. Of course, there were often safeguards, as slaves were separated from their families and fellow members of a tribe and clan in order to
make communication among them difficult. However, because many of the
languages of West Africa had similar patterns, enslaved persons were able
to overcome the separation and concoct ways of communicating with each
other. The other thing to keep in mind is that the size of the plantation and
the reality of absentee ownership did not mean that the terror of slavery was
lessened in the islands of the Caribbean. It seemed that the relative freedom
allowed slaves to take more risks, both in terms of rebellions and of running away. In both contexts there were severe penalties for these infractions
of plantation culture and etiquette. "Slaves had staged plenty of rebellions
in American plantation societies and would carry out many more, but few
thwarted the planters and their troops as long and insistently as those on St.
John. Word was circulating around the Caribbean that a small, poorly armed
band of rebels had taken an entire island and was taunting the colonizers.
In South Carolina, the only North American colony in which enslaved
blacks outnumbered whites, anxious readers attuned to the threat of slave
unrest could follow the revolt in the *Slave Carolina Gazette*."[39] Throughout
the Caribbean slaves often lost a leg or an ear as the price for running away.
"Three of them were burned at the stake on three different plantations on
St. John. . . . 'One was burned to death slowly, another was sawed in half and

a third was impaled. The two Negro women had their hands and heads cut off after all five had been tortured with hot pincers in the town.' "[40]

Churches and Slavery

In the face of this inhumanity of the planter class to enslaved persons, it is appropriate to ask, what was the response of the clergy? What, if any, was the role of the plantation church, both in terms of the Colonial and African expressions of church? The truth is that several Christian churches voiced their unease with slavery and were instrumental in giving substance to the anti-slavery societies. "Most eighteenth-century Southern churches, with the notable exception of the Quakers, raised few questions about the morality of holding slaves. The egalitarian doctrines of the American Revolution and the Great Awakening created, however, a sizable abolition party in Southern churches. . . . In 1789, for example, the Virginia Baptist General Committee, denouncing slavery as a 'horrid evil' and 'violent deprivation of the rights of nature,' called for its abolition. Kentucky Baptists followed suit, organized local associations of Baptist churches committed to emancipation, and several Baptist clergy men preached against slavery from 1790s to 1820s."[41] Presbyterians in Kentucky during the same period declared slavery a moral evil and worked for its overthrow. "In 1809 the Baltimore Conference of the Methodist Church forbade the buying and selling of slaves by its members, throughout the antebellum period the Conference forbade its ministers to hold slaves."[42] It is clear that in the nineteenth century the Methodist revivals had a positive and powerful effect on slave masters, as many of them in the state of Maryland released their slaves from bondage. In the South several masters followed the lead of planters in Maryland. Both religious planters and clergy began to sense that slavery was a sin against humanity. Gradually, many of the slaveholding class came to see the evil embedded in the practice of slavery. "There is overwhelming convincing evidence that a substantial number of Southern slaveholders never rested easy with their black species of property. While guilt was neither the South's biggest nor smallest crop, it grew to sizable proportions among women allied to slaveholding families."[43] If several planters and masters saw slavery as an evil which was out of step with the law of love or the highest ideals of Christianity, then a majority saw it as a necessary evil which was a political and not a religious institution. "As antislavery Northern clergymen pushed their Southern co-religionists to acknowledge slavery as a sin and to excommunicate slaveholders, planters began forbidding ministers to talk to their slaves. Accused of being abolitionists, Southern clergymen launched a campaign in the 1830s to convince the planters that they held orthodox views about the peculiar institution. Practically every state convention of Southern churches held during this period ended with the blistering attack on fanatical abolitionists bent on increasing insurrections."[44] If the planters fought back to protect their enslaved property, the clergy and churches fell in line as churches preached that slavery was a political institution and anti-slavery ministers were seen as the enemy. Many churches followed the 1836 doctrine of the Hopewell Presbytery:

> "Slavery is a political institution, with which the church has nothing to do, except to inculcate the duties of Master and Slave, and to use lawful, spiritual means to have all, both bond and free, to become one in Christ by faith." By the 1840s, the propagandists had largely succeeded in silencing the churches. Torn between their eighteenth-century abolition heritage and their desire to remain as viable institutions in nineteenth-century Southern society, the churches carefully avoided any action which might be interpreted as an attack on slavery. Calls for emancipation were muted.[45]

Many churches began to preach that slavery was a divine institution that would benefit both slave and master. Churches began to teach that the Christianizing of the slave would make him dutiful. Indeed the best slave a master could have would be a Christian slave. Along these lines masters were encouraged to allow their slaves to receive religious instruction as a Christian slave would work harder than a non-Christian slave. "For his own salvation and his profits, the planter had a responsibility to give religious instruction to his slave. . . . The Scriptures look to the correction of servants, and really enjoin it, as they do in the case of children. We esteem it the duty of Christian masters to feed, clothe well, and in the case of disobedience to *whip well*."[46] On both sides of the Christian spectrum, whether Catholic or Protestant from the second half of the nineteenth century the church claimed that the enslavement of Africans was the means for their conversion. But already the paradox of slave and Christian began to bother the conscience of some Christians and there was nervousness that the baptism of a slave could mean that he was no longer in bondage. This seems to place Christianity on a collision course with the economic interest of the master class.

> If this were true, baptizing a slave would in effect free him, contrary to the slave owner's economic interest. Colonial legislators solved the problem by passing decrees that baptism had no effect upon the status of the baptized in regard to slavery or freedom. Despite the legislation,

British American slaveholders remained suspicious of teaching Christianity to slaves because they believed that becoming Christian would raise the slave's self esteem, persuade them that they were equal to the whites, and encourage them to become rebellious. Religious assemblies might present slaves with the opportunity to organize resistance, and teaching slaves to read the Bible would have the dangerous effect of making them literate.[47]

Other concerns had to do with enslaved persons being aware of their place at the bottom of the social/economic pyramid. Would admission into membership of the Christian church blur their cultural and social distinctions in relation to the dominant culture? These were some of the questions that came to the fore as the church had to deal with the issue of Christian instruction, Christian education—which included learning to read the Bible—membership and fellowship in the Christian church. The Society for the Propagation of the Gospel in Foreign Parts (SPG), founded in London in 1701, encouraged and required its missionaries to offer religious instruction to slaves, insisting that the gospel would not foment rebellion or insurrection but instill a docile disposition. In an attempt to assure masters that the Bible did not teach equality of slaves in relation to their masters, the Scripture "slaves be obedient to your masters," from St. Paul's letter to Ephesians, was emphasized. The influence of the Society for the Propagation of the Gospel in Foreign Parts was mediated throughout the American and Caribbean colonies. It is important to highlight that in the second half of the nineteenth century preachers were not at this time advocating abolition of the institution of slavery. What was highlighted was the political dimension of slavery and its importance as an economic institution. However, there were many preachers, even if they owned slaves, who pressed for an amelioration of the conditions of slavery rather than the abolition of the system. This, of course, had the effect of making and securing their peace with the planter class. "While trying to restrain the cruelty of masters, white ministers were attempting to make slaves submissive. Many slaves testified that the white ministers, dedicated to preserving slavery, tried to promote good behavior, contentment, industry, and humility in the quarters and to discourage stealing, lying, and rebelliousness. Indeed, the Bible verses the white ministers quoted frequently admonished slaves to be orderly and dependable workers devoted to their owner's interest, to be satisfied with their station in life, to accept their stripes patiently, and to view their faithful service to earthly masters as service to God."[48] There was no attempt by preachers to differentiate the will of the masters from the will of God as they provided religious instruction for slaves. In fact, slaves were taught that they should honor their masters as they honor God. Service to the master was equated as service to God. There were many sermons that emphasized that God in God's wisdom had set earthly masters over enslaved persons, and gratitude to God should be expressed in service and unconditional obedience of the master.

> White ministers often taught the slaves that they did not deserve freedom, that it was God's will that they were enslaved, that the devil was creating those desires for liberty in their breasts, and that runaways would be expelled from the church. Then followed the slaves beatitudes: blessed *are* the patient, blessed *are* the faithful, blessed *are* the cheerful, blessed *are* the submissive, blessed are the hardworking, and above all, blessed are the obedient.[49]

Missionaries discovered that enslaved persons whether in the Caribbean or in the North American colonies did not take kindly to the notion of obedience to their masters. They saw through the hypocrisy and divided loyalties of the missionaries, and often not only voiced their displeasure but as a group would walk out of church. Howard Thurman tells the story of his grandmother who had been a slave and had to listen to White preachers enjoin slaves from St. Paul's letters to be obedient to their masters. When he enquired of her why she would tell him where to read from the Bible and deliberately exclude the Pauline Epistles, she pointed out to him that she promised herself as a slave that if she ever learned to read she would never read from Paul's letters. "For instance, one Georgia minister reported that when he 'insisted upon fidelity and obedience as Christian virtues in servants and . . . condemned the practice of *running away,* one half of my audience deliberately rose up and walked off . . . some solemnly declared . . . "that it was not the Gospel"; others, "that they did not care if they ever heard me preach again.' "[50] This practice of slaves questioning the veracity of missionaries preaching was also true throughout the Caribbean. There, it was often the case that slaves went to church without any intention of listening to the preaching of White preachers. After church, they would ask the medicine man or the Black preacher what the White preacher said, and he would interpret and edit. It points to the political and spiritual genius of Black people that they would go to the White church without any intention of listening to the White preacher. White preachers became aware of enslaved persons' dislike for sermons about obedience and therefore would keep them to a minimum. Enslaved persons understood the politics that the missionary had to please the master. Favorite topics of White preachers were sin, the need for prayer, Christology, and the grace and mercy of God. The truth is that Black people were not impressed by Christian doctrine but were concerned how the teachings of Jesus or the life of Jesus translates into strategies for liberation. On the other hand, White preachers were primarily concerned that their preaching and teaching made Black servants and slaves compliant to the wishes of the master and the ethics of the plantation. In 1859 the *Southern Episcopalian* published the "Plantation Catechism" in which the following questions and answers were presented for slaves to memorize and practice:

Q: What is the fifth commandment?
A: Honor thy father and thy mother, that thy days may be long in the land which the Lord thy God giveth thee.
Q: What does this commandment require you to do?
A: This commandment requires me to respect and to obey my father and mother, my master and mistress, and everybody that has authority over me.

The Power of Slave Religion

While White ministers emphasized memorization of the Lord's prayer, the ten commandments, and various passages that highlighted obedience and submissiveness, for enslaved persons their love for church and religious services had to do with their love for singing, dancing, praying, and possession of the spirit, and later on when they had their own church they included preaching and drumming. There were different agendas and quite often there was a misunderstanding on the part of the White preachers. For example, Blacks would join the churches and become faithful in attendance and in their participation, and White preachers would understand this as Blacks conforming to church doctrine and polity, while Blacks understood this as a journey to equality with Whites, and freedom for them and their children. This was often why there was a rush to baptism and, where possible, church membership. For Black people there was a joining of the theological and the political. Baptism and church membership were about freedom, equality, and an affirmation of African ways of being and believing.

One of the reasons that enslaved persons survived on plantations in the New World in spite of the long hours and brutality was their ability to adapt their religious practices and beliefs to a Christian frame of reference without losing the essentials of their native beliefs. They found ways of maintaining the integrity of their religious beliefs while at the same time they were open to the change that a new sociological and theological environment imposed on them. "The African spirits, called *lwa* in Haiti, and *santos* in Cuba, might take

on new identities across the Atlantic, or new spirits might be revealed. . . .
Altars, covered with images of the saints, enabled the congregation to offer
food and drink to please their gods. Priests also sacrificed animals to the spirits because blood contained the power of life that strengthened the *lwa* and the
santos. Then the congregation cooked and ate the animals' flesh in a service of
communion that gave the people assembled a share in the spirit's power. Each
member of the Vodou or Santeria community had a special patron spirit, a
relationship established by initiation ceremonies which, in some cases,
'wedded' a person and a spirit together in a life of mutual responsibility and
care."[51] "Missionaries had little success with African-born slaves because many
of them never learned English well enough to understand instructions in
Christianity. American-born slaves, who understood the language and the
customs of the whites, made better candidates for conversion."[52] Because they
made the connections with their religion from Africa, enslaved persons were
free to risk, adapting and making substitutions as they appropriated the new
religion to their needs. This was somewhat easier in the islands of the Caribbean, where the ratio of clergy to enslaved persons was so vast that slaves were
able to practice their religion unhindered by White supervision. In this context, the memory of Africa informed and shaped their faith.

> Becoming Christian involved a lengthy process of learning, memoriza-
> tion, and moral testing. During the first 120 years of black slavery in
> British North America, little headway was made in converting the slave
> population to Christianity. The conversion of slaves in large numbers
> was a product of a period of religious revivals that swept parts of the
> colonies beginning in 1739. These extended meetings of prayer and
> preaching stirred intense religious emotion among crowds of people
> and led many to experience conversion. Leaders of the revivals made
> special mention of the fact that blacks attended their gatherings in
> larger numbers than before. Some were allowed to attend by their mas-
> ters; others risked punishment to attend without permission. Not only
> did free blacks and slaves attend revivals, they also took active part in
> the services, praying, exhorting, and preaching.[53]

It is quite understandable that as a consequence of settler colonialism, in
which the owner of the plantation often lived in close proximity to slaves,
churches in the North American colonies especially in Virginia, Maryland,
and the southern colonies would have greater success in the conversion of
enslaved persons than in the Caribbean. Throughout the Caribbean during
the eighteenth and nineteenth centuries, the Christian church had given in to

a materialist and capitalistic way of life. The church had never advocated a change of the structures of slavery, but only an amelioration of that system. Part of the reason for this was that the church owned slaves and in some cases priests began to whip and brutalize slaves as did the overseers on plantations. This was understandable, as in many instances missionaries were invited to the islands by the planter class and became a part of the ruling class. The situation in Barbados was even more far-reaching, as there the Anglican Church was given hundreds of acres on the Codrington plantation with several hundred slaves and had to be responsible for the production of sugar cane and the management of slaves. In this instance, the church was more invested in the production of sugar than in the saving of souls. The church did not merely capitulate to the demands of the planter class but was won over by the allure of profit made possible by the brutalizing of Black bodies. Because of the common capitalistic ethos that informed life on plantations—whether in Virginia, North Carolina, or Barbados—enslaved persons were likely to hear the same kinds of sermons in these places. These sermons enjoined them to obey their masters, or to be submissive to those whom God had placed in authority over them, being aware that if they would bear their earthly hardships they would receive great rewards in heaven. However, we must keep in mind that although enslaved persons in Virginia, South Carolina, and Cuba were likely to hear the same kinds of sermon, one difference in the Caribbean was the lack of contact with the clergy because of the size of the plantations and the ratio of clergy to Blacks. This provided Black sacred space for the retention of Africa's memory. Even as enslaved people merged Christian and African views, their hermeneutical key was, where do we stand in relation to Africa? They interpreted their new faith in the light of an African frame of reference.

5

The Making of the Black World

IN THE LAST chapter we looked at the world that confronted Black people in European colonies both on the North American mainland and throughout the Caribbean. A number of realities applied to Black people whether here on the mainland or there in the Caribbean. It was noted that all Black people had a number of similarities in their lives: they were all of African ancestry and were regarded by the master class as inferior. There was an ethos of subjugation and subordination that suffused plantation life. Enslaved persons were rootless, informed that they had no history and no family, and therefore they needed the master not only for their survival but also to subsist in a context in which violence against the Black person was the order of the day. But there are differences between how African Americans in the Caribbean and their peers on the American mainland are understood and perceived. "In the Caribbean region, however, the operation of racial bias has generally been more subtle and more complicated than in the United States. Moreover, the Caribbean region, with its more than fifty island and assorted mainland societies, embraces a wide range of local codes of race relations. Even a casual observer will be struck by the differing tenor of social relations in, say, Puerto Rico, Haiti and Jamaica; were one to add Trinidad and one of the very small, historically somewhat untypical islands . . . the picture would even be more complex."[1] Sidney Mintz goes on to point out that throughout the Caribbean Black people are part of the social and political majority, and when this is coupled with linguistic differences and a different emphasis on race relations, one must be careful and mindful not only of the ways cultures and histories in Afro-Americana merge but ways in which they diverge. "To begin with, in many Caribbean societies—in Haiti or Jamaica, for instance—phenotypically black people *are* the majority. Again, great variations exist in local codes of social assortment by which persons of intermediate appearance are perceived and treated as members of one social segment rather than another, and in no Caribbean case may one confidently assume a bipolar 'racial' system—white' and 'Negro'—of the sort operative for white North Americans."[2]

According to W.E.B. Du Bois in *The Negro Church*, another constant that confronted Black people whether here on the American mainland or there in the Caribbean was the loss of rights for women, the emergence of the new polygamy in which there were no rules governing sexual relationships for women and girls, coupled with the absolute rule of the White man and the loss of the home as a place of protection for the family. The truth is, the Black family was lost as the master had the right to sell, mutilate, or dispose of Black persons as he deemed fit. The slave had no name to protect or pass on to children. There was no family to protect. Enslaved persons would see the master whip a spouse or sibling almost to death and could not lift a hand or voice in protest in fear of his or her own life being threatened. Forbidden to speak his own language or use his own name, enslaved persons were required by law to submit to the will of the master. And yet, as many scholars point out, it is a failure to understand Africans caught up in the terrible inferno of slavery to believe that the European could totally impose his will on them. Eugene Genovese helps us understand that no human being can be the total extension of another's will:

> The humanity of the slave implied his action, and his action implied his will. Hegel was therefore right in arguing that slavery constituted an outrage, for in effect, it has always rested on the falsehood that one man could become an extension of another's will. If one could so transform himself, he could do it only by an act of that very will supposedly being surrendered, and he would remain so if he chose to. The clumsy attempt of slaveholders to invoke religious sanction did not extricate them from this contradiction. The Christian tradition, from the early debates over the implications of original sin through the attempts of Hobbes and others to secularize the problem, could not rationally defend the idea of permanent and total submission rooted in a temporary precise surrender of will. The idea of man's surrender to God cannot be equated with the idea of man's surrender to man."[3]

Acculturation—Search for Center

W.E. B. Du Bois agrees that the support system that would have helped Black people affirm and exercise a measure of human transcendence in relation to the grinding suffering engendered by slavery seems at first glance to have been obliterated by the vicious system of slavery itself. "At first sight it would seem that slavery completely destroyed every vestige of spontaneous social movement among Negroes; the home had deteriorated; political authority and economic initiative was in the hands of the masters, property as a social institution, did not exist on the plantation, and, indeed, it is usually assumed by historians and sociologists that every vestige of internal development disappeared, leaving the slaves no means of expression for their common life, thought, striving."[4] Writing sixty years after Du Bois, E. Franklin Frazier, in *The Negro Church in America,* disagrees with the conclusions arrived at by Du Bois that it was through the ministry and agency of the "Negro priest" expressed in Vodou and Obeah that the power of New World slavery was broken and African retentions and culture provided the means for the transcendence of the human spirit. According to Frazier, a number of things must be noted: (1) The manner in which slaves were captured and enslaved contributed to the loss of their culture and retentions. Africans brought to the New World as slaves were practically stripped of their heritage. Further, although the area in which they were captured in West Africa reflects cultural homogeneity, this did not spill over into their enslaved conditions as they were often separated to enhance the control of the slave master over them. "The capture of many slaves in inter-tribal wars and their selection for the slave markets tended to reduce to a minimum the possibility of retentions and the transmission of African culture."[5] (2) Africans captured in intertribal wars were usually males and those chosen for the slave market were usually young and extremely vigorous. "One can get some notion of this selective process from the fact that it was not until 1840 that the number of females equaled the number of males in the slave population in the United States."[6] Frazier concludes that young males are poor bearers of one's cultural heritage. (3) The way in which enslaved persons were held while awaiting the ships from Europe to arrive to transport them across the Atlantic to plantations in the Americas also influenced the retention and transmission of the culture from their home environment. "They were held in baracoons, a euphemistic term for concentration camps at the time, where the slaves without any regard for sex and family and tribal affiliation were kept until some slaver came along to buy a cargo for the markets of the New World. This period of dehumanization was followed by the 'Middle Passage,' the voyage across the Atlantic Ocean to the slave markets of the West Indies and finally the indigo, tobacco, and cotton plantations of what was to become later the United States."[7] Frazier reminds us of the nature of the dehumanization in the Middle Passage in which enslaved persons were shackled aboard ships two by two, the "right wrist and ankle of one to the left wrist and ankle of another" and packed like sardines in the bottom of the ship. All enslaved people were required to sleep without covering on the floors of the ship. It was not unusual for 600 to 700 slaves to be crowded into a ship, "The men standing in the hold ty'd to stakes, the women between decks and those that are with child in the great cabin and the children in the steeridge which in that hot climate occasions an intolerable stench."[8] According to Frazier, slavery in the New World was not just occurrences of unfortunate Africans being captured or kidnapped and taken to plantations in the Americas; it was a carefully designed system, in which the end result was the total dehumanization of Black people. Frazier puts it this way:

> In the New World the process by which the Negro was stripped of his social heritage and thereby, in a sense dehumanized was completed. There was first the size of the plantation, which had a significant influence upon the extent and nature of the contacts between slaves and the whites. On the large sugar and cotton plantations in the Southern States there was, as in Brazil and the West Indies, little contact between whites and the Negro slaves. Under such conditions there was some opportunity for the slaves to undertake to re-establish their old ways. As a matter of fact, however, the majority of slaves in the United States were on small farms and small plantations.[9]

Frazier's main thesis is that the system of slavery was organized and to a large extent succeeded in stripping enslaved Africans of their heritage. But it is interesting that he leaves the door open for cultural retentions on large farms and plantations in the colonies both on the American mainland and throughout the Caribbean. However, it seems that while he is somewhat hopeful that what did in fact take place in the Caribbean because of the large size of many of the plantations and the added reality of absentee ownership, he was not so inclined to posit this in the majority of plantations in the American mainland. "In some of the upland cotton regions of Alabama, Mississippi, Louisiana, and Arkansas the median number of slaves per holding did not reach twenty; while in regions of general agriculture based mainly upon slave labor in Kentucky, Maryland, Missouri, North Carolina, South Carolina, and Tennessee the median number of slave holdings was even smaller."[10]

Additionally, the loss of African languages was a crucial ploy of the enslaver in ensuring control over the enslaved. There were heavy penalties for speaking one's native tongue and this included using one's African name or even attempting to name one's child without the master's name. Slaves who were broken in to the plantation system were counted on to acculturate fresh shipments of slaves from Africa. "Then slaves freshly imported from Africa were usually 'broken in' to the plantation regime. New slaves were 'made to bathe often, to take long walks from time to time, and especially to dance; they are distributed in small numbers among old slaves in order to dispose them better to acquire their habits. . . . These new slaves with their African ways were subjected to the disdain, if not hostility, of Negroes who had become accommodated to the plantation regime and had acquired the ways of their new environment.' "[11]

The way forward then, according to Frazier, was accommodation and acculturation to the language, religious worldviews, and skills necessary for sugar cane and cotton production. "On the small farms very often the slaves worked in the fields with their white owners. On the larger plantations they were under the strict discipline of the overseers, who not only supervised their work but who also in the interest of security maintained strict surveillance over all their activities."[12] It was also understood among the slave population that there were penalties to be exacted for the assembly of five or more slaves without the presence of a White man. This was particularly true of gatherings for religious purposes.

The bottom line then for Frazier was that the way in which slaves were captured and enslaved and acclimated to "the plantation regime tended to loosen all social bonds among them and to destroy the traditional basis of social cohesion. In addition, the organization of labor and the system of social control and discipline on the plantation both tended to prevent the development of social cohesion either on the basis of whatever remnants of African culture might have survived or on the basis of the Negroes' role in plantation economy. Although the Negroes were organized in work gangs, labor lost its traditional African meaning as a cooperative undertaking with communal significance."[13] For Frazier, the historical record was not merely broken but lost. This losing of the African record by Black people caused a disconnection from the myths, religious institutions, and practices of their native land. Plantation slavery was not merely an economic institution, according to Frazier; it was equally a political institution designed to produce a disciplined and dependent slave. The plantation became a primary method and means of European colonization, and survival and decolonization did not reside in the memory of Africa, its ancestors, gods, and religious beliefs. Survival and decolonization resided in adaptation and accommodation to a new environment with the master's book, the Bible, being the source of social organization and the means of survival in an alien land. The plantation was designed to teach the Black person his or her place at the bottom of the society, in the order of life in the New World. According to Frazier, the bottom line is that the Black person was without a heritage, and the way forward was with tools granted to him by the master, the main tool being the Bible. The critical question was whether the Black person could free herself or himself with tools provided by the master.

> The slave plantation served simultaneously as an agent of European colonization, a means of staple agricultural production within an expanding world capitalist market, and the incubator of a highly stratified system of race relations and a unique African-American culture. Because of the peculiarly authoritarian character of plantation slavery, the interdependence of the modes of political, economic, and cultural domination . . . was the problem . . . of plantation societies: their compulsive need for a disciplined, dependent labor force.[14]

Frazier points to the exceptional case of Black people on the Sea Islands along the coasts of South Carolina and Georgia being able to preserve forms of "the Negro dialect known as Gullah. But the very social isolation of these Negroes is an indication of the exceptional situation in which some remnants of aspects of black culture have survived, granted the isolation of the Gullah speaking peoples of the Sea Islands from the white man's culture." I recall as recently as the 1980s having a student at Emory University in Georgia, from Daufuskie Island who shared with me that as a child of twelve he visited Charleston, South Carolina, for the first time, and it was then that he first saw White people. It was quite an emotional experience for him. I was also quite taken with the similarities between the Jamaican dialect and that of the Daufuskie island.

Frazier's point is that apart from these exceptional cases on the American mainland, the loss of language among Africans coupled with the restrictive organization of slavery contributed to the loss of cohesion among peoples of African descent in the New World. It is beyond dispute by serious students of the history and sociology of slavery that enslaved people shipped to plantations in the New World suffered a common lot, that of losing control over their lives and in the process not being treated or respected as human beings. I agree with Frazier that the mode of transportation to plantations in the Americas—Africans forced to travel in cramped and suffocating conditions tied to the holds of ships—challenges the very limits of what it means to be human. Added to this, as Frazier points out, are the psychological effects of being torn away from family, friends, spirits, institutions, forests, and land and forced to work, live, and die, in an alien place that redefined their life. The greatest trauma that enslaved people had to deal with on plantations was not physical, as terrible as this was, but the Gethsemane-like experience of being betrayed and sold by people of their own race to another race who spoke strange languages and stripped them of their dignity and their future.

The question that Frazier raises—and he is joined in debate by W.E. B. Du Bois and by Melville Herskovits in *The Myth of the Negro Past*—is this: did this new reality that enslaved people endured on plantations in the New World render them a people without a heritage, and if so, how then did they find social cohesion and transform and change the world they faced on plantations in the Americas? Frazier calls attention to an alternative position advocated by W.E.B. Du Bois. He writes, "For example, DuBois evidently thought that social cohesion among the slaves was not totally destroyed. For in one of his studies of Negro life he makes the assertion that the Negro Church was 'the only social institution among the Negroes which started in the African forest and survived slavery' and that 'under the leadership of the priest and medicine man' the church preserved the remnants of African tribal life. From the available evidence, including what we know of the manner in which slaves were Christianized and the character of their churches, it is impossible to establish any continuity between African religious practices and the Negro Church in the United States."[15] According to Frazier, the destruction of myths and kinship organizations were too complete for Black people in the United States to find meaning in their native symbols and institutions.

Enculturation—African Churches

We turn now to the position advocated by Du Bois that the context in which African culture and institutions survived in the New World was the Black church. DuBois is quick to point out that this was not at first a Christian church but an African church immersed in heathen rites of Obeah and Vodou worship. It was the missionary interference with these religious practices that gave these rites the feel of Christian faith. According to Du Bois, it took about two centuries for these African religious practices to become Christian, "with a simple Calvinistic creed, but with many of the old customs still clinging to these services. It is this historic fact that the Negro Church of today bases itself upon the sole surviving social institution of the African fatherland, that accounts for its extraordinary growth and vitality . . . the Church became the center of amusements, of what little spontaneous economic activity remained, of education, and of all social intercourse."[16] What then are the marks of this church which was not at first a Christian church? Du Bois reminds us that Africans had a strong respect for Nature worship and strong proclivities toward witchcraft. There were many who came to the New World with some sense of the presence of a higher being coupled with religious ideas.

A substantial number of enslaved persons were Mohammedans, and many had also been exposed to the Christian faith. According to Du Bois, there was a religious basis for the creation of church granted with a measure of variety and plurality, as religions as diverse as Islam, Christianity, and African traditional faith were all present among Africans who were brought to the New World in chains. The key for Du Bois was the presence of African priests who saw the need for equilibrium in the culture and practiced their art of religion, Obeah. He cites at length a comment by the West Indian historian Bryan Edwards:

> As far as we are able to decide from our own experience and information when we lived in the island, and from the current testimony of all the Negroes we have ever conversed with on the subject, the professors of Obi are, and always were, natives of Africa, and none other; they have brought the science with them from thence to Jamaica, where it is so universally practiced, that we believe there are few of the large estates possessing native Africans, which have not one or more of them. The oldest and most crafty are those who usually attract the greatest devotion and confidence; those whose hoary heads, and a somewhat peculiarly harsh and forbidding aspect, together with some skill in plants of the medical and poisonous species, have qualified them for successful imposition upon the weak and credulous. The Negroes in general, whether African or Creoles, revere, consult and fear them. To these oracles they resort, and with the most implicit faith, upon all occasions, whether for the cure of disorders, the obtaining revenge for injuries or insults, the conciliating of favor, the discovery and punishment of the thief or adulterer, and the prediction of future events. The trade which these imposters carry on is extremely lucrative; they manufacture and sell their obeis adapted to different cases and at different prices. A veil of mystery is studiously thrown over their incantations, to which the midnight hours are allotted, and every precaution is to conceal them from the knowledge and discovery of White people.[17]

Du Bois is quite correct in highlighting the mischievous character of Obeah and reminding us that it was brought to the West Indies by African priests who were usually older Africans. But Du Bois seems to be unsure that Obeah as religion inspired and practiced by the priests within the "Negro Church" provided equilibrium for the society and social cohesion for enslaved persons in an alien land. In the *Negro Church* Du Bois missed the significance of the practice of Obeah in Jamaica as the attempt of Black people to adapt African

religious practices to their enslaved condition and to use religion as a tool to
dismantle the house of bondage. There were few tools oppressed people had
to fight their oppressor in slavery, and one such tool was religion. Du Bois
seems to know this intuitively and yet seems to indicate a bias for Christianity
as a superior religion as he moves to dismiss Obeah as witchcraft. He was
unduly influenced by the English aristocrat from Jamaica, Bryan Edwards.

The Jamaican historian of religion, Leonard Barrett explains how Obeah
flourishes contextually yet dangerously in Jamaica.

> In Africa, although witchcraft exists and the sorcerer is one of the reli-
> gious functionaries of the religious system, his work is considered dan-
> gerous to society. If he is discovered, he is generally killed or driven out
> of the community. There are built in controls by which his polluting
> influence can be counteracted. In the social and religious system, the
> evil power of the sorcerer is always in conflict with the powers of the
> traditional priest. . . . Whenever the society is in equilibrium, that is,
> when the society is under proper control, there is little need for witch-
> craft. On the contrary, when the society is in an unstructured state,
> whenever there is cultural confusion or social disorientation, witchcraft
> is likely to flourish. This being the case it is easy to see why witchcraft
> became dominant in slave societies.[18]

Obeah flourished not only because the society had lost its equilibrium and
was in a state of disorientation but because there was a void for a religious
practitioner. So great was the confidence in the Obeah person that Black Jamaica believed he or she had the ability to leave his or her body, to fly at night
and to cause great harm to befall the enemy. The traditional African priest had
lost his power in this alien society, and as he joined forces with the Obeah
practitioner they became a formidable force to reckon with in slave society.
There were strict laws in Jamaican society forbidding Jamaicans to engage in
this practice, as Obeah was regarded as off limits. The bottom line was that
the Obeah practitioner was able to offer enslaved Jamaicans and all who would
seek their help protection against the cruelty of the master who had the right
to flog, sell, or mutilate any enslaved person as he pleased. There are many
folktales in Jamaican culture of how Obeah works and its importance in maintaining a sense of balance in the society as oppressed Jamaicans often sought
the help of the Obeah practitioner in confronting the reckless power of the
oppressor. M. G. Lewis, in his *Journal of a West Indian Proprietor*, in 1816
refers to Christianity as White Obeah in an attempt to counteract the Black
Obeah of Adam who had placed a curse on Bessie because she thwarted a plan

of Adam to poison an attorney through the practice of Obeah. Lewis was of the impression that the superior religion of the master, Christianity, would neutralize Obeah and provide relief for Bessie who had lost four children and was herself quite ill. Bessie was comforted that if she did good, when she dies she would see her children again who are now alive with God beyond the blue. Lewis in his *Journal* indicates that his approach did not succeed, as Adam continued to put on display his powers to punish those who were out of step with the religionist goals for the community. In the end, Lewis expresses the belief that the Christian church should baptize the Obeah man, as baptism would be an antidote for Obeah. Lewis explains, "in short, I know not what I can do with him, except indeed make a Christian of him! This might induce the Negro to believe that he has lost his infernal power by the superior virtue of the holy water, but perhaps he may refuse to be christened. However, I will at least ask him the question and if he consents, I will send him—and a couple of dollars—to the clergyman—for he will not have so great a distinction as baptism from Massa's own hand—and see what effect 'White Obeah' will have in removing the terrors of this professor of the Black."[19]

Most scholars of the Black experience in the Americas point to the fact that prior to 1770s, Black people were not exposed to much Christian teaching or preaching. It was not until the second Great Awakening that Black people in any meaningful numbers were able to attend religious services with the proviso from the missionary that conversion or baptism would not mean freedom or equality for enslaved persons. It is clear that the religious practices and beliefs brought over by the slaves did not constitute a formal unified religion, yet there were religious beliefs they were able to adapt to this strange and alien world that confronted them on the plantations.

The various components of their religion complemented and reinforced each other. The Bible, in fact, could be used to prove the efficacy of sacred folk beliefs. "Does I believe in spirits?" Charles Hayes asked, "Sho I does. When Christ walked on the water, de Apostles was skeered he was a spirit, but Jesus told dem dat he warn't no spirit, dat he was as live as dey was. . . . He tol' 'em dat spirits couln't be teched, dat dey jus' melted when you tried to. So, Mistis, Jesus musta meant dat dere was sich a thing as spirits." Thomas Smith of Georgia made the same point more forcefully when he insisted that the magic power used by Moses to turn his rod into a snake before Pharaoh still exists among Negroes. "Dat happen in Africa duh Bible say. Ain dat show dat Africa wuz a lan uh magic powuh dince duh beginning uh histtry? Well den, duh descendants ub Africans hab duh same gif tuh do unnatchul ting."[20]

This kind of blending of African beliefs with the Christian narrative and an attempt to make it relevant to the new situation that confronted enslaved persons seem to get at what Du Bois had in mind when he talked about the Black preacher/medicine man as the main link between Africa and plantation life. Speaking of the African preacher/medicine man Du Bois stated, "He early appeared on the plantation and found his function as the healer of the sick, the interpreter of the Unknown, the comforter of the sorrowing, the supernatural avenger of wrong, the one who rudely but picturesquely expressed the longing, disappointment, and resentment of a stolen and oppressed people."[21] To understand the role of the African preacher/medicine man one had to look to African ways of understanding the world, spirits, ancestors, and gods. Life for the African was comprised of events that were related and were meant to be interpreted by human beings. Everything fit within a purposeful framework called destiny. Freedom and destiny were intertwined and in the service of humanity. There was no sense in African cosmology that events were random or arbitrary. There was always the notion that events as they unfolded would be part of the common destiny of the tribe or clan. Professor Levine sums up the main tenets of African beliefs that confronted the African preacher/medicine man in his new environment.

> The ethos prevailing in the African cultures from which the slaves came would have little use for concepts of the absurd. Life was not random or accidental or haphazard. Events were meaningful; they had causes which man could divine, understand, and profit from. Human beings could "read" the phenomena surrounding and affecting them because Man was part of, not alien to, the Natural Order of things, attached to the Oneness that bound together all matter, animate and inanimate, all spirits visible or not. . . . Survival and happiness and health depended upon being able to read the signs that existed everywhere, to understand the visions that recurrently visited one, to commune with the spirits that filled the world: the spirit of the Supreme Being who could be approached only through the spirits of the pantheon of intermediary deities; the spirits of all the matter that filled the universe— trees, animals, rivers, the very daily utensils and weapons upon which Man was dependent.[22]

It is this blending of the secular and the sacred, finding the sacred in all things, that positioned the African preacher/medicine man to lead the charge against plantation life and the inhumanity of slavery. In a profound sense we could say that the new element that the African preacher/medicine man brought to the world of slavery was his or her understanding of spirit. It was this confidence in spirit that suffuses the world but is present in a unique way in ancestors, the deities, and the world at large that enabled enslaved persons trapped on plantations in the Americas to explode the cruel myths of inferiority and hegemonic worldviews that were aimed at Africans by their oppressors. Certainly one way in which we may speak of the homogeneity of Africans in the diaspora has to do with their confidence in spirit and the indestructible capacity of spirit that pointed to the presence of the sacred. The presence of spirit, in trees, in water, in the child, in the adult, in all things pointed to the presence of the sacred. The loss of spirit would point to the loss of the sacred. In African cosmology there was no loss of the sacred because there was no loss of spirit. It was the notion of spirit that transformed religion to the source of life and meaning for Africans because spirit was life giving and liberating. The connection between the animate and inanimate, the family and God is made possible by the spirit who makes all things sacred and worthwhile. According to Du Bois, the shock of captivity and slavery in the New World drove enslaved persons through the African priest to return to their traditions and there find spirit-power as the way of challenging the evils of slavery through running away or through rebellions aimed at changing the structure of slavery itself. Africans in the New World embraced "a hermeneutic of return" as they found in their own traditions and beliefs, resources for dismantling the oppressive system of slavery. On many plantations the only religion that was permitted was Christianity, and perhaps because of this enslaved persons ingeniously blended African traditional religions with Christianity. They were able to appropriate Christianity from an African frame of reference. "For the slave convert to Christianity there was as much concern about relating to the ancestors as to a Christian God. Yet the slave's dramatization of devotion and his quest for union with invisible forces was an African ideal. . . . It was transformed in the light of American experience: 'Sprung from the African forests where its counterpart can still be heard, it was adapted, changed, and intensified by the tragic soul-life of the slave, until under the stress of law and whip, it became one expression of a people's sorrow, despair and hope.' "[23] Sterling Stuckey reminds us that for Du Bois the tragic soul-life of the slave became the point of departure for dealing with the Black experience during slavery in which the Black preacher functioned as priest who not only connected enslaved persons to the power of the ancestors and other spiritual forces, but navigated the delicate balance between this world and the next. The African priest during slavery not only served the function on the plantation of helping people make it from day to day and as much as possible gave the enslaved population the confidence that "Massa" did not have all the power or the last word in relation to people's lives, but as priest, he would also mediate between the living and the dead and serve as the symbol of hope. The genius of the priest was not only to point to the unjust circles of inequality and injustice in plantation life but to represent hope in the daily struggle to survive. He could divine the present and the future because he lived so to speak on the boundary between the worlds of the living and the dead. In a profound sense he helped people discover Africa in the Americas and affirm waves of continuity with their new experience in an alien land. The African priest in Black churches mediated two worlds, the world of the master and the world of the slave, in which something new emerged from the crucible of slavery. An Afro-American cosmology emerged in which enslaved persons voiced their disgust and frustration with slavery and through which songs of hope and prayers of liberation articulated their longing for freedom. "In the context of their struggle for freedom and their fight to maintain their humanity, black women and men created an extensive moral value system that included elements of their African heritage and addressed their specific needs as an enslaved people. . . . Over a period of two centuries of pain, suffering and struggle, slaves fashioned and shaped their beliefs into a religion of their own."[24]

It is widely agreed that during a large portion of the eighteenth century the majority of Black people, whether in the Caribbean or in the colonies in North America, did not attend traditional Black churches. Throughout the Caribbean the majority of Black people adapted African religions to their local situation and knew instinctively that they were not welcomed in the White man's church. James Phillippo, the British missionary to Jamaica, commenting on the state of prejudice and race relations between Black and White people in Jamaica within the context of the established church, writes:

> Not only were they oppressed and bowed down by the operation of unjust and cruel laws, but there was yet another circumstance connected with the condition of the colored and black population, in some respects still more painful. The most inveterate prejudice existed against them on account of their color. Hence they were universally prohibited all intercourse of equality with whites, and if of such an opprobrious distinction they ventured to complain, they were often insultingly told that they were "the descendants of the ourang-outang," that their mothers hunted the tiger in the wilds of Africa; and that but for the generosity of their sires, in place of possessing freedom and

property, their lot would have been to dig cane-holes beneath the discipline of the driver's cart whip. At church, if a man of color, however respectable in circumstances or character, entered the pew of the lowest white man, he was instantly ordered out. At any place of public entertainment designed for the whites, he never dared to make his appearance. With people of color, indeed, the whites, like the Egyptians in reference to the Israelites, held it an abomination even to eat bread. This senseless prejudice haunted its victims in the "hospital where humanity suffers, in the prison where it expiates its offences, and in the grave-yards where it sleeps the last sleep." In whomsoever the least trace of an African origin could be discovered the curse of slavery pursued him, and no advantage of wealth, talent, virtue, education, or accomplishments, were sufficient to relieve him from the infamous prescription.[25]

It is not surprising then that enslaved people not only preferred to worship among themselves but often resented having to worship with Whites because of the ways religion was used to reinforce the subjugation and subordination of Blacks in relation to White people. "Many slaves resented having to attend church services conducted by whites. They hated repeatedly being told 'Obey de Massa, obey de overseer; obey dis, obey dat,' while their masters and overseers oppressed and physically abused them. They disliked having to sit in the rear of the church or in galleries set apart exclusively for them. They cherished meetings of their own where they could relax and enjoy the form of worship that pleased them and uplifted their spirits."[26] Because there were some plantations where Blacks were not allowed to have their own worship services or to preach, they would steal away into the woods and meet in what they called the invisible church, or the brush arbor where they constructed meeting places made from the branches of trees or gather in secret in their cabins. Blacks preferred to worship among themselves and they craved preaching from their own. With Black preaching they heard an interpretation from the Bible in their own tongue and shared in an experience in which they were free to dance and sing and often worship with the drum as they could call on the ancestors and their deities who were also in exile in slavery. "On the plantation in Walker County, Texas, where Carey Davenport resided, no blacks were permitted to preach. The only preaching that Davenport's master allowed was that done by white Methodist circuit riders who occasionally passed that area. Therefore, Davenport and the other slaves had to slip away into dugouts or hollows to hold their own services. They sung songs that came 'a-gushing up from the heart.' To protect themselves from discovery by their masters or patrollers, slaves often turned a kettle upside down. They believed that the pot would catch the sounds of their singing and shouts before they came within the hearing range of whites who might punish them."[27] Where ever Black people were they had an irrepressible need, a desire to worship in their own way. But it is clear that the planter class thought enslaved people would use religious gatherings as space for planning revolts or occasions to run away. Because of this fear there were laws on both sides of the Atlantic forbidding the gathering of four or five Black persons without White supervision. Black people got around the laws forbidding their gathering by planning secret meetings. These secret meetings, the "invisible institution," not only provided space for enslaved persons to meet outside the gaze of White people but ensured a setting in which the virtues of respect, cooperation, compassion, hope, and faith would create a basis for them to carry on another day as they enjoined the help of ancestors through dancing, singing, and praying. "These religious communities had their own belief systems and styles of worship. According to the testimony of some slaves, clandestine religious services were held in various places on the plantation—swamps, woods, ravines, and cabins. Open-air meetings were referred to variously as 'hush arbors,' 'bush arbors' and 'brush arbors.' Della Briscoe, formerly enslaved on a large plantation in Puntam County, Georgia, recalled that because of the irregularity of worship services at her master's church, 'brush arbor meetings were common. This arbor was constructed of a brush roof supported by posts and crude joists. The seats were usually made of small saplings nailed to short stumps.' In these meetings out of the sight of their masters, slaves emphasized their belief in a God of justice, a liberating God, who would deliver them out of bondage."[28] Down in the brush arbors, enslaved people would sing, "'Go down Moses, way down in Egypt's land. Tell old pharaoh to let my people go' 'On Jordan's stormy banks I stand and cast a wistful eye,' ' My God delivered Daniel,' and other songs. . . . Interestingly, the spiritual 'Go down Moses' originated at a baptismal service following the Nat Turner revolt."[29] There was a wonderful sense in which enslaved persons throughout the American colonies related their faith in the divine to the negative history of slavery. Enslaved persons learned early to gather to worship and strategize under the cover of night or under the cover of the woods where a redefinition of their status took place. Many enslaved persons did not see themselves as slaves, as property, or as chattel but as children of God who would take responsibility for their lives and seek to make life a little better for their children. Religion which assured them of the help of the ancestors and the God of Christianity and the gods of Africa was in the service of survival. Perhaps at first the passion and focus was not liberation or freedom but "survival with dignity."

Nannie Helen Burroughs—a leader in the national Baptist Convention's Woman's Convention in the twentieth century—recalled the stories her grandmother Maria related about her experience during her enslavement in Virginia. Maria was what she called a "an F.F.V. Slave," a First Family of Virginia Slave. According to Burroughs, Maria's self-esteem was remarkable. The slave experience neither diminished Maria's sense of self nor made her feel inferior. She was imbued with her faith in God. Her motto was "Don't look down, look up at God." Speaking about Maria's attitude toward slavery, Burroughs stated that Maria proudly asserted, "Yes, honey, I was IN slavery, but I wasn't no slave. I was just in it, that's all. . . . We kept on saying 'deliverance will come.' "[30]

Faith and History

The last word, the decisive word for enslaved persons, was not the negative history or the negative world of slavery. It was their African faith adapted to the new situation that indicated the way ahead. It was precisely at the point where history meets faith that faith illustrated the capacity to transform history. And the church of enslaved persons provided the context and content of their hope for deliverance. We should not forget that there were difficulties associated with enslaved persons on both sides of the Atlantic being exposed to the master's religion. There were many slaves, especially fresh shipments from Africa in the second half of the eighteenth century, who did not speak English or care to learn it, or their knowledge of the language did not facilitate their exposure to Christianity. Additionally, there were masters or overseers who themselves did not have much confidence in the efficacy of the Christian religion either for themselves or for enslaved people. Then there were persons from the master class who were conflicted concerning the dangerous possibility of a religion that preached the equality of all persons before God in spite of status. Would the notion of the equality of bondspeople before God mean their freedom? Can one be Christian and slave at the same time? When enslaved persons became Christian, would they have to learn and be encouraged to read that dangerous book the Bible? Many masters regarded the Bible as a dangerous book because of its teaching concerning the equality of persons before God in spite of the earthly status of being in bondage. This undoubtedly was the reason that slaves began to talk about being in slavery but not being slaves and the articulation of the confidence that in spite of the horrors of slavery "deliverance would come." Of course, one way in which the missionaries allayed the fears of the master class on both sides of the Atlantic was to point out that conversion to Christianity did not change the status of the enslaved person. According to the missionary, conversion to Christianity or Christian baptism made enslaved persons docile and obedient. The missionaries attested that the best slaves were baptized slaves who were expected to serve their masters as they served God. Slaves who caught on to the ambiguous dilemma of Christianity and freedom went along with the church's program, entered into Christian conversion, and did not give up their African beliefs. The truth is that very few churches indicated any desire to change the system of slavery. The most faithful of churches were involved in the structures of slavery, as they were often beholden to the planter class, and in many cases the preachers themselves owned slaves. Saving the souls of slaves did not mean changing the system that reduced them to the status of chattel or of making a connection between body and soul. It was felt that if the soul belonged to God then the body belonged to the master. "As the ruling classes considered it dangerous to give religious instruction to slaves, in the 17th–18th c. the religious domain was effectively left in the slaves' own hands. And the churches, deeply involved in the slave system, had no real interest in evangelizing the blacks. There is a long list of Catholic and Protestant missionaries who owned a large number of slaves in the region. All this explains the development of Afro-Antillian religiosity. This has evolved into numerous forms such as Vodou in Haiti, Santeria in Cuba, Shango in Trinidad, Obeahism in Jamaica."[31]

Laws were put in place to underscore the place of slaves in plantation economy. If on the one hand religious instruction emphasized that slaves were created to make a crop and to serve their masters as they served God, on the other hand there were laws in place enforced by police to ensure that enslaved persons were clear that their lot in life was to serve their masters. The sociological and theological principle that the law upheld and enforced was that there were two classes of people, masters and slaves. Gradually, the economic arguments were phased out to be replaced by racial arguments that people of African ancestry were ontologically inferior to White people. With the badge of color being the defining mark of Black people, the churches began to teach that conversion to Christianity meant freedom not from the control of masters but freedom in the next life. To be Black was to be slave and to be White was to be free. This was especially the case for the children of the enslaved: to be born Black was to be slave for life while to be born White was to be free. Toward the latter part of the seventeenth century, the primary reason for enslavement was the badge of color, the race of the people, and not their status as pagan or heathen, which was the case at the beginning of slavery in the

New World. The economic argument that Africa held an inexhaustible supply of labor for plantations began to give way to religious arguments that God made Black people "to make a crop" and to serve White people, but this highlighted the Black experience as the context for reflection on their newfound faith. It was newfound in the sense that it was a faith that exemplified on the one hand an unwillingness to give up their African beliefs, and on the other hand an embrace of the Christian teaching by the missionaries. In navigating the cruel world of slavery that the master designed for Black people they appropriated the teachings of the master's religion, which at times confused the missionary into thinking that Black people were "becoming Christian"—that is, setting their African worldviews aside as they embraced the teachings of the missionary. This was the case in Jamaica when membership in Methodist churches nearly doubled between 1831 and 1841. Baptists grew from 10,000 to 34,000 during the same period. With this success in membership and large attendance of Black people at worship services, it is understandable that church leaders assumed that African religious beliefs were obliterated and that Christianity as taught by the missionaries had won the day. With the addition of new members to their rolls, church leaders were convinced that Christianity was in the ascendancy, the time of Christian freedom had arrived, and the long night of African beliefs and unchristian practices had ended. "The revelries attending births and deaths have given place the decencies and properties of Christian life," declared one church leader. "Licentiousness and discord have been displaced by the sanctity of matrimony, and the harmony and comforts of the domestic circle. Revolting and degrading superstition has vanished before the light and influence of truth as 'mists before the rising sun.'"[32] The missionaries mistook church attendance for assimilation and had to learn that although Black people were open to the new Christianity as taught by the missionaries, they had not and would not abandon African religious practices. Black people were willing to function on two tracks, so to speak: on the one hand they were intrigued by the new that confronted them in Christianity as they saw parallel beliefs between Christianity and their African worldviews, and on the other hand they were willing to allow both faiths to coexist and to interpret Christianity from the perspective of African religious practices. This was especially so during the eighteenth century when the African community in the New World was constantly reenforced with new imports of Africans from the homeland who kept the traditions alive and fresh. When the slave trade was abolished in 1807 and new shipments of enslaved persons were not as numerous as during the peak period of the 1770s, there was more of an adaptation, especially by slaves who were born in the New World and perhaps did not feel as obligated to practice the African religion taught by their parents. An adaptation of the Christian worldview to accommodate African beliefs and rituals may be seen in a practice among the Methodists and Baptists throughout the Caribbean during the nineteenth century. The practice was called the ticket-and-leader system. In it, the congregation would be divided into groups to represent the regions from which the Black families who attended church came. Every class represented a region, and for each class there was a leader, and every member received a ticket that represented membership. The ticket-and-leader system appealed to Africans and people of African ancestry because they could adapt it to African ways of thinking. The class leader was a member of the Black community who had power to call meetings, to visit class members, to reprimand, to preach—in short, to be an African priest. The ticket became a charm that each member carried as a fetish to drive away evil spirits. Churches that would grow had to tolerate the merging and blending of African religious practices with Christianity. The truth is that the gap between African beliefs and the Christian religion could not be bridged. Africans in the New World insisted on carving out their identity and their new faith their way. They refused to reject completely the missionary's teaching of Christianity, and were willing to blend African beliefs with the missionary's teaching. This caused the church to attack "concubinage, drumming, dancing, the Christmas festival and Sabbath breaking. This practically covered the field of Negro amusements, and immoral behavior in one of these respects was grounds for expulsion from the church. The Christian churches were especially strict in respect to marriage and discouraged baptism of illegitimate children. This meant in practice that 70 percent of the population was barred from church. In spite of decades of missionary training, Jamaicans would not get married. Young women felt marriage was a form of slavery."[33] Black people throughout the Caribbean became increasingly dissatisfied with the mission church as the churches outlawed drumming, dancing, and African sexual practices. Increasingly, Black people came to associate the mainline churches with slavery, believing these churches were invested in the system; even when they felt that the missionary might be sympathetic with their plight, he could not fully appreciate their need for their own preachers and their need to embrace African ways of being in the world. After slavery was abolished in the British colonies in the Caribbean in 1838 the further Black people went from the slavery era, the less they felt they needed the mission church. Walter Hark in *The Breaking of the Dawn* reminds us of the resurgence of African religious practices between 1840 and 1860 in Jamaica. What is interesting here was that at first the mission church thought there was a revival of Christianity among the African populace and later discovered there was really no Christian faith to revive. The revival had turned

African. "As soon as darkness set in they assembled in large crowds in open pastures, most frequently under large cotton trees, which they worshipped and counted sacred; and after sacrificing some fowls, the leader began his song in a wild strain, which was answered in chorus; then followed the dance, growing wilder and wilder until those who participated were in a state of mad excitement. Some would perform incredible evolutions while in this state, until utterly exhausted, they fell senseless to the ground, when every word they uttered was received as divine revelation."[34] It is important to note the essential position of nature in worship; the worship experience was outdoors in the pasture and under large cotton trees. Throughout the Caribbean, special reverence is given to cotton trees as they are regarded as sites of the indwelling of the spirits of ancestors. The worship at the cotton tree highlights the symbolic representation of the tree as the tree points beyond itself to the spirit that infuses all of reality. In a recent visit I made to a number of older Black churches in south Georgia, after the Sunday morning worship service deacons called my attention to the fact that several of the churches which had replaced brush arbors were located in close proximity to rivers or smaller streams. According to these deacons, proximity to a river or stream was a requirement for the location of the meeting place for enslaved persons in south Georgia as the river/stream indicated their proximity to the spirit that the stream represented. It was through worship that Africans were able to invoke the presence of gods for protection and healing. This once more points to the crucial role of the African priest in mediating between the human and the divine. One could not make it from day to day without the guidance and direction of good spirits and it was the medicine man/priest who is able to provide access to these spirits. Certainly there was much more leeway for enslaved persons practicing their faith in the Caribbean and Latin America than in the colonies in North America. But even here enslaved persons in the North American colonies were left to depend on their own religious practices until the 1770s, and even then there were questions regarding the wisdom of encouraging Christian conversion and instruction. "Thus in the last half of the eighteenth century it is common to find Protestant ministers still lamenting the hold that non-Christian religious practices continued to have upon the slaves. In 1756, Samuel Davies wrote enthusiastically of his own missionary efforts among the slaves in Virginia but complained of the otherwise 'almost universal neglect of the many thousands of poor slaves . . . who generally continue Heathens in a Christian Country,' and in South Carolina during the Revolutionary War the Reverend Alexander Hewatt observed that the slaves, 'a few only excepted, are to this day as great strangers to Christianity, and as much under the influence of Pagan darkness, idolatry and superstition, as

they were at their first arrival from Africa.' "[35] Professor Levine points out that
as late as 1842 Charles C. Jones observed that the enslaved people among
whom he preached the gospel believed "in second sight, in apparitions,
charms, witchcraft, and in a kind of irresistible Satanic influence. The superstitions brought from Africa have not been wholly laid aside."[36] What has
emerged in more recent research is that African slaves were not as dependent
on European religious beliefs as may have been indicated by scholars such as
E. Franklin Frazier. There is a sense in which Africans would parrot beliefs
the master expected them to believe for the sake of pleasing the master. It has
been observed that there were times when Africans would attend church without any intention of really listening to what the preacher—the White
preacher—said. After the service they would ask the African priest or the class
leader to tell them what the preacher should have said. This has been illustrated in slaves' response to sermons about obedience and the recitation of
instruction that "God made black people to make a crop." Enslaved people saw
through the hypocrisy of the plantation preacher and would sing while look-
ing in the direction of the master's house, "Everybody singing 'bout heaven
ain't going there."

A Plurality of Options

Because of the lack of control enslaved people had over their lives and the
confrontation with the seemingly unlimited power the master had over them,
they were forced to seek help and answers from supernatural means. They
sought the divine in all things, including the Christian religion. They did not
have to choose between African expressions of faith and Christianity; when
exposed to Christianity they were willing to test the rituals and search the
Bible for answers and signals of hope. For Africans, the universe was not constructed in terms of either/or approaches to life, but a plurality of options in
which whatever worked and aided the search for survival and freedom was
sacred. "For slaves, who were much closer to a traditional world view and far
more exposed to forces over which they had minimal control, magical folk
beliefs were a central and necessary part of existence. They were no less important to the slave than his Christian myths, which they supplemented and
fortified. Both were crucial sources of strength and release. Both allowed the
slaves to exert their will and preserve their sanity by permitting them to
impose a sense of rationality and predictability upon a hostile and capricious
environment. Christianity helped to accomplish this by providing assurance
of the ephemeral quality of the present situation and the glories and retribu-
tion to come, both in this world and in the next, by solidifying the slave's sense

of communality, and by reinforcing their feelings of self-worth and dignity."[37] This line of reasoning is very helpful as it gets at the thorny question, how could enslaved people turn to the religion of their captors and oppressors? One answer of course is that they were curious and open to the new, even if they wondered about their presence in an alien land on plantations in which the authority of the master class over them seemed complete. They were open to the new provided it contributed to their freedom and liberation. The key to keep in mind is that Christian myths and ways of being in the world were understood from an African frame of reference and if enslaved people could not abandon African ways of understanding the world, neither were they prepared to ignore Christianity. "Drumming, blowing of conches, dancing. . . . Verily, this is more like heathen Africa than Christian Jamaica. . . . People could meet to read the Bible; none of them could read, but they hired a man to do it for them; they listened attentively; they endeavored to remember what they heard; one of them offered prayer in the usual way; then the leader would call; 'now let the spirit speak!' And what a scene followed. . . . They became excited; they howled, and screamed, and fell into convulsions. These people professed to be the salt of the earth."[38]

Vodou

We have noted that despite a number of differences there are some common themes in religions in the New World. The basic principle is that the world is peopled with spirits. There are the spirits of ancestors, the spirit of the high creator God, and the spirits of the intermediary deities. It is more than a trinity of spirits as we tend to find in Christianity. There is a community of spirits that is indispensable for the practice of religion.

> The term Vodou, which meant "spirit" or "sacred energy" in the AdjaTado group of languages spoken in Arada, was brought to Haiti from Ouida or (Whydah), on the west coast of Africa, at the height of the eighteenth-century slave trade. The word—and indeed most of the lexicon associated with Vodou temple (*ounfo, oungan, manbo,* and *ounsi*)—is a legacy of the Fon kingdom of what is now Benin and was once Dahomey. So are the names of African-born Rada spirits served by Vodou devotees: Danbala, Ayida Wedo, Ezili Freda, Legba, Azaka, Gede, and the names of the sacred drums that summon them to join the congregants in ritual dances. Although in its most restricted sense it refers only to Arada rites, the word Vodou has over the years come to stand for all African-derived religious practices in Haiti.[39]

Vodou is one of the most feared and misunderstood African-derived religions in Haiti and Louisiana and in many ways it is quite similar to Obeah in Jamaica and Trinidad and Santeria in Cuba. Like these religions, its main rituals and liturgy revolve around a community of spirits known as the *loa* or *lwa* who combine a gathering of African and Creole spirits, the spirits of ancestors departed, and Catholic saints. It was noted earlier that one of the marks of African-derived religions in the Caribbean was their hiding behind the icons and beliefs of Christianity as ways of disguising their African beliefs and commitments to African gods. This was especially the case in the practice of Vodou which was replete with Catholic iconography and the veneer of the Catholic faith. And in many cases there is in more recent years a cooperation between Vodou adherents and the Roman Catholic church in Haiti. Of course, a part of the challenge for the Catholic Church after seeking to root out Vodou in Haiti in the second half of the nineteenth century and much of the twentieth is the realization that the majority of the culture embraces Vodou as a faith and that for Haitians, as for Caribbean people in general, to subscribe to Christianity does not negate belief in the spirits and the gods of Africa. Europeans were often confused by African faith claims, as Afro-Caribbean or Afro-Americans crowded their churches with a multiplicity of icons and liturgies. Africans were willing to try whatever would work and provide a respite to the horrors of oppression.

As a young pastor in a Baptist church in rural Jamaica during the 1960s, I needed some time to understand that more than half of my congregants, after celebrating at my church in singing hymns and showing evidence of the presence of the spirit, would in the evening attend the Revival Church and dance to drumming and possession of the spirit all night, and it was not uncommon for them to fall in a trance for several days after being possessed by the spirit. It was natural for the parishioners to navigate both worlds of the Baptist and Revivalist Church in which Jesus had no special powers but was understood as a good friend and an important prophet. There were times when the leader of the Revivalist Church would ask me to perform a wedding ceremony or, on a special occasion like harvest festival, to preach, but I knew that real church began after I left.

In 2009 I had a comparable experience on a field trip in Western Haiti. Accompanied by six students, I spent two weeks in Jolivert as guest of a female leader in the community. Our project, which got us into many homes in the village, was to advocate clean water and demonstrate how a group of neighbors could own a water-purifying machine. While we were there, a brother of our host died, and along with the students I attended the funeral. I was quite intrigued to see the common threads that ran through the funeral experience. There was a homemade coffin, placed in the back yard under trees on chairs, and there was an extremely large gathering of the community, in which everyone seemed to be in their best suit and dress. What I found noteworthy was that the first part of the funeral ceremony was conducted by a priest from the local Roman Catholic Church. I later learned that both the sister of the deceased and the deceased attended that church. But the rites performed by the church were brief, and after the priest left it seemed that the real ceremony began. The singing, handclapping, shouting, and lining of hymns with call and response picked up momentum. And as they were about to take the deceased to the top of a nearby hill for burial, people began to tear off the branches of trees. When I asked what this meant, my neighbor explained that the man who had died was a priest of the Vodou church and the breaking of branches was both a sign of reverence and affection. All this time (from the ceremony performed by the Catholic Church) there was a man who was foaming at the mouth and seemed to be possessed by a spirit that was in total control. He was often rolling in the dust, clearly not in control of his faculties, and yet there were four women who were trying to calm him by throwing water on him, forcing him to drink; and as the procession made its way up a steep climb to the top of the hill for the burial, the women took charge of this man and saw to it that he made it to the burial site. It was explained to me that this man had wronged the Vodou priest and the spirit of the priest had entered the man and would grant him peace only when he confessed his wrong. I was told that there were many times when the spirit of the deceased would demand that a debt which was owed be paid.

On top of the hill, the burial ceremony was taken over by fellow Vodou priests, who announced that the grave was too small and they were in need of tape measures. To my surprise, almost everyone had a tape measure. I later learned that the spirits of the departed are afraid of tape measures, and so most people brought them for protection. Learning that the grave was too small, I wove my way through the crowd to see this grave for myself. Just as I arrived at the grave, I noticed that the homemade coffin was there, and to my horror a man I later learned was a priest opened the coffin; the Vodou priest, who was lying there and seemed quite alive, winked at me. Filled with feelings of dread, I fled and ran down the hill and enquired of my host what was going on. I was informed that Vodou priests can't die. The Vodou priest had experienced a *small* death so that the community whom he served as priest would experience a *large* resurrection. Soon after, the people were asked by the priests to return to the foot of the hill so they could continue the ceremony. The deceased priest was ready for resurrection.

Everyone said that night the *lwa* (spirits) would fly low and it was wise to stay indoors. Usually in the evenings the children in the village would come to sing and play games at the guest quarters where the students and I stayed. That evening none came. All of us, people of the village and visitors, were filled with dread, a sense that spirits of ancestors were all around us and that this power could be used for good or ill.

It was this feeling of dread that was at the heart of the Haitian revolution in 1797, as the early leaders—Boukman from Jamaica and Makandal a Haitian—were skilled oungans (priests) "reputed to be powerful oungans whose knowledge of the powers and poisonous properties of herbs had helped mount a campaign of terror and death among French planters in Saint Dominigue. It was with the blessing of the lwa that slaves gathered in the Bois-Caiman, in the north of Haiti, on the night of the 14 August 1791. In a Vodou ceremony that included the sacrifice of a wild boar, they swore their sacred oath to overthrow the French slave masters."[40] There was a coming together of many traditions in the forging of resistance and press for liberation against the French slave masters. It is interesting that one of the early leaders of the Haitian revolution, Boukman who hails from eastern Jamaica, the parish of St. Thomas (where I was raised as a child), is noted for the large numbers of Africans who were leaders in Obeah. This means that the quest for liberation had the Vodou ritual at the center with its confidence and belief in spirits, conjoined with Boukman's leadership in Obeah, in which practitioners were skilled in the poisonous properties of herbs—and of course all of this was hidden behind the veneer of Roman Catholic rituals and practices. The Catholic Church left Haiti in 1805 in protest against the Haitian revolution and did not return until 1860. This provided a Black sacred space for Vodou to take its place among the populace as the people's religion.

> The destruction of Saint Domingue's plantation economy had momentous repercussions for the development of Haitian Vodou. The consolidation of the Revolution, and the land grants to former slaves it made possible, transformed Haiti into a rural nation of subsistence farmers working their small plots. This new peasantry organized itself around small villages that functioned as extended family compounds. Known as *lakous*, they opened a new space for the preservation of African-derived Creole religions.[41]

With the new peasantry owning their plots of land, being able to grow their own food, and having no resistance from outside authorities, Vodou flourished in Haiti and became the religion of the people. With the people having their own plots of land coupled with the freedom to go and come as they pleased, the organizational polity of Vodou contributed toward the spread of the religion. Like most of the African-derived religions that took root in the New World, there is no central belief system or liturgical praxis in Vodou. What exists in Vodou are foundational principles that any leader may adapt to the existential situation that will make room for the perceived needs of the people. "So while there are many informal ties among various communities of Vodou practitioners, each ounfo follows its own preferences and guidelines in matters of ritual and belief. As a result, practices vary (sometimes greatly) from one congregation to another, as do the nature and attributes of the lwa."[42] With the absence of the Roman Catholic Church from 1805 to 1860 there were no competing churches in Haiti to slow the growth of Vodou. Vodou thrived throughout Haiti as, in ingenious ways, Vodou priests were able to merge and blend Vodou spirits and Roman Catholic saints in the crafting of the new faith on Haitian soil.

Denmark Vesey

A similar expression of religion took hold in Charleston, South Carolina, in 1822, as Denmark Vesey, a leader in an African church, led a conspiracy for change in the social conditions that were impeding the spiritual growth of Black people. "There an essentially African religion was being practiced, with blacks, slave and free, gathering to worship. Since the majority of blacks in South Carolina came from regions of Africa, like Congo-Angola and the western slave coast, in which the ring ceremony was prominent, the shout could hardly have been practiced less fervently there in 1820s than in the 1860s, the decade in which New Englanders entered the state to find it performed on innumerable occasions, day and night."[43]

Caribbean culture and religion spilled over into South Carolina with the Vesey Conspiracy, since Vesey was purchased on one of Captain Vesey's voyages between St. Thomas and San Domingo, at the age of fourteen. "He [Vesey] was 'for 20 years a most faithful slave,' during which time he accompanied his master, as a cabin boy, to the West Indies, which once again provided him with the opportunity to observe Africans from many parts of Africa and to relate to the variegated sweep of their ethnicity. . . . Indeed, he lived among men and women in South Carolina and in the West Indies who had experienced the Middle Passage and retained memories of the complexities of African culture."[44] Vesey was ideally suited to lead a movement for the overthrow of slavery and the liberation of Black people in South Carolina. Although a member of the African Methodist Church, he did not relinquish his African roots and consciousness. He read the Bible from an African frame of reference that emphasized liberation for his African brothers and sisters from the yoke of slavery. His approach to Christianity was a melding and fusing of African and European perspectives. It is reported that Vesey was preoccupied with the Bible, believing in its liberatory power to set African people free, including many of his children who were still in bondage. He gave particular value to the story of the children of Israel in Egypt, likening the plight of Africans to that of the children of Israel. His hermeneutical key was Joshua, chapter 4: 21: "And they utterly destroyed all that was in the city, both man and woman, young and old, and ox, and sheep, and ass, with the edge of the sword." He was also fond of reading Zechariah 14. Often when he addressed Black people in the Charleston area he would mention Joshua 4:20–21 pointing out that the God of their fathers would lead them out of bondage. Vesey's more radical Christian approach was complemented by the African approach of Gullah Jack, who preached the conjurer's doctrine of invincibility and gave courage and confidence to all who would participate in the revolt. But the plot was betrayed to slave masters. "William, 'a Negro man belonging to Mr. John Paul,' testifies against Gullah Jack, saying that 'all those belonging to the African Church are involved in the insurrection, from the country to the town—that there is a little man amongst them who can't be shot, killed or caught.' . . . Secrecy shrouded the services of the African Church and the religion of the two churches of the African Association, secrecy born of the exigencies of planned revolt, secrecy natural to slaves worshipping in a town like Charleston."[45]

> He also held up the example of Toussaint L'Ouverture and the rebels of San Domingo. . . . One of his most trusted companions was Gullah Jack, . . . who worked through a group known as the Gullah Society, which met regularly and whose members were bound to Jack "by a shrewd combination of magic and discipline." Jack himself was a native African sorcerer who had the reputation of being invulnerable. He instructed those who joined the conspiracy to eat nothing but parched corn and ground nuts on the fateful day and to keep a piece of crab claw in their mouths as a protection against harm during the attack.[46]

In the aftermath of the betrayal of the plot, thirty-five Blacks were hanged and more than forty were sent to the Caribbean or to Africa. Black churches in South Carolina had become dangerous spaces as it was demonstrated that plots against the master could be hatched in these churches. For some time in South Carolina after the Vesey plot, class meetings, in Black churches were disbanded and even Bible study and teaching Blacks to read was mainly discontinued after 1822. There were some Blacks who accompanied their masters to church, but by and large even missionaries gave up preaching to Blacks in the coastal regions after 1822, and they were left to the ministry of slave preachers.

Gabriel Prosser

Slave masters on plantations in the New World must have feared that the fate meted out to oppressors in San Domingo by Toussaint L'Ouverture would come to their plantation. "A young man of twenty-five named Gabriel, . . . whose plantation was just outside the City of Richmond, Virginia, was moved to strike the first blow for liberty in the new century. A man of impressive physical and mental capacities, Gabriel was also a student of the Bible and was strongly drawn to lead an insurrection among the slaves by religious convictions."[47] His favorite biblical character was Sampson, and like Sampson he took the Nazarite vow seriously, wearing his hair in imitation of Sampson. In his study of the book of Judges he felt that God had called him to lead his people in Virginia out of slavery, and that the election of Sampson by the Spirit of God was also on his life, as his mandate was to lead enslaved people out of Henrico County to a new Black kingdom in Virginia with him serving as king. It is clear that in melding African ways of being with biblical perspectives he felt that he could do in Virginia what Toussaint L'Ouverture had done for enslaved people in the Caribbean island of Haiti,[48] using the following as his biblical focus:

> And when he came to Lehi, the Philistines shouted against him: and the Spirit of the Lord came mightily upon him, and the cords that were upon his arms became as flax that was burnt with fire, and his band loosed from off his hands. And he found a new jawbone of an ass, and put forth his hand and took it, and slew a thousand men therewith. . . . And he judged Israel in the days of the Philistines for twenty years. (Judges 15: 15–15, 20)
>
> Gabriel saw himself as a black Sampson who with the help of about one thousand blacks aimed at dismantling slavery in Virginia. It so happened that on the very day they were to attack white people and protest slavery a hurricane struck Virginia causing much confusion among the people and the belief that perhaps the hurricane was a sign from God telling them to stay their hand against the enemy. "The Gabriel plot was probably the first well-planned, consciously

revolutionary attempt in the long history of slave revolts on the mainland. . . . Gabriel himself was given the title General. Undoubtedly, the Haitian revolution was the model, but religious factors played a more important role in the Gabriel insurrection than in the uprising led by Toussaint L'Ouverture.[49]

The die was cast, as even before the hurricane struck, two members of the Black community, Tom and Pharaoh, apprised their masters of the impending plot. Early in September members of the conspiracy were arrested by the militia and on September 12 five were hanged, with a final number of thirty-five persons being hanged. Gabriel was executed October 7.

It is clear there was great unrest throughout plantations in the West Indies and in the North American colonies. "Testifying to the uneasiness of the master class there appear numerous precautionary measures for the purpose of overawing, or further restricting the activities of the slave population (which, in turn, very likely stimulated discontent), and, as a last resort, in order to assure the speedy suppression of all evidences of slave insubordination."[50]

Nat Turner

In *American Negro Slave Revolts* Herbert Aptheker reminds us that it was into this context that Nat Turner raised his dark hand against the scourge of slavery in Virginia, summer of 1831. Like Vesey before him, Turner was steeped in the Bible and immersed in African religion which he blended with Baptist faith. "Turner became convinced that he 'was ordained for some great purpose in the hands of the Almighty.' In the spring of 1828, while working in the fields, he 'heard a loud noise in the heavens, and the Spirit instantly appeared to me and said the Serpent was loosened, and Christ had laid down the yoke he had borne for the sins of men, and that I should take it on and fight against the Serpent, for the time was fast approaching when the first should be last and the last should be first.' "[51] Much like Vesey before him he believed in and took signs from God seriously, and a sign came to him in the solar eclipse of February 12, 1831. "Then apparently for the first time, he told four other slaves of his plans for rebellion. All joined him, and these American Negroes selected the Fourth of July as the day on which to strike for liberty."[52] Gayraud Wilmore points out that one cannot emphasize enough the importance of Nat Turner and his family blending African customs and religious beliefs with their newfound faith in the teaching about the God of justice in the Methodist Church at Turner meetinghouse, where his master, Benjamin Turner, allowed and included enslaved persons in prayer meetings on his plantation. It was believed by family members and the African community that Nat was born for a special purpose and this was underscored in the evangelical community that gathered for prayer on Benjamin Turner's plantation. "At a very early age it was obvious to everyone who came into contact with him that Nat was a precious child. This belief was fortified in the mind of his mother and father by certain birthmarks which, according to African custom, indicated the unusual mental capacities associated with a 'witcheh-man.'"[53] Emboldened by his paternal grandmother, who told him he was born for a special purpose, he combined a confidence in African custom with Christian beliefs, convinced that nothing but blessing would attend his fight for justice on behalf of his compatriots. The childhood memory of his father running away from Turner's plantation was always with Nat, coupled with family and fellow slaves telling him that he was better than being a slave. Like his father, he ran away to the woods for thirty days. But unlike his father, he returned to the plantation as a consequence of meditating on his favorite scriptural passage Luke 12: 35, 39–40, 49–51. "It is well to note that shortly after Nat returned to the plantation, he had a remarkable vision in which white spirits and Black spirits were engaged in a great battle, with blood flowing in streams. The voice that spoke out of that vision reminded him that the lot had fallen to him to suffer what had to be suffered in obedience to his calling. 'Such is your luck,' said the voice, 'such you are called to see, and let it come rough or smooth, you must surely bear it.'"[54]

The plans that were carefully laid out for July 4 did not materialize, as Nat Turner was ill, and his adherents saw that as another sign that their plans were not ready for execution. But the spirit prevailed, and along with friends he began in Southhampton to reenact the Exodus story in which Black people felt that their sojourn in America was the experience of slaves in Egypt. They were the true Israelites, their captors were the Egyptians, and God through the spirit had authorized their liberation. Turner clues us into his thinking: "Having soon discovered to be great, I must appear so, and therefore studiously avoided mixing in society, and wrapped myself in mystery, devoting my time to fasting and prayer—By this time, having arrived to man's estate, and hearing the scriptures commented on at meetings, I was struck with that particular passage which says: 'Seek ye first the kingdom of Heaven and all things shall be added unto you.' . . . As I was praying one day at my plough, the spirit spoke to me, saying 'Seek ye the kingdom of heaven and all things will be added unto you.'"[55] It is interesting that the recorder of Turner's confessions did not ask him what he meant by the kingdom of Heaven or how he understood kingdom but what he meant by spirit. Turner related his understanding of spirit to the Old Testament prophetic tradition of justice. Like his father before him, he escaped, staying in the forests for thirty days. On his return to the plantation he had a vision in which he saw White spirits and Black spirits engaged in battle in which thunder rolled in the heavens and blood flowed in streams.

It is clear that this movement of the spirit was not limited to Nat Turner. Black people seemed to have known intuitively that a change in the old order of plantation life required justice made possible by bloodshed. This was confirmed by a White woman who overheard a prayer by her housekeeper, Aggy, whose daughter had been brutally whipped by the master:

> Thar's a day comin'! Thar's a day comin' . . . I hear rumblin' ob de chariots! I see the flashin' ob de guns! White folks blood is a runnin' on de ground like riber, an' de dead's heaped up dat high! . . . Oh, Lor'! hasten de day when de blows, an' de bruises, an' de aches, an' de pains, shall come to de white folks, an' de buzzards shall eat 'em as dey's dead in de streets. Oh, Lo'! roll on de chariots, an'gib de black people rest an' peace.[56]

Perhaps Aggy had heard of the revolution in Haiti and of the Gabriel Prosser revolt in 1800 and the Denmark Vesey plots in 1822. In any event, Turner had returned to the plantation after running away for thirty days to carry out the will of his master, as the spirit had instructed him that he needed to keep his eyes on the things of the kingdom of Heaven, and not on the things of the world. It seems that Turner understood the spirit's instruction as a renewal of his call to make a difference by allowing the spirit to guide him back to the purpose that the community enjoined on him. Turner states in his confession:

> And now the Holy Ghost had revealed itself to me, and made plain the miracles it had shown me. For as the blood of Christ had been shed on this earth, and had ascended to heaven for the salvation of sinners, and was now returning to earth again in the form of dew . . . it was plain to me that the Savior was about to lay down the yoke he had borne for the sins of men, and the great day of judgment was at hand.[57]

Turner indicates that his vision of a world beyond slavery included bloodshed. Although he grounds his argument in the sacrificial death of Christ and inspiration from the Holy Ghost, these warrants could also have been from African ways of thinking, that change in the social order requires guidance of the ancestors and the offering of sacrifice. He was led by the spirit to the water for baptism. In preparation for the sacrifice of lives that would serve he believed as a means for justice making on his plantation, Turner and close friends observed "a last supper." "On Saturday evening, the 20th of August, it was agreed between Henry, Hark, and myself, to prepare a dinner the next day for the men we expected, and then to concert a plan, as we had not yet determined on any. Hark, on the following morning, brought a pig, and Henry brandy, and being joined by Sam, Nelson, Will and Jack, they prepared in the woods a dinner, where about three o'clock, I joined them."[58] Turner was very suspicious of Will's motive for attending. He enquired of him what was his purpose for being there. Will assured him that he too was willing to lay his life down for a just cause. With the group being satisfied that Will was no Judas, after the meal on August 21, 1831, like angels of death they entered the homes of their oppressors and struck what they perceived as a blow for justice and freedom. There were about seventy enslaved persons who were involved in this uprising and about fifty-five Whites were killed. The local militia was engaged and finally brought the uprising under control. Of the many prisoners taken, twenty were tried and executed with about 100 innocent Blacks murdered by vigilante groups in later weeks. Turner was found guilty and hanged. The work of Black churches became more difficult as the plantocracy now sought to control the religious life of Black people.

It was clear to both masters and slaves that Black people's appropriation of Christianity was radically different from that of the White missionary and master class. Something new had emerged; the terror and beauty of the Bible and religion now informed their search for freedom within and without, externally and internally. Enslaved people spent much time in prayer and Bible study, but religion was in the service of liberation. Prayer, Bible study, and conversion experiences were ways of getting ready for protest against the vicious circle of slavery and oppression. There was a hermeneutic of freedom that informed their reading of the Bible and their understanding of church. While it was clear that in many instances the White church had made peace with slavery and extolled slavery as a Christian institution for the emergent Black church, on both sides of the Atlantic, Christianity and slavery were antithetical. Blacks wanted freedom not only in their souls but for their bodies. The body was also a site for freedom and liberation. And so unlike White Christians, Black folks would sing:

> *O freedom! O freedom! O freedom over me!*
> *An' befo' I'd be a slave, I'll be buried in my grave,*
> *An' go home to my Lord an' be free*

And at other times they would sing:

> Slavery chain done broke at last, broke at last, broke at last,
> Slavery chain done broke at last, Going to praise God till I die
> Way down in-a dat Valley, Praying on my knees;
> Told God about my troubles, And to help me ef-a He please
> I did know my Jesus heard me, 'Cause de spirit spoke to me,
> And said, Rise my child, your chillum, And you shall be free.

Black churches throughout Black Americana merged history and eschatology in their appropriation of the terrible and the beautiful work of the spirit. Their history of oppression in the terrible inferno of slavery was redeemed by the breaking of a new order in which they had glimpses of freedom, human dignity, and a sense of being sons and daughters of God. With Mary the mother of Jesus they dreamed of a new day:

> He has brought down the powerful from their thrones, and lifted
>   up the lowly;
> He has filled the hungry with good things, and sent the rich away
>   empty
> He has helped his servant . . . in remembrance of his mercy,
> According to the promise he made to our ancestors.
> (Luke 1:52–56. NRSV)

6

Toward a Creolized Ecclesiology

IN A POIGNANTLY argued article, St. Clair Drake, who lived both in the Caribbean and in the United States, points out that people of African descent in the United States never developed an African American culture in the sense that people in the Caribbean have done. He claims that what transpired in the United States context was that Afro-American culture emerged as a subculture of the dominant White culture and the main cause was the Christianization of African Americans and the marginalization of their culture. The Christianization of Africans and their culture was employed as a means of social control and a clever way to de-Africanize a people and rob them of the very essence of their culture—religion. This Christianization of the African church, according to Drake, did not occur in the Caribbean except for Barbados, one of the smaller islands in the Caribbean. One reason is that Barbados did not have many mountains and forests to which slaves could escape and practice African culture. Another factor in Barbados was the active presence of the Society for the Propagation of the Gospel. This organization, with authorizing agency in Great Britain, had an enormous influence on the lives of enslaved persons from as early as 1710. Drake recognizes other factors that contributed to the cultural differences between Afro-Americans and Afro-Caribbean people, but he sees Christianization as the main tool in placing Black culture in a subordinate role to Euro-American culture.

> Of the many factors that account for the difference—economic, demographic, and acculturational—perhaps the most important was the decision of the masters to encourage the Christianization of Africans as a means of social control to an extent that occurred nowhere else in the New World except in Barbados. . . . The basic kinship unit of West African society was not preserved or reconstituted in the New World, the

lineage that binds together brothers and sisters . . . into a tight-knit
social group and which forms the basis of the ancestor-cult, the keystone
of West African religion. . . . With the disintegration of the lineage, religious beliefs and practices based upon the solidarity of a group of kinsmen did not become part of the evolving African-American culture.[1]

According to Drake, there was no group of preachers anywhere in the Caribbean similar to those who emerged throughout the United States during the
Great Awakening. "In the French and Spanish areas there were no black
Christian religious leaders at all. The priests were all white. . . . Unlike the
situation in the United States, free men of color stood completely aloof from
the black slaves, supplying no leadership for them. . . . In 1791, the blacks of
Haiti rose up against both the whites and free persons of color and a 12-year
armed struggle began that ended with the proclamation of the Republic of
Haiti in 1804."[2] It is interesting that since Christianity was the only religion
allowed by masters on plantations in the American South, a consequence of
this imperial imposition was that Black people in the United States were more
exposed to Christian missionary teaching than to African religious practices.
Albert Raboteau supports Drake at this point. "In fact, in the United States
African religions and Christianity came to be more closely and inseparably
interwoven than in any other slave society. Religions like Vodou in Haiti and
Santeria in Cuba adopted Catholic imagery but remained fundamentally African in character. . . . The parish church remained distinct from the Vodou or
Santeria house of worship. In the United States, on the other hand, Christian
conversion and the ring-shout occurred in the same prayer meetings."[3]

A central reason for the difference in the practice of African religions on
plantations, or in local meeting places among African Americans, in contrast
to the Caribbean region, according to Raboteau, may be explained by the dis-
tribution of Africans imported into the Caribbean and the United States. Of
the twelve million enslaved persons who came to the New World, only about
4.5 percent were brought to North America. Haiti imported more than twice
that amount, "and Cuba received more slaves in the first half of the nineteenth
century than the United States did overall. Also, slaves in these Caribbean islands were concentrated in small geographic areas, as opposed to the wide
dispersal of slaves in the United States. . . . In the United States, large concen-
trations of slaves were comparatively rare and the slaves lived amidst a white
population that was equal or larger in size, with the exception of Louisiana,
and the coastal areas of Georgia and South Carolina."[4] Another important key
piece of evidence to keep in mind as we seek to make sense of the difference
between the religious practices of enslaved persons in the United States and

the Caribbean has to do with what Raboteau refers to as the "higher rate of natural increase" in the United States. In contradistinction to the United States, the Caribbean had a very high mortality rate which exceeded the overall birth rate. In order to maintain a robust slave population, slaveholders imported slaves continually from Africa. One of the benefits of this constant importation was that the African community was constantly re-Africanized. "On the other hand, most Africans brought to the United States arrived between 1750 and 1808, the year the slave trade officially ended. . . . [T]heir numbers were nowhere near the size of the African population imported into Cuba, . . . until the 1860s."⁵ In the United States the birth rate far exceeded the death rate, and because of this, during the nineteenth century the great majority of enslaved persons in the United States were native-born, among a relatively small number of native-born Africans. We must probe further to discover what this difference in population meant for the religious life of enslaved people in the United States and in the Caribbean.

Many historians point out that missionary preaching did not thrive among slaves who were born in Africa, as the language barrier posed a real problem. There was a roadblock to understanding on both sides because communication was very limited. Hope for the evangelization of enslaved persons in the New World rested with slaves who were born in the colonies and had a grasp of the English language and an introduction to the customs of the master. Much of the frustration that missionaries expressed about the futility of instruction to enslaved persons was directed at those who were born in Africa. One of the implications of the claims made by Raboteau and Drake is that the loss of religion signaled the loss of other aspects of the culture, as religion is often its most enduring aspect. Drake explains:

In Haiti and Brazil where the proportion of Dahomean and Yoruba slaves was high, the emerging Creole culture institutionalized the high status of two sets of holy persons, equally revered. There were priests and monks and nuns, predominantly white, who "knew" the Creator God in which all Africans already believed, and his sacrificed son about which the white man told them, but which fitted no religious concepts in their own societies. (Where human sacrifice did exist, outsiders, not kinsmen, were the victims.) But there were also black priests and priestesses who "knew" the other gods of Africa, including both those in the official pantheons who controlled rain and war, and the smelting of iron, and the personal gods, *orishas* and *loas*, who, upon occasion entered into their bodies and transformed them into oracles, soothsayers and diviners.⁶

While many of the beliefs of African religion disappeared because of the controlling effect of Westernization and Christianization, Drake admits that what persisted and survived in most slave societies in the New World was the presence of the diviner-healer and sorcerer who became key players on plantations in the New World. In earlier chapters, we noted that W.E.B. Du Bois refers to this aspect of leadership on plantations as the African church. Du Bois pointed out that this was the case in most slave societies for the first 200 years of slavery in the New World. Drake agrees:

> What Africans today call the "juju man," West Indians, the "Obeah man," and American Negroes, the "hoodoo man" performed the function of allaying anxiety, assuring good-luck, and of confounding enemies. And some of them were believed to have power of wreaking destruction upon a client's enemies. . . . All such practitioners were defined as "agents of the Devil" by Christians, and traffic with them as sin. New World Negroes continued to deal with them, however—or at least believe in their powers—even when they became Christians.[7]

Speaking of the advent of the African in the New World Du Bois supports the claims of Drake that the roots of the Black church did not begin in the Americas but in Africa.

> These foundations we can find if we remember that the social history of the Negro did not start in America. He was brought from a definite social environment,—the polygamous clan life under the leadership of the chief and the potent influence of the priest. His religion was nature worship, with profound belief in invisible surrounding influences, good and bad, and his worship was through incantation and sacrifice. The first rude change in his life was the slave ship and the West Indian sugar-fields. The plantation organization replaced the clan and tribe, and the white master replaced the chief with far greater and more despotic powers. . . . It was a terrific social revolution, and yet some traces were retained of the former group life, and the chief remaining institution was the Priest or Medicine-man. He early appeared on the plantation and found his function as healer of the sick, the interpreter of the Unknown, the comforter of the sorrowing, the supernatural avenger of wrong, and the one who rudely but picturesquely expressed the longing, disappointment, and resentment of a stolen and oppressed people. . . . And under him the first church was not at first by any

means Christian nor definitely organized; rather it was an adaptation and mingling of heathen rites among members of each plantation, and roughly designated as Voodooism.[8]

Du Bois is emphatic that it was the association of enslaved persons with master and missionary that gave the theology and practice of the African church the "veneer of Christianity." But over the years something new happened, especially in the United States, the African church became a Christian church. It is important to note a nuanced distinction between the approach of Du Bois and Drake. Drake suggests that there was Christianization and de-Africanization of African Americans in large measure because of the decision of the masters to introduce Christian preaching and teaching on plantations as a tool of social control. Du Bois does not suggest or imply that African Americans became Christians and as a consequence lost the memory of Africa or what was distinctive about African culture. Du Bois, who had studied the music of African Americans and the role of the spirit and the "shout" in their religious practices, affirmed the distinctiveness and uniqueness of African American culture. "Careful scholar that he was, DuBois did not say that the slaves became Christian, simply that the slave church was Christian, and he did not say precisely when it became so. . . . DuBois realized that the African component made slave culture vastly superior to that of the slave-holder."[9] The conversation between Du Bois and Drake leads us to enquire what percentage of enslaved persons during slavery in the United States became Christians. Sterling Stuckey suggests about 250,000 and asks, what faith did those who were not Christians embrace? Did all Africans abandon Africa? Did Africa cease to provide the controlling metaphor and the hermeneutical key in the creation of a "Black sacred cosmos"? Did the question, where do we stand in relation to Jesus? preempt the earlier question, where do we stand in relation to Africa? Could it be that Drake's suggestion, that African culture disappeared under the fervor of Christianization, imply that he underestimated the power and durability of African culture?

Factors that Shaped Black Church Culture

Melville Herskovits who made the most in-depth study of these questions frames the issue for us: "What caused the differences between the several parts of the New World in retention of African custom? Though the answer can only be sketched, . . . yet the effective factors are discernible. They were four in number: climate and topography; the organization and operation of the plantations; the numerical ratios of Negroes to whites; and the extent to which the contacts between Negroes and whites in a given area took place in rural or urban setting."[10] We focus on the first three of these factors and note that throughout the book the fourth question is addressed.

We begin with the environmental factor because we are reminded that the environment was a decisive influence for Africans who were forcibly brought to the New World to work on plantations, irrespective of the tribe or country where they originated. To begin with the environment is, in many ways, to begin with the doctrine of creation. Africans believe that the created world is peopled with spirits and the land does not belong to the high God but to the ancestors. John Mbiti reminds us that Africans take their religion with them to the fields, the market, and that religion suffuses all of life. Throughout the Caribbean this is translated in terms of the understanding of "yard." The house is where we sleep. Everything else happens in the yard—worship, meeting visitors and friends, games, and socializing. When I was on a field trip with students to Haiti, they were quite surprised when a local pastor invited us to meet in his office under a tree in his yard. We had a conference there and were served refreshments.

Herskovits points out that Africans brought to the tropics did not experience the same challenges of acculturation and adjustment as enslaved persons who were taken to colder climates. "In the United States, for example, a man's life on the rice plantations of the Carolina coast or in the cotton country of Alabama and Louisiana was quite different than if his lot made him the property of a master interested in the production of turpentine or one whose farm was in the uplands."[11]

The contrast is even more sharply drawn when the enslaved person works and lives in the Caribbean or in South America and is required to work on sugar plantations. Most of the contact is with other Africans on a plantation, where the nature of the crop and its harvesting required many slaves. In order to supply the world market with sugar, many plantations were large, because small farms were inefficient. "The encouragement given by such an environment to large scale agricultural production thus made for the concentration of large numbers of Africans and of persons of African descent in natural settings where the greatest possible use could be made by them of their aboriginal cultural heritage."[12] One argument is that to be in the natural environment and to have one's primary contact with other enslaved persons allowed for some form of community to emerge, as enslaved persons had opportunities to assess possibilities of escape. "It is clear that individual escapes were more likely to be made good where natural obstacles to pursuit were the most severe; in the United States, swamps always invited running away, permitting the slave a measure of protection. . . . In the tropics, dense jungles aided revolters, both because of the similarity between the conditions of life the runaways had to meet in these forests and the setting of their lives in Africa."[13] The mountains always seemed to invite enslaved persons to make a run for freedom as their jungles and forests provided covering for them along with communion of ancestors who were ever present with them. This was the case in Guyana, Haiti, Jamaica, Brazil, and Surinam. "It is striking that in smaller, less heavily forested islands such as Barbados, St. Vincent, and the Virgin islands, or in the United States (with the one exception of the Maroons of Florida, whose salvation lay in their joining the Indians rather than through their own unaided efforts), serious revolts were put down."[14] The point so artfully alluded to by Herskovits is that escape from the plantation, where the only religion permitted was Christianity, meant that through escape to the forests and mountains there was an opportunity to avoid Westernization and Christianity as opportunities for enculturation—the practice and preservation of African rituals and customs were embraced. In some countries like Surinam, Jamaica, Guyana, Haiti, and Brazil, Maroon communities were able to survive and African cultural practices were passed on to succeeding generations. In several of these countries there were reinforcements of Africans through fresh shipments of slaves who enhanced the possibility of the retention of African beliefs and customs.

The second factor that must be considered as we examine questions of enculturation and acculturation in the New World is the way in which plantations were organized and operated. Herskovits points out that because all plantations had the same goal—maximizing profits as they produced for world markets—they were rather similar in management style. This meant that "unskilled labor had to be directed toward growing the principal crop in which the plantations of a given area specialized. Sugar in the West Indies and South America and cotton in the United States were most important, but some plantations and some regions were devoted to growing other major crops, such as coffee and tobacco and rice and indigo."[15] There were similar routines in field preparation, in recruiting skilled labor, and in providing assistantship for a White overseer. "Some slaves had to be trained to provide such special tasks, but everywhere careful and constant supervision assured that all aspects of the work went forward, the white overseers being assisted by slaves who were charged with supervising the labor of a smaller group than the white superintendent could effectively control."[16] The point being made is that whether we look at the plantation system in the Caribbean or in the United States, they were operated and managed in similar fashion. "Planters coming to South Carolina from Barbados, Jamaica, Antigua and St. Kitts brought with them the ideas of the plantation regime with slavery as the basis of the labor system."[17]

We noted in earlier chapters that there was a constant exchange of ideas between countries on the American mainland and among nation-states in the Caribbean because both enslaved and master class would compare notes of slave revolts, and economic and political practices in plantation culture. The main point Herskovits wants to establish is that special skills were required on the plantation which required enslaved persons to be in close contact with the master, almost a parallel situation between the White missionary/preacher and the Black preacher, who within the context of the Christian church had to be licensed and authorized by the White preacher/missionary; yet the constant contact between them did not mean that the enslaved person would necessarily copy the ways of the European. African culture did not disappear in the wake of its contact with European culture. Herskovits elucidates:

> It does not follow, however, that the training of those who operated and repaired sugar mills, or acted as house servants, or otherwise followed a routine different from that of the great body of field hands was in itself sufficient to cause them to give up their African modes of behavior. Though greater personal contact with the masters was the direct route to greater taking over of European modes of behavior, the manner of life led by the whites, certainly in the West Indies, was not such as to inculcate either love or respect for it on the part of those who viewed it closely . . . the slaves closest to the masters were those most exposed to their caprice; and the situation of the house slave, if not involving as hard and continuous physical labor as that required of the ordinary field hand, had serious drawbacks in the constant exposure to the severe punishment that followed, even unwitting conduct that displeased the ever-present masters.[18]

We are told that those who were most active in the Underground Railroad were those who had the greatest opportunities to learn the ways of the White master. There are similar expressions of close contact with the White people throughout the Caribbean and an equal commitment to dismantle slavery and secure the freedom of those in bondage. "On the basis of studies made in the United States, it is generally held that European habits were most prevalent among the free Negroes. Yet though this might be true in the United States . . . in the rest of the New World it by no means follows. Thus, in Brazil, it was just among those Negroes who, either for the account of their owners or because they had purchased their own freedom, followed specialized callings, that the stream of African tradition was kept free flowing to reach in relatively undiluted form to the present day."[19] A similar claim is made for the leaders of the

Haitian revolution, who were conversant with European life and warfare and used that skill against their imperial masters. Herskovits exposes one of the myths that provide a basis for our judgment of ancestors who worked on plantations in the New World that closeness with the master class invariably meant a rejection of African ways of being and an embrace of European worldviews. This view does not take into account a number of variables. On the one hand, many enslaved persons were practiced in saying what they thought the master wanted to hear. Enslaved persons were often heard to say, "I have two minds, one for the master and one for me." We noted in earlier chapters that enslaved persons both in the Caribbean and in the American South would attend Christian churches without any intention of listening to the preacher, and often after church they would ask the class leaders what the White preacher said. What they thought and felt was often in contradistinction to what they expressed. There was a level of freedom to their thinking and feeling that placed these emotions beyond the reach of the master, just as was the case in their songs. Their songs, feelings, and thinking were truly theirs and hence truly free. Often oppressed people would sing while working:

> *Ten poun' hammer kill John Henry,*
> *Somebody dying ebery day*
> *Tek de hammer and give it to the worker,*
> *Somebody dying ebery day*
> *When me go home me will tell me mother,*
> *Somebody dying ebery day*
> *Me no born yah (here), me come from yondah,*
> *Somebody dying ebery day*[20]

The case was made earlier that Denmark Vesey, the architect and enforcer of the rebellion in South Carolina in 1822, was a close worker with his master, often working in the home and accompanying him on trips to the Caribbean. Throughout the Caribbean those most responsible for poisoning the master and embodying the powers of Obeah were those closest to the master—house servants. They often chose freedom in relation to land and people rather than life in the big house, albeit a house of bondage.

In an attempt to further highlight the influence and impact of White ways of thinking on Black behavior, Herskovits examines the ratio of enslaved persons to the master class. At one level a central question has to do with the level of syncretism that took place in the contact between Africa and Europe. It is difficult not to suggest that Europeans had the edge and advantage over enslaved persons, considering that the master class often had police and military as means of enforcing their wishes and cultural habits. They would often use death as a threat for refusal of their way of life and the acceptance of their ideas. Herskovits's contribution, at this point, concerns the nature of the contact. Constancy and the enduring quality of the contact were a basis for the patterning of the behavior of enslaved people. In the previous section we noted the impact of close relationships between slave and master, and it was observed that being in the same space or place was not sufficient basis to posit an axiom: those who were closest to the master surrendered their African ways of thinking and being. At one level this seems to be Drake's thesis, that contact with the master by enslaved Africans provided an openness for the embrace of the master's religion—Christianity. But we enquire whether Drake, too, easily posits the disappearance of African culture in contact with European ways of life.

One question debated is, what does it mean to be African or an African church, broadly understood, in a culture of epistemic violence? Another important question is, what does it mean to be an African people (congregation, church) in a context of being a political and sociological minority or majority? Does it matter if Africans were a majority or minority?

It was noted that the racial ratios varied throughout the New World, and that in the United States, the vast number of farms were small, with large plantations being the exception. Herskovits illustrates:

> According to the census of 1860, for example, one-fourth of all the slaves in the United States were held in parcels of less than ten slaves each, and nearly another fourth in parcels of from ten to twenty slaves. This means about one-half of the slaves had a distinct facilitation in obtaining an appreciable share in the social heritage of their masters. . . [T]he very fact that the Negroes were slaves linked them as a whole more closely to the whites than any scheme of wage-labor could well have done.[21]

It is this informal contact between masters and enslaved people on small farms throughout the continental United States that explains the greater incidence of African retentions in the Caribbean and South America. He explains the American phenomenon:

> In the earliest days, the number of slaves in proportion to their masters was extremely small, and though as time went on thousands and tens of thousands of slaves were brought to satisfy the demands of the southern plantations, nonetheless the Negroes lived in constant

association with whites to a degree not found anywhere else in the New World. That the Sea Islands of the Carolina and Georgia coast offer the most striking retention of Africanisms to be encountered in the United States is to be regarded as but a reflection of the isolation of these Negroes when compared to those on the mainland.[22]

The problem enslaved persons on small farms of ten to fifteen persons faced was the close scrutiny by their masters and the added difficulty of preserving their aboriginal traditions, especially if there were no forests, swamps, or mountains to shield them from the constant gaze of the master. In many instances enslaved persons in the United States lived in close proximity to the master. Frederick Douglass alludes to this when he tells of masters hiding in the bushes in an attempt to ensure that enslaved workers took no breaks while working on their farms. "How might the specialists in technology, in magic, in manipulating the supernatural powers carry on their work among such small groups existing, as these had to exist, under the close scrutiny and constant supervision of slaveowners?"[23]

The scene changes when we turn to the Caribbean and South America where numbers were far more disproportionate. In most instances, Whites were in the minority; in some cases there would be a single family of Whites in charge of a couple hundred Black people. Herskovits points out that there was seldom the presence of "poor whites," as "the white man with but a few slaves was seldom encountered. The requirement of conformity to the plantation system was far more stringent than in the United States where a certain degree of economic self-sufficiency was sought after, no matter to what extent the raising of a single crop was the major objective."[24] He cites the example of a White farmer in Haiti who complains of the isolation of his family of five who have more than 200 slaves, of which thirty are domestic. "From morning to night, wherever we turn, their faces meet our eyes. No matter how early we awaken, they are at our bedsides, and the custom which obtains here not to make the least move without the help of one of these Negro servants brings it about not only that we live in their society the greater portion of the day, but also that they are involved in the least important events of our daily lives."[25] Numbers matter, as the paradigm shifts, and Whites in the Caribbean discover that they "live, and move and have their being" in a Black cultural ethos.

Another point of contrast between the Caribbean and the United States has to do with the adjustment of masters to their setting. In the tropics they were always thinking of home in Europe, and in many islands a majority of masters resided in Europe; those who lived in the islands were always longing for home, in part because of climate, tropical diseases, and the fear of Obeah as it took form in poison. Thinking of home in Europe did not help their acculturation process in the Caribbean. In the United States what existed was settler colonialism. Europeans had come to the United States to build their homes and their way of life, and they secured the free labor of enslaved people to help them in this task.

The bottom line is that closer contact between slave and master in the United States made for greater familiarity with European customs and the openness of Black people to include these customs in their behavior. "Nothing could contrast more to this than the situation as it affected the slaves where greater numbers of Negroes lived a life on estates which removed them from their masters far more than on the North American continent. . . . One can set off the United States from the rest of the New World as a region where departure from African modes of life was greatest."[26] It is clear then that Africa survived in all areas of the New World to different degrees and as Herskovits reminds us we should not imagine that Africans in the New World were passive agents in the face of European contact, but that their culture was a living reality which they adapted to their new and alien world of slavery. Throughout the New World the master resisted various aspects of African culture among enslaved people as it was believed that African customs and patterns of behavior could unify enslaved people and make rebellions and other forms of resistance more difficult to control and anticipate.

Plantation life under the regimented rule of the master destroyed family life and the relationship to kinship ties, and it is precisely at this point that the Black church as the African church emerged as the center of social and cultural life for Black people. Religion proved to be one of the more durable aspects of African culture. It did not survive in whole as it was brought from Africa but became a living reality as it took root in new soil embracing new traditions. One of the remarkable traits of African people in the New World was their openness to new ways of being including worship, the embrace of the God of their captors, without relinquishing African roots. "In West Africa, it was common for both conquerors and conquered to take over one another's gods and how, in the course of a man's everyday experience, it was deemed more advantageous for him to give way to a point of view against which he could not prevail than to persist in that attitude."[27]

Does a Righteous God Govern the Universe?

Drake points out that the seeming death of the gods of Africa caused Black people in the trauma of slavery to begin to question their relationship to Africa and their understanding of faith and life. Unlike European questions pertaining to faith and reason, the questions of Africans during the holocaust of New

World slavery made connections between faith and life. Drake reminds us that Africans believed in a form of the debate between fate and destiny that was not far from Calvinistic understandings of predestination. The central question was, could a people be carted from their homes, taken across the Atlantic to distant and alien lands in chains as beasts of burden, outside of the will of their gods? Sister Kelly a slave from Columbia, Tennessee, frames the issue for us:

> Well, Chile, I tell you, my mind ain't on old times today but I'll tell you what I kin. When the War broke out I had three little children. You know when I come along we didn't know our ages nor nothing. They stealed just like they stealed now . . . you kin take that from sister Kelly. The white folks throwed the book what had our ages in it in the fire to keep us from having it, and none of us ever knowed just how old we was. When I was about 12 years old, just look like one day the stars was falling, and it just got as dark as it could be. If you wants me to tell you what a hard time the po' ole slave had working and getting whupped, and sech like that, I knows about that, yes sir, and I ain't forgot neither. I will never forget none of that this side of the grave. I have plowed many a field honey. Sometime, we was in the field time it was daylight, and sometime even before day broke; we would work there all day, then we had to shell corn at night when it was too dark to bend yo' back any longer in the field. . . . When Christmas come . . . all the white folks would come from New York and places, and there was sho' nuf fine times. The ole red-headed yaps would bid us off to the highest bidder and we couldn't do nothin' but pray. Yes, fine time for them, but awful for us po' niggers. Yes'm, they would cry you off to the highest bidder for the next year. One by one, we had to get up on that block, and he bid us off.[28]

Frederick Douglass joins Sister Kelly in raising questions concerning fate, destiny, and predestination in the African Diaspora in the New World.

> I held my Sabbath school at the house of a free colored man. . . . We loved each other. . . . When I think that these precious schools are today shut up in the prison-house of slavery, my feelings over come me, and I am almost ready to ask, 'Does a righteous God govern the universe? And for what does he hold the thunders in his right hand, if not to smite the oppressor? . . . Rev. Daniel Weeden . . . owned, among others a woman slave. . . . This woman's back, for weeks, was kept literally raw, made so by the lash of the merciless, *religious* wretch.[29]

Drake indicates that Africans, while embracing the broad concept of fate and destiny, that the gods allowed their captivity and enslavement in the Americas, agreed that this did not obviate personal and collective responsibility for their lives in the midst of suffering. The embrace of their suffering and at the same time a refusal to make peace with the conditions of that suffering was certainly a reason for enslaved persons to find strength in the cross and suffering of Jesus. Jesus knew the way through the valley of suffering and as friend would guide them through, and if Jesus did not act in haste to help them through this painful vale of suffering, appeal was made to other spirits. There was no conflict here, as Jesus was seen as one of the spirits, even if for some he became their favorite spirit. Grafted into the concept of fate and destiny was the doctrine of Divine Providence. Drake suggests that the question of the mystery of the evil of slavery forced both missionary and slave to find comfort and relief in notions of the providence of God or the gods. The lived reality of radical evil forced enslaved people, trapped in the quagmire of slavery, to posit faith in their gods who had not abandoned them, who would see them through, and who had willed good for them. Sister Kelly speaks from her experience as a slave in support of notions of divine providence helping her to make it through the long night of slavery:

> Well, we used to have little singing and praying like good ole time revival; and we would take pots and put them right in the middle of the floor to keep the sound in the room; yeah, keep the white folks from meddling. Yes'm, the sound will stay right in the room after you do that. Well, we allus used these old house wash pots like you boil clothes in, you know. Just turn one down in the middle of the floor, that was sufficient. . . . Well, chile, I got happy and I jest went up and down, jest shouting and praying and crying for dear life. . . . I stopped right still and started thinking, and seemed like a loud voice said, "You is jest in God's hands, and you must praise and bless God all the time." Well, honey, you know I was young, and I knowed no more about it than this here rock, but I sho' felt something and I heard something, too.[30]

For Sister Kelly, God's world is one of freedom; therefore, it was all right to be in God's hand. The God who loves freedom wills freedom for all God's children. Sister Kelly did not spend time debating whether or not God exists. This was not a concern for African peoples. Their concern was, do God and the ancestors care, and even in the face of the radical evil of suffering and slavery, Sister Kelly says: "You is jest in God's hands, and you must praise and bless God at all times."

Sin, Guilt and the Afterlife

St. Clair Drake points out that the new elements Christianity introduced to Africans caught in the inferno of slavery in the New World were sin, guilt, and the afterlife. "The belief in divine providence was grafted onto African belief. However, concepts of sin and guilt that affected the afterlife of individuals or the destiny of groups did not exist in West African societies, and could offer no explanations of why people had been enslaved or what God or the gods had planned as the destiny of tribes and nations. Nevertheless, the trauma of The Diaspora forced reflection on these aspects of Man's Fate, and those slaves who became Christians were exposed to eschatological doctrines."[31] We are grateful to Drake for the reminder that there were no notions of original sin in African theologies. In African theologies people were not born sinners but were born whole, and sin entered the human story as an intrusion—an intruder from outside. When one sinned, a sacrifice was offered, sin was forgiven and one went on with one's life. Here we see parallels with Old Testament understandings of sin and African religions. According to Drake the doctrine of sin was especially central in the preaching and teaching of Baptist and Methodist churches which were flocked to by enslaved persons. These doctrines were also very central in Negro spirituals, the sorrow songs of enslaved people. "In North America, where evangelical Protestantism of the Baptist and Methodist variety was deliberately taught to many of the slaves, a body of folk-music, the 'spirituals,' came into being which voiced the hope of an ultimate apocalyptic deliverance for the people of the Black Diaspora with the experience of the Jews as a paradigm. . . . The concept of the Western African 'high god' who did not interfere in human affairs was replaced by that of a God 'who's got the whole world in his hands' and who, at the end of time, will judge all men."[32] Drake alludes to the differences between Caribbean and African American approaches to Christianity. He uses a thesis statement, that Christianity, as presented by the missionaries on plantations in the United States, de-Africanized the culture of enslaved persons and this leaves them with a subculture inferior to Euro-American culture. It is important, at this point, to note that Negro spirituals are not indigenous to the Caribbean. Drake's logic seems to imply that one reason for the absence of slave songs in the Caribbean when compared to the Negro spirituals, is that enslaved people in the Caribbean did not embrace the Christian concepts of sin and the afterlife, which are main keys of Negro spirituals. It is precisely at this point that Drake reminds us that one of the motivations for the crafting of these songs was the camp meetings that were occasioned by the Great Awakening, which began in the United States in

1739, and according to Love Henry Whelchel Jr., impacted Black people especially during the Second Great Awakening, 1780–1830.[33]

There was no parallel to the Great Awakening in the Caribbean and as was noted in the previous chapter, when African American preachers came to the Caribbean in 1783, after the American War, their version of Christianity was placed in the matrix of African religions and a new church emerged, the Native Baptists. Throughout the Caribbean, during slavery, concepts of sin, guilt, and the afterlife originated with orthodox Christianity and not to churches with an African ethos. There is ample evidence that in African religions, as they took root in the Caribbean and were ignited by a hermeneutic of freedom, Christian doctrines of sin, guilt, and the afterlife took root much later and were inspired by the missionary's church. A majority of Caribbean people who were born in Africa during slavery were steeped in African notions of wholeness that did not make room for sin and guilt. Later, when these doctrines found currency among enslaved people in the Caribbean, they were cast in an African framework. Therefore, they associated teaching about the afterlife with their return to Africa after death.

On both sides of the Atlantic enslaved persons were able to recognize notions of sin and sacrifice because there were parallels in their own religion. The point being made is that Caribbean people acknowledged that human beings are sinful but do not self-define as sinners. This self-definition of African Americans as sinners was a direct consequence of their playing out the implications of the question, "Where do we stand in relation to Jesus?" Christian faith in many iterations taught that human beings who were estranged from God were lost and that they were held in contempt by God. They were on their way to hell and therefore in need of divine salvation. African Americans were taught to acknowledge sinfulness, divine contempt, and the desire to be accepted through the love and sacrifice of Jesus. Jesus was often seen as one of the lesser deities who mediated between the human condition of sinfulness and the divine life of grace and mercy.

But one way in which the plantation, through the missionary, kept Black people in their place as unequal to White people is that there was this terrible sense of worthlessness and unworthiness that came with one's relationship to Jesus. In the act of seeing Jesus as worthy, one saw oneself as unworthy and condemned in that state until the church mediated divine forgiveness and grace. The journey to divine acceptance was not automatic. It was mediated by the church in terms and conditions stipulated by the church. It is in this sense that the posture of enslaved persons to Jesus opened the door for the church to use Christian faith as a means of social control. The end sought by enslaved persons—equality and freedom—were constantly moving goalposts as they required subordination and subservience in plantation culture. The problem was compounded for many enslaved persons in that Christian churches, during slavery, taught that acceptance by Jesus meant that sin and condemnation were relaxed. It also meant acceptance by the master. Enslaved persons were taught that the way to please Jesus was to please the master. Obedience to the master was equated with obedience to Jesus. It is fair to say that during the era of slavery more harm and wrongs were committed in the name of obedience to Jesus and master than in enslaved people's refusal to acknowledge the Christian faith.

The genius of slave religion, as expressed in Obeah, Vodou, and Santeria, is that the locus of power and authority was often outside organized religion, as was the case in Haiti, South Carolina, Virginia, Jamaica, and in several other places where rebellion was authorized by religious forces outside orthodox Christianity. The bottom line is that churches, during slavery, had to take sides, and it was clear they could not pledge allegiance to master and freedom at the same time

There were some limited yet important gains that came from one's allegiance to the Jesus who was controlled by the church. Although Richard Allen's conversion has the marks of the sinful condition and a sense of condemnation, he found comfort in the knowledge that Jesus died for him. He was able to go on, within the context of the church, to assist enslaved persons to freedom. His church became a center for the Underground Railroad. Additionally, the church was a place of expression, where enslaved persons danced, testified, preached, and often controlled their space, and interpreted the Good Book in terms of equality and freedom

Richard Allen speaks of himself as sinner. "I was awakened and brought to see myself, poor, wretched and undone, and without the mercy of God. . . . I cried to the Lord both night and day. . . . [A]ll of a sudden my dungeon shook, my chains flew off, and glory to God I cried. My soul was filled. I cried, enough—for me the savior died."[34] He went on to found a church and become a leader of his people.

Life on plantations in the New World was an existential expression of bondage from which enslaved persons sought to be delivered, and religion provided the impetus and means of this sought-after deliverance. There is a distinction between how Whites viewed their existence in the New World and how Africans, taken there in chains as beasts of burden, saw theirs. If Europeans understood themselves as the New Israel in the Promised Land, enslaved Africans saw themselves as the children of Israel in Egypt in need of divine liberation. The New World was their Egypt and their prayer to the gods was for Exodus from slavery in Egypt. This self-understanding places the emphasis

not on Africans as the primary agents of sin or some sense of them committing sin but sin being committed against them. Sin was outside of them as an
alien force and when it invaded their personality, all the spirits were summoned to extricate it from their being. Although sin was viewed as private and
personal, it was also social and corporate. Often in the experience of Africans
on both sides of the Atlantic the Christian spirits were no match for the perni-
cious trauma that sin engendered, and African spirits had to be summoned to
"cast them out." This was often the case in the need for healing or the rever-
sals of misfortune and tragedy.

Strategies of Liberation

Liberation included solidarity and strategies of resistance as Africans organized for healing and exodus from traditions that demean and diminish the
self. Early after his relocation to Jamaica, George Liele was placed in prison
for preaching on Romans 10:1 "Brethren, my heart's desire and prayer for
Israel is that they might be saved." The charge brought against Liele for
which he was imprisoned was that "he was exciting the slaves to rebellion."[35]
Liele, while in prison, equivocated between notions of survival and liberation. Should he speak out against the evils of slavery and challenge the forces
of oppression to let God's people go free or should he work within the system
of slavery and cooperate with the status quo? The choice was between survival with dignity or liberation. The story of the role and function of the
Black church as the midwife of healing and survival has always highlighted
the need not only to make decisions in relation to enculturation and acculturation but also in relation to issues of survival and liberation. It is clear that
St. Clair Drake sees acculturation as a way of survival and enculturation as
liberation. For Drake to embrace African culture and allow that culture to
frame the response to violence against the enslaved Africans is clearly a path
to liberation. And yet, much of life in the New World for African people has
not always presented a clear choice between enculturation and acculturation, but a fusing of African and European ways of thinking and being, and
the church has often led the way in this form of creolization. When Africa
and Europe met in the New World the choice between two ways of thinking
and being were not always clear. This is noted in the response of leaders as
diverse as Richard Allen, Denmark Vesey, Nat Turner, Sister Kelly, and
George Liele.

Liele's choice, while in prison was to opt for survival rather than to press
for Exodus from slavery. This choice sheds light into his character, as a leader
among his people in Savannah, Georgia, and Kingston, Jamaica. George Liele,

one of the first Black persons to introduce Christianity to enslaved persons in the United States and the Caribbean, represents an interesting model of one who was committed to the survival of his people and his own family. His own story of his conversion to the Christian church lends credence to Drake's thesis that survival of enslaved persons in the southern colonies in the United States meant the embrace of missionary teaching and a willingness to frame life with the question "Where do I stand in relation to Jesus" rather than "Where do I stand in relation to Africa?" This was not an easy or straightforward choice for enslaved persons in the United States. One of the assumptions that enslaved persons often had to work with was that conversion to Christianity would raise their social profile and perhaps even place them on social parity with the master. There was some suspicion that the church's book, the Bible, taught the equality of colonizer and colonized before God. Several enslaved persons believed that Christianity offered the best path to freedom, even if spiritual freedom was seen as a necessary step toward physical freedom. The truth is that often masters and missionaries alike were disappointed with the result of the conversion of enslaved persons, as they would often combine Christian and African practices. In many instances they were not willing to abandon Africa nor were they willing to ignore Europe. Africa and Europe competed for the souls of Black folks. On the other hand, the missionary hoped that a Christian slave would be industrious, would not run away or "rob Massa." When slave life was seen from the perspective of missionary teaching, Jesus meant conformity, obedience, and even an acknowledgment of subordination and subservience to the master. One aspect of the logic of proffering this ethic of love for Jesus was that it would save both master and slave from conflict and the need for the master to brutalize the slave. The net result is that it would make for a better master-slave relationship. In the case of the founder of the African Methodist Church, Richard Allen, we note that he and his brother, Samson, used their conversion to Christianity to impress their master of the superiority of the Christian way of life by working hard on their master's farm, exposing him to Christian teaching, and then bargaining for their own freedom. Their strategy was to use Christianity and their own conversion as tools for liberation and eventual freedom. This seems to have been the exception rather than the rule. The sad news is that for many enslaved persons who took missionary teaching too seriously, although conversion to Christianity meant that they were allowed to go to church, pray, testify, and dance, this was all within the world of slavery. One answer to the question, "Where do I stand in relation to Jesus?" was survival within the context of slavery. Jesus softened the harshness and terror of slavery. Jesus did not yet mean freedom or liberation from the chains of slavery. If spiritual chains were removed from their "souls," chains remained in their minds and on their feet.

One lesson that George Liele teaches us is that the answer to the Jesus-Africa question, namely, "Where do I stand in relation to Jesus?" or "Where do I stand in relation to Africa?" was contextual for enslaved persons. Of course there were enslaved persons who chose to return to their master after the American Revolution. We noted an example of Jesse Peters whose pragmatic and contextual theology left the door open for him to return to slavery after the American War, an action that he deemed was in his best interest. Although he had an opportunity to leave the United States for the Caribbean or Nova Scotia like others of his colleagues, he chose to remain in bondage and work for the Galphin plantation and expand the work of the Black church in Augusta, Georgia. But for the most part, Black people were committed to a hermeneutic of freedom, and survival with dignity was interpreted as an aspect of that freedom.

I Have Two Minds, One for the Master and One for Me

George Liele is often written off as an Uncle Tom, or one who too easily embraced a missionary theology of subordination and subservience to the master while discarding the question of his people, "Where do we stand in relation to Africa," in preference to the missionary's question, "Where do we stand in relation to Jesus." It is clear that in the context of slavery in Georgia his decision to convert to Jesus gave him opportunities to preach at both the White church, of which he was a member, and on plantations along the Savannah River that took him as far afield as Silver Bluff, South Carolina, where he had an impact and influence on the formation of the first Black Baptist Church in the world. It points to Liele's commitment to his people, that during the American War, he spent much of his time at Tybee Island, where a majority of enslaved persons, caught in the cross-fire of the American War, lived as refugees. It is difficult to argue that Liele did not see the Christian gospel as providing a liberating message of freedom and equality for enslaved persons in this context. But his theology was contextual. It took shape in terms of both the city in which he lived and the need for survival with dignity. The renowned church historian Walter H. Brooks wrote:

How well these slaves understood and appreciated the proffered boon, may be inferred from a letter, which was written by Mr. Stephen Bull to Col. Henry Laurens, President of the Council of Safety, Charleston, S. C., March 14, 1776. In that letter he says: "It is better for the public, and the owners, if the deserted Negroes who are on the Tybee Island be shot, if they cannot be taken." By this means, as he informs us, he hoped to "deter other Negroes from deserting"—their masters. . . . Rev. George Liele, although not a runaway slave, appears to have some liking for the Tybee River, as a place of abode, and it is probable that when he could no longer visit Silver Bluff, . . . he resorted to Tybee Island to preach the Gospel of Christ to the refugees there assembled. At any rate, when Liele appears in Savannah, Ga., as a preacher of the Gospel, his biographer declares that "He came up to the city of Savannah from Tybee River."[36]

Liele's commitment to the refugees on Tybee Island with whom he spent much time comports with his naming his church in Jamaica the Ethiopian Baptist Church, and his use of Romans 10:1 for his incendiary sermon in that country in 1783. And yet this first African American who would preach a sermon that would land him in jail in Jamaica and name his church in a way that remembers Africa says of his own conversion in 1774 under the preaching of a White preacher, Matthew Moore:

> He unfolded all my dark views, opened my best behavior and good works to me, which I thought I was to be saved by, and I was convinced that I was not in the way of heaven, but in the way to hell. This state I labored under for the space of five or six months. The more I heard or read the more I [saw that I] was condemned as a sinner before God until at length I was brought to perceive that my life hung by a slender thread, and if it was the will of God to cut me off at that time, I was sure I should be found in hell, as sure as God was in heaven. I saw my condemnation in my own heart, and I found no way wherein I could escape the damnation of hell, only through the merits of my dying Lord and Savior Jesus Christ; which caused me to make intercession with Christ, for the salvation of my poor immortal soul; and I full well recollect, I requested of my Lord and Master to give me a work, I did not care how mean it was, only to try and see how good I would do it.[37]

It is quite clear that there were no straightforward ways in which enculturation and acculturation functioned for George Liele. One wonders to what extent Black people often said what they felt the master wanted to hear or do what they needed to do in order to survive in the cruel world of slavery. Within a relatively short time after he was licensed to preach and given some freedom to travel as an itinerant preacher, Liele staked out a theological position declaring where he stood in relation to Jesus, and this helped secure opportunities for him to enjoy a measure of freedom. One is also led to wonder if there is a double entendre in his claim: "I requested of my Lord and Master to give me a work, I did not care how mean it was, only to try and see how good I would do it." Was this his way of suggesting that there was a master above his earthly master, one who would call the activities of his earthly master into question? Was this a clever way of using the master's language and theology to call into question the master's claim of authority and right to the enforced labor of Black people? Was this his way of saying, I seek work from a greater master, one to whom I am ultimately accountable, and whom I seek to please while at the same time show respect for the role of the master?

In December 1777, Liele founded a Black church in Yama Craw, on the outskirts of Savannah, Georgia. He linked this church through a covenant to the one founded in Jamaica, 1783, which he called the Ethiopian Baptist Church. I will list this covenant in full as it is the first such document produced by a Black church and in this case spanning the Atlantic as it joins two regions and two churches together.

After his experience in prison in Jamaica, for preaching from Romans 10:1, Liele produced a church covenant titled, "The COVENANT OF THE ANABAPTIST CHURCH" begun in America, December 1777, and in Jamaica, December 1783.

(I)   We are of the Anabaptist persuasion, because we believe it agreeable to the Scriptures. Proof: (Matt.iii. 1–3; 2Cor.vi.14–18.)

(II) We hold to keep the Lord's Day throughout the year, in a place appointed for Public Worship, in singing psalms, hymns, and spiritual songs, and preaching the Gospel of Jesus Christ. (Mark xvi. 2,5,6; Col.iii.16.)

(III) We hold to be baptized in a river, or in a place where there is much water, in the name of the Father, and the Son, and the Holy Ghost. (Matt. iii.13,16,17; Mark xvi.15,16; Matt.xxviii.19.)

(IV) We hold to receiving the Lord's Supper in obedience according to his commands. (Mark xiv. 22–24; John vi. 53–57.)

(V)   We hold to the ordinance of washing one another's feet. (John xiii.2–7.)

(VI) We hold to receive and admit young children into the Church according to the Word of God. (Luke ii.27–28; Mark x.13–16.)

(VII) We hold to pray over the sick, anointing them with oil in the name of the Lord. (James v. 14,15.)

(VIII) We hold to laboring one with another according to the Word of God. (Matt. xviii. 15–18.)

(IX) We hold to appoint Judges and such other Officers among us, to settle any matter according to the Word of God. (Acts vi. 1–3.)

(X) We hold not to shedding of blood. (Genesis ix.6; Matt. xxvi. 51–52.)

(XI) We are forbidden to go to law one with another before the unjust, but to settle any matter we have before the Saints. (1 Cor.vi. 1–3.)

(XII) We are forbidden to swear not at all [sic]. (Matt. v. 33–37; Jas. V.12.)

(XIII) We are forbidden to eat blood, for it is the life of a creature, and from things strangled, and from meat offered to idols. (Acts. xv. 29.)

(XIV) We are forbidden to wear any costly raiment, such as superfluity. (1 Peter iii. 3, 4; 1 Timothy ii. 9–10.)

(XV) We permit no slaves to join the Church without first having a few lines from their owners for good behavior. (1 Peter ii. 13–16; 1 Thess. iii. 13.)

(XVI) To avoid fornication, we permit none to keep each other, except they be married according to the Word of God. (1 Cor. vii.2; Heb. xiii.4.)

(XVII) If a slave or servant misbehave to their owners they are to be dealt with according to the Word of God. (1 Tim. i.6; Eph. vi.5; 1 Peter ii. 18–22; Titus ii.9–11.)

(XVIII) If anyone of the Religion should transgress and walk disorderly, and not according to the Commands which we have received in this Covenant, he will be censured according to the Word of God. (Luke xii. 47–48.)

(XIX) We hold, if a brother or sister should transgress any of these articles written in this Covenant so as to become a swearer, a fornicator, or adulterer; a covetous person, an idolater, a railer, a drunkard, an extortioner, or whoremonger; or should commit any abominable sin, and do not give satisfaction to the Church, according to the Word of God, he or she, shall be put away from among us, not to keep company, nor to eat with him. (Cor. v. 11–13.)

(XX) We hold if a Brother or Sister should transgress, and abideth not in the doctrine of Christ, and he or she, after being justly dealt with agreeable to the 8th article, and be put out of the Church, that they shall have no right or claim whatsoever to be interred into the Burying-ground during the time they are put out, should they depart life; but should they return in peace, and make a concession so as to give satisfaction, according to the Word of God, they shall be received into the Church again and have all privileges as before granted. (2 John i. 9–10; Gal. vi. 1,2; Luke xvii. 3,4.)

(XXI)   We hold to all the other Commandments, Articles, Covenants, and
        Ordinances, recorded in the Holy Scriptures as are set forth by our
        Lord and master Jesus Christ and His Apostles, which are not written
        in this Covenant, and to live to them as nigh as we possibly can,
        agreeable to the Word of God. (John xv. 7–14.)[38]

It is rather difficult to identify several of these articles of the covenant as representing the customs or interests of Afro-Jamaicans during the latter part of
the eighteenth and early decades of the nineteenth centuries. The logical conclusion to be drawn from the disconnect between the ideals and provisions of
this document, which Liele informs us was read once per month at worship
service, is that it was imported from his congregation in Georgia and ratified
by the congregation in Jamaica, which at first was predominantly of fellow
African Americans who migrated with him to Jamaica. The document as cir-
culated by Liele raises the question of whether it was intended primarily for
the master and missionary as a tool to satisfy them that Liele's church was
committed to the terms and conditions of slavery as practiced in Jamaica.
John Parmer Gates puts it succinctly:"George Liele was probably the first
person to do religious work among the slaves in Jamaica. Up to this time there
was not very much effort expended to preach the Gospel even to whites. . . .
Some of the Negroes were undoubtedly not far removed from their primitive
state, . . . Not infrequently drums were heard that beat out the rhythm for
crude sensual dances which, to the whites at times, were dangerously sugges-
tive of earlier African drum beats in preparation for going on the war path.
Belief in witchcraft, the use of charms and other superstitions were common
among them. . . . Even after he was relatively well established as a local
preacher he was charged with teaching sedition and thrown into prison. After
being loaded with irons and put into stocks, during which time he was not
permitted to see his family, he was tried for his life and acquitted. It seems he
had preached on the text, "Brethren, my heart's desire and prayer for Israel is
that they might be saved" (Romans 10:1).[39] It is clear that what was at stake in
the articles of this covenant was the survival of Liele and his church. According to Gates, Liele was tried for his Life, and this covenant was one reason for
his acquittal as it was first submitted to the Jamaica legislature for their approval prior to its adoption by Liele's church. Liele went to extraordinary
means to secure a bell for his church not so much to inform parishioners of
times when church service would commence but to inform masters and overseers when church services would begin and end. "As a result Liele won the
confidence, not only of masters and overseers, but of several influential men

in Kingston. One of these was Stephen Cooke, a member of the Assembly, who, although he preferred the discipline of the Methodist Church, contributed to the building of Liele's sanctuary and later wrote to Dr. Rippon in London in order to help Liele secure funds from the England Baptists."[40] What are we to infer of Liele's catering to the people in power, who were committed to keep slavery in its place? Did he place his own survival above his own people's freedom from slavery? Was the covenant a smokescreen to throw the planter class off guard, while Liele knew full well that his parishioners would not abide by the conditions of the covenant?

There are two ways to understand how this first covenant, produced by an African American preacher, functioned in the Caribbean. The first thing to keep in mind is how Caribbean people functioned in relation to what they would have perceived as a church that had the confidence and blessing of the dominant culture. The church planted by Liele was not an African church, which was concerned primarily with the question of keeping alive African traditions and religious practices in Jamaica. The name of the church, the Ethiopian Baptist Church, and his sermon from Romans chapter 10:1 give an indication that there was an early attempt by Liele to combine the questions, "Where do we stand in relation to Jesus?" with the African question, "Where do we stand in relation to Africa?" This approach not only sought to merge issues of enculturation and acculturation, the search for survival with that of liberation, but it meant that the church combined questions of salvation and social justice. It is clear that Liele began a new tradition in Jamaica and through his disciples in the Bahamas and Trinidad. This was noted in the previous chapter. He introduced something new—how to make the church available to people in the Caribbean as a center for worship and the practice of African ways of being in the world. Perhaps he joined issues of salvation and social justice without meaning to threaten the system of slavery in Jamaica. Did his change of heart, placing his own survival above the liberation of his own people from the clutches of slavery, indicate that the gospel of Jesus became for him a tool of social control?

The hard question is why his people would endorse or support his capitulation to the status quo. One answer is that Caribbean people in general and Jamaicans in particular have always had membership in two churches. On the one hand, they have always supported the church that highlights, "Where do I stand in relation to Jesus?" This church has always represented status for them as it has always been aligned with the dominant culture. Jamaicans have always been proud to identify themselves as Baptist, Methodist, or Anglican although they know full well that these churches, during slavery, often sabotaged and actively worked against their best interests. It is very important to understand the double entendre at work in Liele's covenant; that on the one hand it was a document intended to satisfy the Jamaican legislature, masters and overseers, and on the other hand a framework for the local populace that they would "take with a grain of salt." Liele's congregation knew that things were not necessarily the way they appeared or in the parlance of Caribbean people, "Things ain't what they seem to be."

One of the important contributions that Liele's church made was to combine church with education. His church provided a school for the children of enslaved persons, and this tradition has continued throughout the years because churches were identified with social services. After emancipation in Jamaica, Liele's church took the lead in purchasing large tracts of lands that were subdivided and sold in small portions to ex-slaves. Needless to say, Jamaicans flocked to this church and other churches that participated in this practice of combining salvation and social justice. Another service that Liele's church provided was stated in article xx—that of providing a "burying ground" or cemetery. This was crucial in Jamaica because the majority of enslaved persons were born in Africa and held tenaciously to the sanctity of burial and the importance of treating the dead with respect. For enslaved persons of African ancestry who did not own lands on which to bury their dead, the promise of sacred space on land owned by the church was important for the ancestors because the bottom line was that the land belongs to the ancestors. The central issue of status, the promise of education for children, and a place where one could visit ancestors elicited a compromise from Afro-Jamaicans who understood that "there was seeing beyond seeing"—the world of appearance was usually different from reality.

But enslaved people may have opted to go along with Liele's program because they knew his "hands were tied," and they may have personally rejoiced that he was off death row and no longer "in irons and in stocks." One can imagine how preacher George Liele, who it is said imitated evangelist George Whitfield, described what it was like being in jail, as he sermonized that he was being tried for his life, with the prospect of being hanged for sedition in Jamaica. Perhaps he pointed out that his situation was worse than that of Paul and Silas because there was no possibility of converting his jailors. The church people would have understood that he had to satisfy his accusers and produce language to appease them and in all probability feign his compliance and acceptance of their worldviews. The eminent Caribbean theologian William Watty expresses with clarity and exquisite beauty the ethos that would have informed the production and adoption of this covenant.

Weak and defenseless, kidnapped and alone, the survival of the black man has been due mainly to a combination of outward conformity to white demands and inward skepticism of white systems. In a situation where those who taught him religion had the same origins and largely the same presuppositions as those who held at his head the loaded pistol, his response was to assent readily and publicly with the necessary "Yes Massa," and to feign acceptance of the ready made imported canons of belief and conduct, but *in camera* he whispered to his fellow captives "but it ain't necessarily so."

Expatriates complain about the practice of Christianity in the Caribbean that there is a marked discrepancy between profession and behavior. From time to time, missionaries have found it necessary to fore-shorten their contract, and negotiate a premature return out of frustration and not a little contempt at this apparent inconsistency. Between creed on Sundays and conduct on Mondays there seems to be a great gulf fixed. . . . A theory is propounded here that when theology is part and parcel of the system of colonial domination, then it is a tribute to a people's resilience to be able to survive the impact of colonialism even if it is by dissembling in matters of religion. It is further suggested that, but for that discrepancy, churches, such as they are, could not have been planted in this region.[41]

What was at stake, according to Watty, was the survival of the church and the circumstances of slavery which dictated that Liele would appeal to a framework in which acceptance was feigned and enslaved persons understood "that it ain't necessarily so." What has to be kept in mind, according to Watty, is that Christianity, as it emerged in the New World in general, and in the Caribbean in particular, was an integral part of colonial domination, supported by an anthropology that argued that the appropriate place for Black people was to serve their master within the context of slavery. Very few leaders within the Christian church made the connection between church as the context of salvation for the souls of Black people and social justice. "It was one thing for the Christian conscience to be profoundly shocked and outraged at the logical end of colonialism in the dehumanization of man by man, it was for them an entirely different question to judge the whole system of colonialism as inherently evil, . . . or the dignity of slaves or their descendants as men equal in capacity to all other men and entitled to the same opportunities of self-hood."[42] It is in this context that one has to understand Liele's covenant; that Black people's priority was survival with dignity, and in a situation in which they understood that everything African was treated with scorn and contempt, they willingly said "Yes Massa," understanding that outward conformity did not excise or cancel out a critical appraisal. As it is often said in the Caribbean, "We stoop in order to survive."

But there is a down side to this approach to life which valorizes caricature and mimicry. The problem, says Watty, is that it was a response to the evil of colonization and European domination. While it functioned as a tool for survival in the context of epistemic violence, it compromised one's humanity, because the penchant to live in the nexus of truth and deceit rendered one imitative and uncreative—a necessary reaction inspired by deceit rather than truth. The challenge is to move beyond this double standard and not allow an evil situation to define us, but as faith is lived in the context of history, to allow that faith to redefine and re-create history. One practice has been to allow the history of oppression to dictate the terms of our response to life and thereby live comfortably with untruth.

One wonders if the practice of saying "Yes Massa" when one was not in harmony with what was asked or requested was how the members of the Ethiopian Baptist Church understood article xx. In it they were admonished to practice Christian marriage, which Africans found oppressive and Europeans spurned. In Jamaica, during the eighteenth and nineteenth centuries, neither Whites nor Blacks had any appetite for Christian marriage. James Phillippo, a missionary who was invited to Jamaica by Liele's church, wrote, "Mr Baillie, a large West Indian proprietor, when examined before a Committee of the House of Lords in 1832, was asked the question—'Can you name any overseer, driver, or other person in authority, who does not keep a mistress?' He replied—'I cannot.' . . . The most shameless adultery was everywhere prevalent. This sin was so common that groups of white and mulatto children, legitimate and illegitimate, were frequently claimed by the same father, and all brought up together under the same roof. . . . Unblushing licentiousness, from the Governor downwards."[43] Phillippo indicated that nine out of ten White men practiced concubinage. This was to become a way of life in Jamaica as African women found Christian marriage a form of tyranny. "Alluding to the people of color," says Phillippo in 1823, "few marriages take place among them. Most of the females of color think it more genteel to be the kept mistress of a White man. They view marriage as an unnecessary restraint. Worse than this;—and it can be heard by Christian parents without a thrill of horror?—in hundred of instances, mothers and fathers gave away in friendship, or sold, their daughters at the tenderest age for the worst purpose, or became the guardians of their virtue for a time only."[44] It is quite clear that missionary Phillippo is seeking to make sense of African customs and traditions as they inform marriage. He supports the point that Christian marriage was almost nonexistent even in 1823, and Liele's covenant was presented and adopted by his church much earlier.

But as Watty explains, it was the ethos of extreme oppression, in which Black people could embrace and adopt a covenant they understood was necessary if the church, as envisioned by Liele, was to survive. They understood "that it ain't necessarily so," outward confession did not mean inner conformity. Enslaved persons had two minds, "one for the master and the other one for me."

But what would have made this possible for Africans in Jamaica to agree with Liele was the knowledge that their membership in Liele's church did not preclude their membership in their African church which interpreted the Jesus question from an African frame of reference. Many of the Afrocentric churches met at nights and in secret, and this was where enslaved Jamaicans understood that the central questions of identity and their plans for liberation were born. Mainline churches were formal and membership was nominal. Attendance at the churches that gave the nod to colonial Christianity offered the appearance that one was in harmony with the worldviews of the master class, even when one was planning to overthrow the world that oppressed them. This was the main context in which Afro-Caribbean people gave their own interpretation of Jesus and Africa responding from an African frame of reference.

A Lasting Legacy—Creolization and Faith

According to Drake the sociopolitical situation between Black churches in the Caribbean and the United States were rather similar until after the American War. Drake explains:

> Among the many circumstances that account for the large-scale conversion of Negroes after the Revolution is the fact that plantation communities had suffered considerable disorganization during the war and a general state of restlessness prevailed, and that among Negroes disillusionment and disappointment was widespread over the fact that while the colonies secured their freedom from Britain the blacks remained enslaved. Their social situation was ripe for revivalism and restoration of a sense of solidarity and hope.[45]

The naming of their churches point to a time when Africa as a central element of their identity was crucial: "First *African* Baptist Church, Savannah, Georgia (1788); *African* Baptist Church, Lexington, Kentucky (1790); *Abyssinia* Baptist

Church, New York City, (1800); Free *African* Meeting House, Boston (1805); First *African* Presbyterian Church, Philadelphia (1807); Union Church of *Africans,* Wilmington (1813); First *African* Baptist Church, New Orleans (1826); First *African* Baptist Church, Richmond, Virginia (1841)."[46] Black people accepted themselves as Africans noting that although the egalitarian language of the Declaration of Independence spoke in glowing terms of humanity, in general, they were not accepted by the dominant culture. The period from 1780 to 1830 was one of extraordinary growth for Christianity in the United States when several slaves and former slaves had opportunities to become converts and preachers of the Christian religion. Albert Raboteau supports Drake's claim that the revival after the Revolution had a lasting effect on African American spirituality:

> After the Revolution, revivals continued to occur in the South and increasing numbers of slaves were moved to convert by the dramatic preaching of the revivalist ministers, especially Methodists and Baptists. The emotional excitement of the revivals encouraged those who attended to express their religious feelings. The sight of black and white converts weeping, shouting, fainting, and dancing in ecstatic trances became a familiar feature of the camp meeting revivals—outdoor gatherings for prayer and preaching that attracted large crowds. . . . In this emotionally charged atmosphere, slaves encountered a form of Protestant worship that resembled the religious celebration of their African homelands. The similarity between African and revival styles of worship made Christianity seem more familiar to the slaves and helped them to make sense of this new religion in terms of their old ones.[47]

The form of evangelical Protestantism that may have stirred memories of Africa had the net result of African Americans making connections between African roots and tenets of Protestant Christianity—the sin and guilt complex and notions of life beyond the sky. If we note a distinction between the Christianity of the master and the slave in their interpretation of the Exodus story in which they disagree concerning the locus of Egypt for enslaved Africans— plantations on which they were enslaved, and the promised land being in Africa—it is clear that regarding notions of sin and guilt and the longing for life beyond the sky, master and enslaved were on the same page. It was the experience of learning from the camp meetings and the preachers of the Great Awakening that caused both master and slave to agree that God required repentance of sin and guilt and that the eternal home of those who are saved is heaven, beyond the sky. It is precisely at this point that Raboteau as an interpreter of Afro-American Christianity points out that when Du Bois alluded to the marks of the Black church as the preacher, the frenzy, and music, he omitted conversion to Christianity. I do not believe Du Bois was ever convinced that Africans in the Caribbean and the American colonies converted to Christianity. Members of African churches embraced a pragmatic theology; they took from colonial Christianity elements that they thought necessary for survival but they never abandoned Africa. African churches never became Christian. In this regard it was often the practice for worshippers in African churches to replace Catholic saints with the names of their gods. This may explain why Du Bois omitted conversion as a mark of Black churches. In the colonial church, there was a requirement of confession of sin; in African churches one was possessed by the spirit, and there it was more appropriate to speak of the fourth ingredient beyond the preacher, the music and the frenzy, as an awakening to African consciousness made possible by reliance on spirit power. Enslaved persons in Black churches who were not accountable to mainline churches and who did not see the need to pattern their theology and worship after colonial Christianity did not experience a conversion to Christianity. Indeed, Black Christianity, the interpretation of Christian forms, rituals, and myths from an African frame of reference—an African understanding of spirit, with an emphasis on dancing, drumming, singing and testifying—resulted in an awakening to African spirits and African ways of being. While both experiences required the presence and control of the spirit, the confession of sin and guilt and the hope for heaven were attached to requirements of colonial Christianity and churches that patterned the colonial approach.

We must ask what, if anything, is the lasting legacy of the religion of enslaved persons, trapped on plantations in the Caribbean and the United States? Beyond the shadow of a doubt their seminal contribution is Black churches—the creation of Black sacred spaces through which they were able to restore their stolen dignity and humanity. Because of the agency of Black churches and the critical roles of the slave preacher and medicine person, enslaved persons won the war waged against their humanity by the master class. Black churches provided the framework for meaning making, healing, and a stubborn refusal to settle for estimates of humanity that demeaned and diminished their high calling as family of the ancestors. The challenge was to make sense of their existence in a strange and alien land among people with strange ways, and this pushed them back to African roots. They questioned their gods and experimented with various forms of their religion. They experimented with expressions of faith that were presented by the missionary and the master, but in these activities they were seeking a faith that would redeem their humanity and allow them to embrace freedom and justice as equality and parity with the master class. Religion—African, Christian, or a blending of both—were always in the service of liberation. We have noted throughout this manuscript that there were times when it was propitious for enslaved people to settle for survival in the midst of slavery, but they were persistent—they kept their eyes on freedom. This meant that they did not place an inordinate attention on doctrine, worrying, for example, about the Council of Nicea, or about the intricacies of the doctrine of the trinity. Creeds, doctrines, and rituals made sense if they pointed to and resulted in freedom not only of the soul but of the body. The meaning of the Black religious experience then is that there was sacred space for the dignity and humanity of each person. There was a place for every ritual and doctrine as long as these were viewed through the lens of African awakening aimed at freedom.

But if it is true that Black churches became Black sacred spaces for dreaming of and protesting for the practice of freedom, it is equally true that Black people were expressive about how they felt, because they remembered Africa, and feeling for them was an important index of what was to become of their humanity. They would walk as a group out of St. Georges Methodist Church to their own sacred space, an African society, because it was important for them to feel welcomed. It was important "to feel like a child of God," or "to feel like somebody." They created Black sacred spaces in which they were welcomed and in which they could learn the truth about themselves, that they were not created to be subordinate or subservient but to be creators of history. We noted that enslaved persons had no name that their children had to honor, no name to pass on to their children; they were seen by the dominant culture as nameless, rootless, and faceless. Black men were called boys and Black women girls, as they got older they were called uncles and aunties. They had no names that others were invited to respect. Black people had to learn to see themselves differently—not as things to be used but persons worthy of love and respect. This means they had to acquire new tools to dismantle "the house of bondage" that was constructed for them by the master. As Drake pointed out earlier in this chapter, one of the enduring problems for the Black family was seeking to dismantle the house of bondage with tools provided by the master. It is something of a truism that the hands that enslave find it extremely difficult to liberate. Bob Marley sums up this line of reasoning, in his Exodus Album: "Emancipate yourself from mental slavery, none but ourselves can free our minds." Black churches provided a new context over against the plantation and the big house, in which the cycle of dependency was broken, and Black people began to depend on themselves, create new worldviews, and take steps to liberate themselves.

Within these Black sacred spaces enslaved persons begin to pray, "lead us not into imitation." Whether in the brush arbor or down by the riverside, they would seek to physically and mentally remove themselves from the cruel world of slavery constructed for them by their oppressors. In this new context they concluded that God is freedom as they remembered Africa and were open to an African awakening. Enslaved persons began to realize that Christianity as presented by the missionaries represented the interests of slave owners and therefore had to be handled with care. We noted in the debate between practices of enculturation and acculturation, or in the choice between Africa and Jesus, that enslaved persons had to keep their gaze on the goal of freedom as Jesus, God, spirits, and ancestors had to meet the test of an African awakening, the freedom to be a son and daughter of Africa. This was crucial in the affirmation of their humanity in a context of extreme dehumanization. They discovered that to be free was to be human, noting that humanity's essence was an awakening to an African consciousness

One of the breakthroughs that occurred in the creation of Black sacred spaces, whether in the Caribbean or on the US mainland, and which accelerated the formation of a Black Christianity in distinction from colonial Christianity, was the realization by enslaved persons that the God of their ancestors was the God of the Bible. This allowed them to read the Bible with confidence from an African frame of reference and to regard the Bible as normative and a source for faith and life. It did not matter whether Black people in Louisanna were practicing Vodou or the Native Baptists of Jamaica were rebelling for freedom, enslaved people sought freedom through their ancestors and the God of their ancestors. While they had confidence in their reading and interpretation of the Bible, they did not always trust the missionary's interpretation of Christianity. Enslaved persons discovered early that most missionaries represented the interests of slave owners. While they acknowledged the God of Black Christianity as the God of their ancestors and would often reference the Christian God as the Great Ancestor, they were often unsure about Jesus, as they became aware that Christian churches would manipulate Jesus and use him as a source of social control. This was one reason that enslaved persons preferred their own preachers, believing that their agendas were more in keeping with that of the Black community.

The journey of enslaved persons to freedom and equality was a byproduct of worshipping and missional communities that included variations of enculturation and acculturation, coming to grips with the role of Africa and Jesus in the construction of worldviews and the creation of meaningful centers of value from which they would draw to shape a new humanity. Black churches became centers for healing, rest-havens for weary travelers on the journey to freedom, and places where they met the God of their ancestors as the God of a Black Christianity who was at work restoring their humanity. In these sacred spaces they created their own meaning, their own sacred cosmos.

Notes

INTRODUCTION

1. Albert J. Raboteau, *Canaan Land: A Religious History of African Americans* (New York: Oxford University Press, 2001), 6.
2. Herbert Aptheker, ed., *The Correspondence of W.E.B. Du Bois*, Vol. 1, *1877–1934* (Cambridge, MA: University of Massachusetts Press, 1973), 263.

CHAPTER 1

1. John Clark, W. Dendy, and J. Phillippo, *The Voice of Jubilee: A Narrative of the Baptist Mission, Jamaica from Its Commencement, with Biographical Notices of Its Fathers and Founders* (London: Baptist Missionary Society, 1865), 74.
2. Malcolm Cowley and Daniel P. Mannix, "The Middle Passage," in *The Atlantic Slave Trade*, ed. Daniel Northrop (Lexington, MA: D.C. Heath, 1994), 99.
3. See R. R. Wright Jr., comp., *History of the Sixteenth Episcopal District of the African Methodist Church* (Philadelphia: Bethel A.M.E. Archives, 1964), 15.
4. Ibid.
5. Ibid., 16.
6. Sidney W. Mintz and Richard Price, *The Birth of African-American Culture: An Anthropological Perspective* (Boston, MA: Beacon Press, 1992), 43.
7. Ibid.
8. Ibid., 43–44.
9. C. Eric Lincoln, "Introduction," in *Mighty like a River* by Andrew Billingsley (New York: Oxford University Press, 2003), xxi.
10. Bartolome de Las Casas, *The Devastation of the Indies*, trans. Herman Briffault (Baltimore, MD: Johns Hopkins University Press, 1992), 3.
11. O. A. Sherrard, *Freedom from Fear* (London: The Bodley Head, 1959), 27.
12. Ibid., 28, 29.

13. Las Casas, *The Devastation of the Indies*, 5.

14. Johanes Meir, "The Beginnings of the Catholic Church in the Caribbean," in *Christianity in the Caribbean*, ed. Amando Lampe (Kingston, Jamaica: University of the West Indies Press, 2001), 6–7.

15. Ibid., 6.

16. Ibid., 11.

17. Ibid., 12.

18. Ibid., 12.

19. Ibid., 13.

20. Lewin Williams, *Caribbean Theology* (New York: Peter Lang, 1994), 10.

21. Lampe, *Christianity in the Caribbean*, 18–19.

22. Ibid., 25–26.

23. Arthur Charles Dayfoot, *The Shaping of the West Indian Church 1492–1962* (Kingston, Jamaica: University of the West Indies Press, 1999), 26.

24. Sherrard, *Freedom from Fear*, 33.

25. Bryan Edwards, *The History, Civil and Commercial, of the British Colonies in the West Indies* (London: Stockdale, 1801), Vol.1, 38–39.

26. Lampe, *Christianity in the Caribbean*, 45.

27. Ibid., 47.

28. Williams, *Caribbean Theology*, 10.

29. Dale Bisnauth, *A History of Religions in the Caribbean* (Kingston, Jamaica: Kingston Publishers, 1989), 11.

30. Herbert Klein, *Slavery in the Americas* (Chicago: University of Chicago Press, 1967), 99–100.

31. Noel Leo Erskine, *Decolonizing Theology* (Trenton, NJ: Africa World Press, 1998), 39–40.

32. Bisnauth, *A History of Religions in the Caribbean*, 81.

33. Walter Hark, *The Breaking of the Dawn* (Kingston: Jamaica Moravian Church, 1904), 28.

34. See W. E. Burghardt Du Bois, *The Negro Church* (Atlanta, GA: Atlanta University Press, 1903).

35. Ibid., 4

36. Bettina E. Schmidt, "The Creation of Afro-Caribbean Religions and Their Incorporation of Christian Elements: A Critique against Syncretism," *Transformation* 23 (October 4, 2006): 238.

37. Ibid., 238.

38. Dianne M. Stewart, *Three Eyes for the Journey: African Dimensions of the Jamaican Religious Experience* (New York: Oxford University Press, 2005), 24.

CHAPTER 2

1. For an excellent review of these stories, see J. Omosade Awolalu and P. Adelumo Dopamu, *West African Traditional Religion* (Ibadan, Nigeria: Onibonoje Press &

Book Industries, 1979). The Yoruba contend that these stories happened in Ile-Ife,the village in which I lived during my sabbatical.

2. Harry Sawyer, *Creative Evangelism* (London: Lutterworth Press, 1968), 14.

3. Ibid., 15.

4. Ibid., 16.

5. Ibid., 18.

6. Ibid., 18.

7. Ibid., 18.

8. John S. Mbiti, *African Religions and Philosophy* (New York: Doubleday, 1969), 28–29.

9. Kwesi Dickson and Paul Ellingworth, eds., *Biblical Revelation and African Beliefs* (London: Lutterworth Press, 1969), 160.

10. Ibid., 161.

11. Ibid., 163.

12. Ibid., 163.

13. Ibid., 165.

14. Ibid., 169.

15. Kwesi A. Dickson, *Aspects of Religion and Life in Africa* (Accra, Ghana:Ghana Academy of Arts and Sciences, 1977), 5.

16. Ibid., 5.

17. Ibid., 6.

18. Ibid., 7.

19. Ibid., 8.

20. Ibid., 8.

21. Ibid., 8.

22. Ibid., 11.

23. Ibid., 11.

24. Ibid., 11–12.

25. Awolalu and Dopamu, *West African Traditional Religion*, 117–118.

26. Ibid., 119.

27. Kwame Gyekye, *An Essay on African Philosophical Thought* (Cambridge: Cambridge University Press, 1987), 107–108.

28. Ibid., 112.

29. Ibid., 114.

30. Ibid., 114.

31. Ibid., 116.

32. Ibid., 116.

33. Dickson and Paul Ellingworth, *Biblical Revelation and African Beliefs*, 41–42.

34. Ibid., 30–46.

35. Ibid., 42.

36. Stephen N. Ezeanya "God, Spirits and the Spirit World," in *Biblical Revelations and African Beliefs*, ed. Kwesi Dickson and Paul Ellingworth (London: Lutterworth Press, 1969), 36.

37. Awolalu and Dopamu, *West African Traditional Religion*, 274.

38. Ibid., 275.

39. Ibid., 276.

40. Ibid., 278.

41. See Vincent Mulago, "Traditional African Religion and Christianity," in *African Traditional Religions in Contemporary Society*, ed. Jacob K. Olupona (New York: Paragon House 1991), 121.

42. Harry Sawyer, *Creative Evangelism* (London: Lutterworth Press, 1968), 29.

43. John S. Mbiti, *New Testament Eschatology in an African Background* (London: Oxford University Press, 1971).

44. Mbiti, *African Religions and Philosophy*, 127.

45. Cited in G. E. Phillips, *The Old Testament in the World Church* (Guildford: Lutterworth, 1942), 6.

46. Kwesi A Dickson, *Theology in Africa*, Maryknoll, N.Y. Orbis Books, 1984. 148–149.

47. Ibid., 156.

48. John W. Blassingame, *The Slave Community* (New York: Oxford University Press, 1972), 66. Blassingame uses the term Latin America rather broadly as he includes not only countries in South America but also Cuba, the Bahamas, and Santo Domingo.

49. Ibid., 67.

50. Orlando Patterson, *The Sociology of Slavery* (London: McGibbon and Kee, 1967).

51. Blassingame, *The Slave Community*, 68.

52. Ibid., 72–73.

53. Philip Curtin, *Two Jamaicas* (Cambridge, MA: Harvard University Press, 1955), 169.

54. Herbert S. Klein, *Slavery in the Americas* (Chicago: University of Chicago Press, 1967), 120.

55. Ibid., 121.

56. Joseph B. Earnest Jr., *The Religious Development of the Negro in Virginia* (Charlottesville, VA: Michie, 1914), 12.

57. W. E. Burghardt Du Bois, *The Negro Church* (Atlanta, GA: Atlanta University Press, 1903), 5.

58. Ibid., 6.

59. Bolaji Idowu, *Towards an Indigenous Church* (London: Oxford University Press, 1965), 7.

60. J. K. Agbete, "African Theology: What It Is," in *Presence, Vol.3*, ed. Bethuel A. Kiplagat (Nairobi, Kenya: World Student Christian Federation, 1969), 7.

CHAPTER 3

1. Henry Louis Gates Jr., *Black in Latin America* (New York: New York University Press, 2011), 2.

2. Barry Chevannes, *Betwixt and Between: Explorations in an African-Caribbean Mindscape* (Kingston, Jamaica: Ian Randle, 2006), 7.

3. Winston James, *Holding Aloft the Banner of Ethiopia* (London: Verso, 1998), 9–11.

4. Ibid., 11.

5. George Reid Andrews, *Afro-Latin America 1800–2000* (New York: Oxford University Press, 2004), 19.

6. Ibid., 67–68.

7. Ibid., 68.

8. Ibid., 69.

9. Ibid., 70.

10. Gates, *Black in Latin America*, 191.

11. Andrews, *Afro-Latin America*, 72–73.

12. George Eaton Simpson, *Black Religions in the New World* (New York: Columbia University Press, 1978).

13. Ibid., 18–19.

14. Ibid., 19.

15. Cited in Kingsley Lewis, *The Moravian Mission in Barbados 1816–1886* (Frankfurt: Verlag Peter Lang, 1985), 53.

16. Ibid., 53.

17. Johannes Meier, "The Beginnings of the Catholic Church in the Caribbean," in *Christianity in the Caribbean*, ed. Armando Lampe (Barbados and Jamaica: University of the West Indies Press, 2001), 42.

18. Charles Joyner, "Believer I Know. The Emergence of African-American Christianity," in *African American Christianity*, ed. Paul E. Johnson (Berkeley: University of California Press, 1994), 22.

19. Ibid., 48–49.

20. Ibid., 49.

21. Philip S. Foner, ed., *The Life and Writings of Frederick Douglass*, Vol.II. *Pre-Civil War Decade 1850–1860* (New York: International, 1975), 197.

22. Harriet A. Jacobs, *Incidents in the Life of a Slave Girl* (Cambridge, MA: Harvard University Press, 1987), 68–69.

23. Ibid., 69.

24. Noel Leo Erskine, "Christologies in the Caribbean Islands: History," in *The Cambridge Dictionary of Christianity*, ed. Daniel Patte (New York: Cambridge University Press, 2010), 221.

25. Jacobs, *Incidents in the Life of a Slave Girl*, 70.

26. Ibid., 70.

27. Ibid., 71.

28. Carter G. Woodson, *The History of the Negro Church* (Washington, DC: Associated Publishers, 1921), 6–7.

29. Ibid., 25.

30. Ibid., 26.

31. Ibid., 30.

32. Ibid., 40–41.

33. Charles Joyner, "Believer I Know, the Emergence of African-American Christianity," in *African-American Christianity*, ed. Paul E. Johnson (Berkeley: University of California Press, 1994), 21.

34. Carter G. Woodson and Charles H. Wesley, *The Negro in Our History* (Washington, DC: Associated Publishers, 1962), 147–148.

35. Albert J. Raboteau, *Slave Religion* (New York: Oxford University Press, 1978), 152.

36. Ibid., 153.

37. Ibid., 162.

38. Ibid., 162–163.

39. Margaret Washington, "Community Regulation and Cultural Specialization in Gullah Folk Religion," in *African-American Christianity*, ed. Paul E. Johnson (Berkeley: University of California Press, 1994), 50.

40. Ibid., 50.

41. Albert J. Raboteau, *Slave Religion* (New York: Oxford University Press, 1978), 213.

42. Mechal Sobel, *Trabelin' On: The Slave Journey to an Afro-Baptist Faith* (Princeton, NJ: Princeton University Press, 1988), 102.

43. Walter Brooks, "The Priority of the Silver Bluff Church and Its Promoters," *Journal of Negro History* 7 (April 2, 1922): 172–196, 181.

44. Walter H. Brooks, "The Evolution of the Negro Baptist Church," *Journal of Negro History* 7. (January 1, 1922): 11–22, 17.

45. Brooks, "The Priority of the Silver Bluff Church," 174.

46. Alfred Lane Pugh, *Pioneer Preachers in Paradise* (Peoria, IL: Versa Press, 2003), 3.

47. John Parmer Gates, "George Liele: A Pioneer Negro Preacher," *Chronicle* 5, no. 3 (1943): 118–129, 118.

48. Brooks, "The Priority of the Silver Bluff Church," 176.

49. Charles O. Walker, "Georgia's Religion in the Colonial Era, 1733–1790," *Viewpoints: Georgia Baptist Historical Society* 5 (1976): 17–44, 31.

50. Ibid., 31–32.

51. Ibid., 33.

52. Alfred L. Pugh, "The Great Awakening and Baptist Beginnings in Colonial Georgia, the Bahama Islands, and Jamaica (1739–1833)," *American Baptist Quarterly* 26, no. 4 (Winter 2007): 357–373, 367.

53. Pugh, *Pioneer Preachers in Paradise*, 12.

54. Pugh, "The Great Awakening and Baptist Beginnings," 369, 371.

55. Ibid., 371.

56. Brooks, "The Priority of the Silver Bluff Church," 185.

57. Ibid., 194–195.

58. Pugh, "The Great Awakening and Baptist Beginnings," 372.

59. Jim Lawlor, "Shadrach Kerr: Priest and Missionary," *American Baptist Quarterly* 26, no. 4 (Winter 2007): 388–402, 392–393.

60. Ibid., 388.

61. Ernest Payne, "Baptist Work in Jamaica before the Arrival of the Missionaries," *Baptist Quarterly Incorporating the Transactions of the Baptist Historical Society*, New Series, 7 (1934–35): 20–26, 21.

62. Leonard E. Barrett, *Soul-Force* (Garden City, NY: Anchor Press/Doubleday, 1974), 66–67.

63. Winston Lawson, *Religion and Race* (New York: Peter Lang, 1996), 25.

64. Philip D. Curtin, *Two Jamaicas* (New York: Atheneum, 1970), 33.

65. W. J. Gardner, *A History of Jamaica* (London: T. Fisher, 1873), 344.

66. Curtin, *Two Jamaicas*, 33.

67. Ibid., 33–34.

68. Hazel Bennett and Philip Sherlock, *The Story of the Jamaican People* (Kingston, Jamaica: Ian Randle, 1998), 214.

69. Ibid., 214.

70. Curtin, *Two Jamaicas*, 86.

71. Bennett and Sherlock, *The Story of the Jamaican People*, 216.

72. John Howard Hinton, *Memoir of William Knibb* (London: Houston and Stoneman, 1847), 118.

73. Trevor Munroe and Don Robothan, *Struggles of the Jamaican People* (Kingston, Jamaica: E.P. Printery, 1976), 6.

74. Gardner, *A History of Jamaica*, 348.

CHAPTER 4

1. W. E. Burghardt Du Bois, *The Negro Church* (Atlanta, GA: Atlanta University Press, 1903), 5.

2. Ibid., 3.

3. Ibid., 4.

4. Ibid., 4.

5. Thomas L. Webber, *Deep like the Rivers* (New York: W.W. Norton, 1978), 28.

6. Ibid., 28.

7. Ibid., 28–29.

8. Ibid., 29.

9. Ibid., 29.

10. Ibid., 30.

11. Ibid., 31.

12. Ibid., 32–33.

13. Ibid., 34–35.

14. Charles F. Jenkins, *Tortola: A Quaker Experiment of Long Ago in the Tropics* (London: Friends Bookshop, 1923), 52.

15. Herbert S. Klein, *Slavery in the Americas* (Chicago: University of Chicago Press, 1967), 38–39.

16. Ibid., 39.

17. Ibid., 40.

18. Ibid., 41.

19. Edward Long, *The History of Jamaica* (London: Lowndes, 1774), Vol. 2, 288–289.

20. Klein, *Slavery in the Americas*, 41.

21. Ibid., 42.

22. Ibid., 43.

23. Ibid., 46.

24. Ibid., 47.

25. Ibid., 51.

26. Webber, *Deep like the Rivers*, 35.

27. Ibid., 36.

28. Ibid., 36.

29. Ibid., 38.

30. Cited by Joseph Augustine Fahy, "The Antislavery Thought of Jose Agustin Cabellero, Juan Jose Diaz De Espada, and Felix Varela, in Cuba, 1791–1823," diss., Harvard University Divinity School, 1983, 22.

31. Orlando Patterson, "The Constituent Elements of Slavery," in *Caribbean Slavery in the Atlantic World*, ed. VereneShepherd and Hilary McD. Beckles (Kingston, Jamaica: Ian Randle, 2000), 32.

32. Ibid., 33.

33. Ibid., 34.

34. Ibid., 34.

35. Ibid., 35.

36. Ibid., 38–39.

37. E. Franklin Frazier, *The Negro Church in America*/C. Eric Lincoln, *The Black Church since Frazier* (New York: Shocken Books, 1974), 10.

38. Jon F. Sensbach, *Rebecca's Revival: Creating Black Christianity in the Atlantic World* (Cambridge, MA: Harvard University Press, 2005), 10.

39. Sensbach, *Rebecca's Revival*, 23.

40. Ibid., 23.

41. John W. Blassingame, *The Slave Community* (New York: Oxford University Press, 1972), 75.

42. Ibid., 75.

43. Ibid., 79.

44. Ibid., 81.

45. Ibid., 81.

46. Ibid., 83.
47. Albert J. Raboteau, *Canaan Land: A Religious History of African Americans* (New York: Oxford University Press, 2001), 14.
48. Blassingame, *The Slave Community*, 84.
49. Ibid., 86.
50. Ibid., 86.
51. Raboteau, *Canaan Land*, 13.
52. Ibid., 15.
53. Ibid., 16–17.

CHAPTER 5

1. Sidney W. Mintz, *Caribbean Transformations* (New York: Columbia University Press, 1989), 21.
2. Ibid., 21.
3. Eugene Genovese, *Roll, Jordan, Roll* (New York: Pantheon Books, 1974), 88.
4. W.E. Burghardt Du Bois, *The Negro Church* (Atlanta, GA: Atlanta University Press, 1903), 5.
5. I.E. Franklin Frazier, The Negro Church in America & C.Eric Lincoln, The Black Church Since Frazier, New York: Schocken Books. 1974. 9
6. Ibid., 9.
7. Ibid., 9–10.
8. Malcolm Cowley and Daniel P. Mannix, "The Middle Passage," in *The Atlantic Slave Trade*, ed. David Northrup (Lexington, MA: D.C. Heath, 1994), 99.
9. Frazier, *The Negro Church in America*, 10.
10. Ibid., 10.
11. Ibid., 10–11.
12. Ibid., 11.
13. Ibid., 11.
14. Eric Foner, *Nothing but Freedom* (Baton Rouge: Louisiana State University Press, 1983), 10.
15. E. Franklin Frazier, The Negro Church in America, 13
16. Du Bois, *The Negro Church*, 5.
17. Ibid., 6.
18. Leonard Barrett, *Soul-Force* (Garden City, NY: Anchor Press/Doubleday, 1974), 64–65.
19. M.G. Lewis, *Journal of a West Indian Proprietor* (Boston, MA: Houghton Mifflin, 1929), 126. For a fuller discussion of Obeah, see Noel Leo Erskine, *From Garvey to Marley: Rastafari Theology* (Gainesville: University Press of Florida, 2005).
20. Lawrence W. Levine, *Black Culture and Black Consciousness* (New York: Oxford University Press, 1977), 57.

21. W.E.B. DuBois, The Souls of Black Folk, New York: Bantham Books,1989. 138

22. Levine, Black Culture and Black Consciousness, 58

23. Sterling Stuckey, *Slave Culture* (New York: Oxford University Press, 1987), 254–255.

24. Betty Collier-Thomas, *Jesus, Jobs, and Justice* (New York: Alfred A. Knopf, 2010), –5.

25. James M. Phillippo, *Jamaica: Its Past and Present State* (London: John Snow 1843; reprinted, Westport, CT: Negro University Press, 1970), 147–148.

26. William E. Montgomery, *Under Their Own Vine and Fig Tree: The African American Church in the South 1865–1900* (Baton Rouge: Louisiana State University Press, 1993), 33.

27. Ibid., 34.

28. Collier-Thomas, *Jesus, Jobs and Justice*, 6–7.

29. Ibid., 7.

30. Ibid., 7.

31. Armando Lampe, "Caribbean Islands and West Indies," in *The Cambridge Dictionary of Christianity*, ed. Daniel Patte (New York: Cambridge University Press, 2010), 171.

32. Philip Curtin, *Two Jamaicas* (Cambridge, MA: Harvard University Press, 1955), 162.

33. Ibid., 169.

34. Walter Hark, *The Breaking of the Dawn 1754–1904* (Kingston, Jamaica: Jamaica Moravian Church Press, 1904), 90.

35. Levine, *Black Culture and Black Consciousness*, 61.

36. Ibid., 61.

37. Ibid., 63.

38. Hark, *The Breaking of the Dawn*, 92–93.

39. Margarite Fernandez Olmos and Lizabeth Paravisini-Gebert, *Creole Religions in the Caribbean: An Introduction from Vodou and Santeria to Obeah and Espiritismo* (New York: New York University Press, 2003). 102

40. Ibid., 103.

41. Ibid., 103.

42. Ibid., 104.

43. Stuckey, *Slave Culture*, 43.

44. Ibid., 44.

45. Ibid., 50–51.

46. Gayraud S. Wilmore, *Black Religion and Black Radicalism* (Garden City, NY: Doubleday, 1972), 82.

47. Ibid., 74–75.

48. Ibid., 75

49. Ibid., 76.

50. Herbert Aptheker, *American Negro Slave Revolts*, New York: International Publishers, 1983. 294.

51. Ibid., 296.

52. Ibid., 296–297.

53. Wilmore, *Black Religion and Black Radicalism*, 89.

54. Ibid., 94.

55. See "The Confessions of Nat Turner," in *Afro-American History*, ed. Thomas R. Frazier (Belmont, CA: Wadsworth/Thomson Learning, 1971), 53.

56. Albert J. Raboteau, *A Fire in the Bones: Reflections on African-American Religious History* (Boston, MA: Beacon Press, 1995), 32.

57. Frazier, *Afro-American History*, 54.

58. Ibid., 55.

CHAPTER 6

1. St. Clair Drake, *The Redemption of Africa and Black Religion* (Chicago: Third World Press, 1970), 19.

2. Ibid., 29.

3. Albert J. Raboteau, *Canaan Land: A Religious History of African Americans* (New York: Oxford University Press, 2001), 53–54.

4. Ibid., 55.

5. Ibid., 55.

6. Drake, The Redemption of Africa and Black Religion, 20.

7. Ibid., 20.

8. W.E.B. Du Bois, *The Souls of Black Folks* (New York: Bantam Books,1989; originally published 1903), 137–138.

9. Sterling Stuckey, *Slave Culture* (New York: Oxford University Press, 1987), 258–259.

10. Melville J. Herskovits, *The Myth of the Negro Past* (Boston, MA: Beacon Press, 1958), 111.

11. Ibid., 112.

12. Ibid., 112.

13. Ibid., 113.

14. Ibid., 113.

15. Ibid., 113–114.

16. Ibid., 114.

17. Ibid., 114.

18. Ibid., 115.

19. Ibid., 115–116.

20. Martha Warren Beckwith, *Black Road Ways: A Study of Jamican Folk Life* (Chapel Hill: University of North Carolina Press, 1929), 208.

21. Herskovits, *The Myth of the Negro Past*, 120.

22. Ibid., 120.

23. Ibid., 120.

24. Ibid., 121.

25. Ibid.,121.

26. Ibid., 122.

27. Ibid., 141.

28. Sister Kelly, "Proud of that 'Ole Time' Religion," in *Afro-American Religious History: A Documentary Witness*, ed. Milton C. Sernett (Durham, NC: Duke University Press, 1985), 70.

29. Frederick Douglass, "Slaveholding Religion and the Christianity of Christ," in *Afro-American Religious History: A Documentary Witness*, ed. Milton C. Sernett (Durham, NC: Duke University Press, 1885), 101, 103.

30. Kelly, "Proud of the 'Ole Time' Religion," 71.

31. Drake, *The Redemption of Africa and Black Religion*, 22.

32. Ibid., 22.

33. Love Henry Whelchel Jr., *Hell without Fire: Conversions in Slave Religion* (Nashville, TN: Abingdon Press, 2002), 63.

34. Albert J. Raboteau, *A Fire in the Bones* (Boston, MA: Beacon Press, 1995), 81.

35. John Parmer Gates, "George Liele: A Pioneer Negro Preacher," *Chronicle* 5, no. 3 (1943): 118–129, 124.

36. Walter H. Brooks, *The Silver Bluff Church: A History of the Negro Baptist Churches in America* (Washington, DC: Press of R L Pendleton, 1910), 8, 9.

37. Mechal Sobel, *Trabelin' On: The Slave Journey to an Afro-Baptist Faith* (Princeton, NJ: Princeton University Press, 1988), 104–105.

38. Ernest A. Payne, "Baptist Work in Jamaica before the Arrival of the Missionaries." *Baptist Quarterly Incorporating the Transactions of the Baptist Historical Society*, New Series, 7 (1934–1935): 20–26, 24–26.

39. Gates, "George Liele," 123, 124.

40. Ibid., 124–125.

41. William W. Watty, "The De-Colonization of Theology," in *Troubling of the Waters*, ed. Idris Hamid (Trinidad, W.I.: Rahaman Printery, 1973), 49–50.

42. Ibid., 62.

43. James M. Phillippo, *Jamaica, Its Past and Present State* (Westport, CT: Negro University Press, 1843), 124–125.

44. Ibid., 148–149.

45. Ibid., Drake, The Redemption of Africa and Black Religion, 25.

46. Ibid., 26.

47. Albert J. Raboteau, *Canaan Land: A Religious History of African Americans* (New York: Oxford University Press, 2001), 18.

Bibliography

Bethuel A. Kiplagat, ed. "African Theology: What It Is." *Presence. Vol. 3*, Nairobi, Kenya: World Student Christian Federation, 1969: 7.

Andrews, George Reid. *Afro-Latin America 1800–2000*. New York: Oxford University Press, 2004.

Aptheker, Herbert ed. *The Correspondence of W.E.B. Du Bois. Vol. 1, 1877–1934*. Cambridge, MA: University of Massachusetts Press, 1973.

Aptheker, Herbert American Negro Slave Revolts, New York: International Publishers, 1983.

Awolalu, J. Omodade, and P. Adelumo Dopamu. *West African Traditional Religion*. Ibadan: Nigeria: Onibonoje Press & Book Industries, 1979.

Barrett, Leonard. *Soul-Fource*. Garden City, NY: Anchor Press/Doubleday, 1974.

Beckwith, Martha Warren. *Black Roadways: A Study of Jamaican Folk Life*. Chapel Hill: University of North Carolina Press, 1929.

Bennett, Hazel, and Philip Sherlock. *The Story of the Jamaican People*. Kingston, Jamaica: Ian Randle, 1998.

Bisnauth, Dale. *A History of Religions in the Caribbean*. Kingston, Jamaica: Kingston Publishers, 1989.

Blassingame, John W. *The Slave Community*. New York: Oxford University Press, 1972.

Brooks, Walter H. "The Evolution of the Negro Baptist Church." *Journal of Negro History*, Vol. 7, No. 1, 1922: 11–22.

Brooks, Walter H. "The Priority of the Silver Bluff Church and Its Promoters." *Journal of Negro History*, Vol. 7, No. 2, 1922: 172–196.

Chevannes, Barry. *Betwixt and Between: Explorations in an African-Caribbean Mindscape*. Kingston: Ian Randle, 2006.

Clark, John, W. Dendy, and J. Phillippo. *The Voice Jubilee: A Narrative of the Baptist Mission, Jamaica from Its Commencement, with Biographical Notices of Its Fathers and Founders*. London: Baptist Missionary Society, 1865.

Collier-Thomas, Betty. *Jesus, Jobs, and Justice*. New York: Alfred A. Knopf, 2010.

"The Confessors of Nat Turner." In *Afro-American History*, ed. Thomas R. Frazier. Belmont, CA: Wadsworth, 1988.

Cowley, Malcolm, and Daniel P. Mannix. "The Middle Passage." In *The Atlantic Slave Trade*, ed. Daniel Northrup, 99. Lexington, MA: D.C. Heath, 1994.

Curtin, Philip. *Two Jamaicas*. Cambridge, MA: Harvard University Press, 1955.

Curtin, Philip D. *Two Jamaicas*. New York: Atheneum, 1970.

Dayfoot, Arthur Charles. *The Shaping of the West Indian Church 1492–1962*. Kingston, Jamaica: The Press University of the West Indies, 1999.

De Las Casas, Bartolome, and Herman Briffault, trans. *The Devastation of the Indies*. Baltimore, MD: Johns Hopkins University Press, 1992.

Dickson, Kwesi A. *Aspects of Religion and Life in Africa*. Accra: Ghana: Ghana Academy of Arts and Sciences, 1977.

Kwesi A. Dickson, Theology in Africa, (Maryknoll, N.Y.: Orbis Books, 1984).

Dickson, Kwesi, and Paul Ellingworth, eds. *Biblical Revelation and African Beliefs*. London: Lutterworth, 1969.

Douglass, Frederick. "Slaveholding Religion and the Christianity of Christ." In *Afro-American Religious History: A Documentary Witness*, ed. Milton C. Sernett, 103. Durham, NC: Duke University Press, 1885.

Drake, St. Clair. *The Redemption of Africa and Black Religion*. Chicago: Third World Press, 1970.

Du Bois, W.E. Burghardt. *The Negro Church*. Atlanta: Atlanta University Press, 1903.

Du Bois, W.E.B. *The Souls of Black Folks*. New York: Bantam Books, 1989.

Earnest, Joseph B. Jr. *The Religious Development of the Negro in Virginia*. Charlottesville, VA: Michie, 1914.

Edwards, Bryan. *The History, Civil and Commercial, of the British Colonies in the West Indies*. London: Stockdale, 1801.

Erskine, Noel Leo. "Christologies in the Caribbean Islands: History." In *The Cambridge Dictionary of Christianity*, ed. Daniel Patte, 221. New York: Cambridge University Press, 2010.

Erskine, Noel Leo. *Decolonizing Theology*. Trenton, NJ: Africa World Press, 1998.

Erskine, Noel Leo. *From Garvey to Marley: Rastafari Theology*. Gainesville: University Press of Florida, 2005 .

Ezeanya, Stephen N. "God, Spirits and the Spirit World." In *Biblical Revelation and African Beliefs*, ed. Kwesi Dickson and Paul Ellingworth, 274–278. London: Lutterworth Press, 1969.

Fahy, Jaul Augustine. *The Antislavery Thought of Jose Agustin Cabellero, Juan Jose Diaz De Espada, and Felix Varela, in Cuba 1791–1823*. Dissertation, Cambridge, MA, Harvard University Divinity School, 1983.

Foner, Eric, ed. *Nothing but Freedom*. Baton Rouge: Louisiana State University Press, 1983.

Foner, Philip S. *The Life and Writings of Frederick Douglass, Vol. 11.* New York: International Publishers, 1975.

Frazier, E. Franklin. *The Negro Church in America*/C. Eric Lincoln, *The Black Church since Frazier.* New York: Schocken Books, 1974.

Gardner, W. J. *A History of Jamaica.* London: T. Fisher, 1873.

Gates, Henry Louis Jr. *Black in Latin America.* New York: New York University Press, 2011.

Gates, John Parmer. "George Liele: A Pioneer Negro Preacher." *The Chronicle*, Vol. 6, No. 3, 1943: 118–129.

Genovese, Eugene. *Roll, Jordan, Roll.* New York: Pantheon Books, 1974.

Gyekye, Kwame. *An Essay on African Philosophical Thought.* Cambridge: Cambridge University Press, 1987.

Hark, Walter. *The Breaking of the Dawn 1754–1904.* Kingston, Jamaica: Jamaica Moravian Church, 1904.

Herskovits, Melville J. *The Myth of the Negro Past.* Boston: Beacon Press, 1958.

Hinton, John Howard. *Memoir of William Knibb.* London: Houston and Stoneman, 1847.

Idowu, Bolaji. *Towards an Indigenous Church.* London: Oxford University Press, 1965.

Jacobs, Harriet A. *Incidents in the Life of a Slave Girl.* Cambridge, MA: Harvard University Press, 1987.

James, Winston. *Holding Aloft the Banner of Ethiopia.* London: Verso, 1998.

Jenkins, Charles F. *Tortola: A Quaker Experiment of Long Ago in the Tropics.* London: Friends Bookshop, 1923.

Joyner, Charles. "Believer I Know: The Emergence of African-American Christianity." In *African American Christianity*, ed. Paul E. Johnson, 22. Berkeley: University of California Press, 1994.

Kelly, Sister. "Proud of that 'Ole Time' Religion." In *Afro-American Religious History: A Documentary History Witness*, ed. Milton C. Sernett, 70. Durham: Duke University Press, 1985.

Klein, Herbert. *Slavery in the Americas.* Chicago: University of Chicago Press, 1967.

Lampe, Armando. "Caribbean Islands and West Indies." In *The Cambridge Dictionary of Christianity*, ed. Daniel Patte, 171. New York: Cambridge University Press, 2010.

Lawlor, Jim. "Shadrach Kerr: Priest and Missionary." *American Baptist Quarterly*, Vol. 24, No. 4, 2007: 388–402.

Lawson, Winston. *Religion and Race.* New York: Peter Lang, 1996.

Levine, Lawrence W. *Black Culture and Black Consciousness.* New York: Oxford University Press, 1977.

Lewis, Kingsley. *The Moravian Mission in Barbados 1816–1886.* Frankfurt: Verlag Peter Lang, 1985.

Lewis, M. G. *Journal of a West Indian Proprietor.* Boston: Houghton Mifflin, 1929.

Lincoln, C. Eric. "Introduction." In *Mighty like a River: The Black Church and Social Reform*, by Andrew Billingsley. New York: Oxford University Press, 2003.

Long, Edward. *The History of Jamaica*. London: Lowndes, 1774.

Mbiti, John S. *African Religions and Philosophy*. New York: Doubleday, 1969.

Mbiti, John S. *New Testament Eschatology in an African Background*. London: Oxford University Press, 1971. Meier, Johannes. "The Beginnings of the Catholic Church in the Caribbean." In *Christianity in the Caribbean*, ed. Amando Lampe. Kingston, Jamaica: University of the West Indies Press, 2001.

Mintz, Sidney W. *Caribbean Transformations*. New York: Columbia University Press, 1989.

Mintz, Sidney W., and Richard Price. *The Birth of African-American Culture: An Anthropological Perspective*. Boston: Beacon Press, 1992.

Montgomery, William E. *Under Their Own Vine and Fig Tree: The African American Church in the South 1865–1900*. Baton Rouge, LA: Louisiana University Press, 1992

Mulago, Vincent. "Traditional African Religion and Christianity." In *African Traditional Religions in Contempory Society*, ed. Jacob K.Olupona, 121. New York: Paragon House, 1991.

Munroe, Trevor, and Don Robothan. *Struggles of the Jamaican People*. Kingston, Jamaica: E.P. Printery, 1976.

Olmos, Margarite Fernandez, and Elizabeth Paravisini-Gebert. *Creole Religions in the Caribbean: An Introduction from Vodou and Santeria to Obeah and Espiritismo*. New York: New York University Press, 2003.

Patterson, Orlando. "The Constituent Elements of Slavery." In *Caribbean Slavery in the Atlantic World*, eds. Verene Shepherd and Hilary McD. Beckles, 32. Kingston: Ian Randle Publishers, 2000.

Patterson, Orlando. *The Sociology of Slavery*. London: McGibbon and Kee, 1967. Payne, Ernest. "Baptist Work in Jamaica before the Arrival of the Missionaries." *The Baptist Quarterly Incorporating the Transactions of the Baptist Historical Society New Series*, Vol. 7, 1934–35: 20–26.

Phillippo, James M. *Jamaica: Its Past and Present State*. Westport, CT: Negro University Press, 1843.

Phillips, G. E. *The Old Testament in the World Church*. Guildford: Lutterworth, 1942.

Pugh, Alfred L. "The Great Awakening and Baptist Beginnings in Colonial Georgia, the Bahama Islands and Jamaica (1739–1833)." *American Baptist Quarterly*, Vol. 26, No. 4, 2007: 357–373.

Pugh, Alfred Lane. *Pioneer Preachers in Paradise*. Peoria, IL: Versa Press, 2003.

Raboteau, Albert J. *Canaan Land: A Religious History of African Americans*. New York: Oxford University Press, 2001.

Raboteau, Albert J. *Slave Religion*. New York: Oxford University Press, 1978. Raboteau, Albert J. *A Fire in the Bones: Reflections on African-American Religious History*. Boston: Beacon Press, 1995.

Sawyer, Harry. *Creative Evangelism*. London: Lutterworth Press, 1968.

Schmidt, Bettina E. "The Creation of Afro-Caribbean Religions and Their Incorporation of Christian Elements: A Critique against Syncretism." *Transformation*, October 2006: 238.

Sensbach, Jon F. *Rebecca's Revival: Creating Black Christianity in the Atlantic World*. Cambridge, MA: Harvard University, 2005.

Shannon, David. ed. *George Liele's Life and Legacy*. Macon, GA: Mercer University Press, 2012.

Sherrard, O. A. *Freedom from Fear*. London: The Bodley Head, 1959.

Simpson, George Eaton. *Black Religions in the New World*. New York: Columbia University Press, 1978.

Sobel, Mechal. *Trabelin' On: The Slave Journey to an Afro-Baptist Faith*. Princeton, NJ: Princeton University Press, 1988.

Stewart, Dianne M. *Three Eyes for the Journey: African Dimensions of the Jamaican Religious Experience*. New York: Oxford University Press, 2005.

Stuckey, Sterling. *Slave Culture*. New York: Oxford University Press, 1987.

Walker, Charles O. "Georgia's Religion in the Colonial Era, 1733–1790." *Viewpoints: Georgia Baptist Historical Society*, Vol. 5, 1976: 17–44.

Washington, Margaret. "Community Regulation and Cultural Specialization in Gullah Folk Religion." In *African-American Christianity*, ed. Paul E Johnson, 50. Berkeley: University of California Press, 1994.

Watty, William W. "The De-Colonization of Theology." In *Troubling of the Waters*, ed. Idris Hamid, 49–50. San Fernando: Trinidad and Tobago: W.I. Rahaman Printery, 1973.

Webber, Thomas L. *Deep like the Rivers*. New York: W. W. Norton, 1978.

Whelchel, Love Henry Jr. *Hell without Fire: Conversation in Slave Religion*. Nashville, TN: Abingdon Press, 2002.

Williams, Lewin. *Caribbean Theology*. New York: Peter Lang, 1994.

Wilmore, Gayraud. *Black Religion and Black Radicalism*. Garden City, NY: Doubleday, 1972.

Woodson, Carter G. *The History of the Negro Church*. Washington, DC: Associated Publishers, 1921.

Woodson, Carter G., and Charles H. Wesley. *The Negro in Our History*. Washington, DC: Associated Publishers, 1962.

Wright, R. R. Jr., comp. *History of the Sixteenth Episcopal District of the African Methodist Church*. Philadelphia: Bethel A.M.E. Archives, 1964.

Index

CPSIA information can be obtained at www.ICGtesting.com
Printed in the USA
BVOW05s0348250914

368098BV00001B/8/P

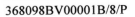

9 780195 369137